Praise for *The Book of Women's Sermons*

"Most of these messages are not fiery or threatening. If there is any common thread in this eclectic group, it's a call for churches—and, more important, for church members—to show compassion and equally welcome all people into their midst. . . . Along the way there is some remarkably good writing." —*Chicago Tribune*

"A great idea, and an overdue one." —Associated Press

"Contributors . . . are women clergy quietly working in regional churches. This book could make you want to tour the country a whole new way." —*Los Angeles Times*

"The tone runs from light-hearted to profoundly scholastic. Some sermons are both." —*Daily News* (New York)

"Dozens of well-educated women, heterosexual and lesbian, young and old, of diverse ethnicity and faiths, encourage us to deeper spirituality. Oh, how liberating to know that all over the United States, women not only are being accepted as church leaders but are telling truths and being listened to." —*Fort Worth Star-Telegram*

"[The] sermons can be a revelation." —*The Sacramento Bee*

"In quick succession, thirty-five women expound on sacred texts and sacred moments. Often their approach is fresh and unconventional. Much of it is controversial." —*The Plain Dealer*

"[A] striking way of visualizing God." —*The San Diego Union-Tribune*

The BOOK of WOMEN'S SERMONS

Hearing God in Each Other's Voices

Edited by

THE REVEREND E. LEE HANCOCK

RIVERHEAD BOOKS

New York

RIVERHEAD BOOKS
Published by The Berkley Publishing Group
A division of Penguin Putnam Inc.
375 Hudson Street
New York, New York 10014

*First Riverhead hardcover edition: June 1999
First Riverhead trade paperback edition: April 2000
Riverhead trade paperback ISBN: 1-57322-783-8*

*The Penguin Putnam Inc. World Wide Web site address is
http://www.penguinputnam.com*

The Library of Congress has catalogued the Riverhead hardcover edition as follows:

*The book of women's sermons : hearing God in each other's voices | edited by E. Lee Hancock.
p.   cm.
Includes bibliographical references.
ISBN 1-57322-059-0 (alk. paper)
1. Sermons, American—Women authors.   I. Hancock, E. Lee
(Eugenia Lee)
BV4241.B57   1999   98-56546 CIP
252'.0082—dc21*

Printed in the United States of America

10   9   8   7   6   5   4   3   2   1

TO MARK,

in whose damp eyes I found the courage to preach

Acknowledgments

Y FIRST DEBT of gratitude goes to the women who contributed to this book. Their willingness to share their sermons and to translate a spoken craft into the written word made this book possible. Without them, it would, undoubtedly, not exist. I am also grateful to those women who cared enough about the project to send me their work even when it did not appear in this volume, and to those who, for various reasons, said no to my request. All manners of response helped to shape this book. It was my intention to include a sermon by So Young Park, but people do not always have complete control over the books they edit.

I owe my dear friend Lauren Artress thanks for sending this project my way!

I am grateful to the staff at Riverhead Books. To publisher Susan Petersen for her openness to my undertaking this project sight unseen, and to Wendy Carlton for her constant and infectious good cheer, even under fire. Special thanks go to Sarah Manges for taking this project to heart. She loved the voices within. Everyone longs for a skilled and caring midwife to facilitate a birth; I was blessed by Sarah.

Richard Newman has always enthusiastically supported my work with constant interest and encouragement. Paul Bernabeo willingly offered his friendship of twenty-five years and his expertise when I needed it.

I want to thank the women whose interest in this book and love for me roped them in to all sorts of tasks. To Kathy Meth, who, with her characteristic industry and generous spirit, lent me her laptop for this project when my computer went on the fritz; Barbara Bedway for her interest and willingness to help out even with an errant footnote; Susan Beckwith who became my ad hoc secretary with grace and that beautiful smile; and especially to Laurie Ferguson for her hours of intellectual and spiritual engagement with me in the creation of this volume.

All love goes to my family, Mark, Hannah, and Sarah, who always knew to find me in the study behind the computer, and encouraged me to be there! For their willingness to help with tasks—Sarah, counting and collating, Hannah, tinkering with the downed computer—and most especially for their pride in, and sustenance of, their mama, I am eternally grateful.

This project was supported by a cloud of witnesses and surrounded by love. Blessed be.

Contents

Introduction

REACHING is a living art form. It is also performed. But although it is performed, it is not about the performer. Preaching relies on the interaction between congregation and preacher, and in that respect, it resembles acting. However, preaching requires a third element. It is unique among the arts for it presumes, even *declares*, that there are other factors, forces, unseen realities at work in this process. It does not depend on its own inspiration; instead, it assumes the presence and the power of the transcendent. We all preach with the hope that the divine will show up; at some times it is more readily felt than others. Preaching *relies* on the transcendent.

The purposes of preaching are to inspire, interpret a text (interpretation is considered a *gift* in the scriptures), motivate, challenge, comfort and console, teach and enlighten, share truth, and make meaning. Preaching is either scriptural, based on a text, or topical. Congregations usually shape preachers—"grow" them, as my mentor, Howard Moody, used to say. Preaching creates relationships; in fact, the best preaching springs forth from the needs and concerns of communities. It is a dynamic triangle: preacher to congregation, congregation to spirit, spirit to preacher. Preaching—the homiletical event—is a living moment. It offers a glimpse, a taste of the divine, of the will, nature, and love of God. No sermon well preached is without the passion of love to fuel and inspire. It is no small order.

Preaching is a craft in which the word is "made flesh" as the passion, tone, and voice of the speaker are alive in each text. This book must be read with an ear for the spoken word. Embodied in these texts are the voices of women from diverse backgrounds, faith traditions, and experiences.

During the past—nearly three—decades, a quiet revolution has taken place in churches and synagogues all across America. As a result of the women's movement, in the early seventies women entered seminaries, theological and rabbinical schools to obtain degrees in unprecedented numbers, irretrievably altering the complexion and the tenor of theological education—and the voice in the pulpit, as well. The disturbingly unfamiliar voices of women were increasingly heard in worship services throughout the country. From the sidelines and basements, out of religious education rooms and kitchens, women began to move from invisible positions of service to command the authority of the word. This was a revolution of sight and sound, and women's voices were often received as discordant in tone and content.

In the first position where I began to preach regularly, Central Presbyterian Church on Park Avenue in New York City, a prominent member of the congregation, a grand and proud matriarch nearing ninety, was not only bothered by my shoes (on a snowy Sunday I wore cowboy boots under my robe instead of regulation black pumps); she was also bothered by my *voice.* "I can't *hear* you," she would declare to my embarrassment and frustration. Even though I was assiduously wired for sound, she could *not* hear me, for mine was a voice she was unaccustomed, even resistant, to hearing. The deep, resonant tones of my male colleague, however, were not only familiar but also received. What I perceived twenty years ago as a judgment upon my skill and experience was really a reflection of the social order. For Letitia, church meant men in the pulpit and women in the congregation. My performance was personalized and problematized.

Power structures have always been embedded in religious institutions. Upon learning my plans to attend seminary, my Southern Baptist grandmother commented, "Why, my dear, *women* let men be up front in the church. Otherwise the men wouldn't participate." Women have always been the backbone of congregations, black and white, Christian and Jewish. But until recently, in most institutions[1] women were not entrusted with handling, or empowered to speak, the Word of God.[2] JoAnne Terrell reminds us in her sermon that women have been considered "incompetent to pastor churches and preach the Word of God!"

Preaching is indeed a political act. Over the past thirty years, women have been rearranging the power structures and reconstructing the expectations of society simply by taking charge of a pulpit for a brief time each week. Since women's presence has often been regarded as profaning, for women to assume the sacred role of entering the pulpit has been, and continues to be in some quarters, a revolutionary act.

Simone de Beauvoir observed that at any given time God does indeed resemble those in power.[3] The converse is also true: Those in power resemble the representations of God worshiped by congregations. This became an organizing principle for feminist and womanist theologies. Professor James Cone's groundbreaking work *Black Theology, Black Power*[4] sharply raised the question Alice Walker so poignantly addresses in her article and in her powerful novel *The Color Purple* (which Joan Hemenway discusses in her sermon). How is it that the God we worship looks like those who oppress us? That question, critically articulated by Cone, was also raised by women in theological education. In response to this question, the women in this book have positioned themselves at various distances in relationship to their traditions.

In addition to race, the gender of God became an issue. Even though we were taught to be suspicious of anthropomorphizing God, it was hard to overlook the fact that God was always referred to as "He." The gendered nature of God is even more pronounced in the Romance languages. In Spanish, God is "El Señor," emphasizing the fundamental identification of God with the male sex. Women began to question the authority of a male God, since gender hierarchy was understood as a source of women's oppression. Language emerged as a critical concern in theological education. Susan Harriss tells a wonderful story about an Old Testament class in which women students brought high heels to class to rap on desks every time the professor referred to humankind as "man." We were told that everyone understood that "man" referred to all humankind, that we were just overly sensitive and unnecessarily reactive. But it had dawned on us that women were required to make a translation that men were not. Unlike men, women were forced to read themselves into so-called generic categories. Liberation movements were beginning to examine the dynamics of power, particularly from the underside. Liberation theologies, informed by the sociology of knowledge, questioned hierarchies and power.

These feminist concerns were often parodied or ridiculed. In congregations, women sometimes found it difficult to raise concerns about inclusive language from the pulpit for fear that their "approval ratings" would suffer. Women had to demonstrate that they were, in short, up to a "man's job." Challenging communities to use inclusive language was tricky business for women who had a tentative grasp on the pulpit and who had to counter their own fears of being seen as frauds or interlopers. Women were torn between their conscience and their desire to participate in a system that was, at best, wary of them. In her sermon, "If You Speak: Burden or Blessing?" Holly Bean addresses the complexity of language and the importance of its careful usage.

But times have changed. Women have begun to accumulate a tradition of active participation and service in churches and synagogues. Enrollment of women is at nearly 50 percent[6] in most mainline, nondenominational, and reform Jewish seminaries. Many women now hold positions of power in religious institutions, and many men accept and utilize inclusive language in their liturgies and sermons. And yet, in some quarters, women are still denied full rights and privileges. The sacred continues to be perceived as threatened with profanation by the presence of women in the pulpit.

The early years of challenge and confrontation produced a legacy of analysis that is basic to an understanding of women in religious institutions. This analysis is about power.[7] It contends that the images used in worship and liturgy reflect the power dynamics in culture and society. The New Testament scholar Marcus Borg writes:

> . . . among the people kneeling at the altar rail was a four-year-old girl, looking up expectantly at my wife's face as she bent down to give her a piece of bread. My wife has a beautiful face and a wonderful smile. As I watched the little girl, I suddenly wondered if my wife's face was filling her visual screen and being imprinted in her mind as an image of God, much as the face of my male pastor from my childhood had been imprinted in mine. And I was struck by the difference: an image of God as a male authority shaking his finger at us versus an image of God as a beautiful loving woman bending down to feed us. Of course, I do not know what was happening in that little girl's mind, but the dif-

ference in images is dramatic. In that difference, something is at stake for both men and women.[8]

A different social vision can be enacted simply by changing the words one uses to address God. This analysis extends beyond gender; race and ethnicity are equally embedded in one's representations of God. Can the message of God be liberating to all when the language, the description, and the likeness of God are at odds with those who are told that they are made in God's image? The hegemonic presuppositions of our society regarding race, class, gender, ethnicity, sexual practice, and ableism are all embedded in and revealed by our images of God and the language we use to talk about God.[9] Several voices in this volume address images or representations of God. Jacquelyn Holland's sermon speaks to a community struggling against internalizing the message that gay men and lesbians are not made in God's image. In "The Motherhood of God," Dorothy Austin offers some creative and provocative images that arose from conversations about God. "God is the baker of chocolate cakes," one young theologian muses. "God Is a Woman and She Is Growing Older" by Rabbi Margaret Moers Wenig challenges the idea of God as static by etching in our minds a detailed vision of God as an old woman, a mother welcoming her children.

The status of women as "outsiders" to religious leadership has both subtly and overtly affected the content of women's preaching; however, the suggestion that there exists something known as a "woman's sermon" smacks of essentialism. The idea of such a genre reduces women's experiences to a set of assumptions. It conjures up a vision of words offered to ensure that women will faithfully fulfill their divinely sanctioned roles as wives and mothers. Women's experience, particularly as it relates to issues of power, is woven throughout this collection. If, indeed, everything in this postmodern world is standpoint dependent, then this generalization extends to biblical interpretation as well. Different interpretations emerge from reading the text in a different light, from a different social location, from the perspective of outsider, or "other." Radically different interpretations emerge when a text is read through the lens of oppression.

In *The Good Book,* Peter Gomes writes:

> The dynamic quality of scripture has to do with the fact that while the text itself does not change, we who read the Bible do change; it is not that we adapt ourselves to the world of the Bible and play at re-creating it as a pageant or tableau "long ago and far away." Rather, it is that the text actually adapts itself to our capacity to hear it. Thus we hear not as first-century Christians, not even as eighteenth-century Christians, but as men and women alive here and now. We hear the same texts that our ancestors heard but we hear them not necessarily as they heard them, but only as we can. . . . In this sense, then scripture is both transformed and transformative; that is to say, our understanding of what it says and means evolves, and so do we as a result. This transformation does not always repudiate what was before, but it does always transcend it.[10]

Gomes also observes that "to read is to interpret."[11] A hermeneutic of suspicion[12] often informs the interpretations in this collection. This is to say that the operating principle of interpretation employed by a preacher when she approaches a passage of scripture assumes that the social and cultural world of the text was oppressive to women. And yet from this hermeneutical perspective, the text often reveals how, in spite of oppression, women triumph. Rather than perceiving these biblical heroines simply as victims or prostitutes or conniving and morally degenerate, their stories pro-

vide clues to the empowerment of women. These sermons celebrate women's strength and spirit.

Given the relative invisibility of women in biblical texts, in the
sermons of women, you can find greater attention given to and
identification with the female subjects of biblical narratives. Ada
María Isasi-Díaz lifts up the Egyptian midwives and the
Syrophonician woman, as does Lynnette Delbridge. In their grap-
pling with the text, both women reveal the particularity of their
lives and context. Vanessa Ochs invites us to consider Tamar's integrity in a situation where she is virtually without options, and
Traci West lifts up the song of Mary as a radical vision of social
justice. In several places in the book, two preachers use the same
text. This device demonstrates the power and possibility of different interpretations. Each woman offers, in her own voice, a fresh
interpretation of the power dynamics within those stories.

Related to the issue of power and the status of women as
"other" is the concept of inclusion. As people historically denied
a place at the table, several of the voices in this volume speak directly to this issue of inclusion. Louise Green addresses homosexuality; Elizabeth Carl, the diversity within community. Barbara
Lundblad raises the question "Who belongs?" when a homeless
man joins her community.

Not only does a preacher's perspective inform the choice of issues and topics her sermons address, but it has an impact on doctrine as well. Based on their experience, women are offering
different interpretations of orthodox theological formulations. Early
in my ministry, I had a conversation with a parishioner that
brought me up short. She was deeply disturbed by the language
of the prayer of confession used in the Sunday service. The prayer
was riddled with apologies for pride, willfulness, and wrongdoing.
In tears, she confessed that she couldn't relate to the content of the
prayer because she didn't feel as if she even *had* a self. Later, I
would refer to this as "worm theology," the declaration of our
worthlessness, our nothingness, our corruption. Hubris has tradi-

tionally been identified as the most significant sin, a denial of God resulting from our self-reliance, grandiosity, and egotism. I heard from this woman what I knew in myself: the concept of sin that I had been taught throughout my childhood simply did not work. In fact, it was injurious to women. In her sermon, "A Charge to the Sisterhood: Love Yourself," Annie Ruth Powell challenges this traditional theological assumption that self-love is sinful. Her text confronts the complexity of how internalized racism and sexism, combined with inappropriate theological application, contribute to self-abnegation.

In this volume, women challenge orthodoxy. Laurie Ferguson takes on the traditional understanding of Jesus as a victim; Donna Berman, the nature of covenant; Sharon Betcher, the meaning of resurrection; and I, the omnipotence of God. Each of these texts offers an unusual and controversial interpretation that grows out of lived experience. The experience of women as expressed in sermons is indeed constructing new theological formulations, and experience has emerged as a crucial factor against which our theological ideas must be measured. Theological concepts shared from the pulpit are usually interrogated by the human condition. When they deliver no meaning or enlightenment they are discarded, declared bankrupt, or there is a collision of theological ideas and lived experience. Donna Berman chillingly refers to the "burning of the children" in the Holocaust as the measurement of our theological honesty and integrity. How can we declare God all good and all powerful when children's lives are destroyed? We must remember that, for women, learning to trust our experience has been a developmental task. Ann Hallstein encourages listeners to embrace their own experience; other preachers, such as Peggy Halsey and Mary Foulke, encourage us to "break the silence" and admit to our experience of the horrors of abuse and violence to initiate healing and justice.

The experiences of women shape the content as well as the point of view in a sermon. After the birth of my first child, I preached a Christmas sermon on "The Innocence of God." It was inspired by my wonder at the innocence of my newborn, and I reflected upon the nature of the God who came to earth as a baby. At the end of worship, an Old Testament professor in the congregation rushed forward to exclaim, "A man could never have preached that story." "Lo Contidiario,"[13] Ada María Isasi-Díaz's conceptualization of the everydayness of life, drifts into women's sermons. Women tell stories about their lives and relationships. Rebecca Edmiston-Lange reflects upon eternity through her relationship with her aging mother; during her mother's surgery, Barbara Bedway muses about inheriting two religious traditions; and Maxine Silverman speaks about simply making the bed, a meditation on the Sabbath.

This book is like a beautiful basket of assorted breads, each one with its own texture, shape, and color—each one with the capacity to nourish. It is like a song sung by a wide variety of voices, each sounding the different notes of social location, experience, and religious tradition. There is widespread interfaith diversity as we hear the voices from the African Methodist Episcopal, AME Zion, Baptist, Methodist, Presbyterian, Episcopal, Moravian, United Church of Christ, Unity Fellowship, Unitarian Universalist, Roman Catholic, and the Conservative and Reformed Jewish traditions. These voices have a distinct urban flavor, and the sermons often reveal how the preacher is situated and the nature of her community. You will hear the voice of a Latina Episcopal priest serving a parish in downtown Los Angeles; a Conservative Jewish laywoman teaching in Charlottesville, Virginia; a Moravian from North Carolina transplanted to a seminary in Berkeley, California; a poet from Harlem on the pastoral staff of one of New York City's largest churches; a film producer ordained as an interfaith minister, self-described as a "Roman Catholic by tradition and a roamin' Catholic by necessity"; and an African-American lesbian from the Pentecostal tradition pastoring a gay-affirming congregation in the heart of Newark.

In certain racial and ethnic groups, preaching is entirely a spoken art. This fact bears multiple meanings. When I requested a
sermon from Sr. Jose Hobday, a Dominican Sister from the
Lakota Tribe, she wished me well with the project but told me that
since her tradition was an oral one, these things were not written
down. In the black and Hispanic churches, preaching rests primarily on the power and inspiration of the Holy Spirit in tandem
with scriptural knowledge and insight. We were fortunate to have
some sermons that were delivered "freestyle" or from a few notes,
preserved on audiotape and made available for transcription.

The women in this book regard preaching not only as a means
to communicate their commitments and their faith but also as
their spiritual food. "Preaching is my spiritual discipline," writes
one author in a note to me; "Preaching is a freeing event," con-
fides another whose tradition has barred women from the pulpit;
"preaching has kept me faithful" is the way Joan Hemenway concludes her biography. For me, the congregations I have served have
"grown" me into a preacher. I am grateful to Central Presbyterian
Church, Judson Memorial, Union Theological Seminary, New
Hempstead and Palisades Presbyterian for their encouragement
and nurture. I hope that in these pages you will find words of encouragement, words that challenge and illumine, and words that
make you cry. I hope you encounter a glimpse, a small taste of the
divine. Within these pages, I pray you will find bread for the journey, soul food served up by women whose lives reflect the glory
of God.

E. L. H.
Advent 1998

THE REVEREND CANON DR. LAUREN ARTRESS

A Feather on the Breath of God: Hildegard of Bingen

On Creativity

ACTS 8:26–40; FIRST JOHN 3:18–24; JOHN 14:15–21

I N the early part of this century, builders in this great Grace Cathedral in San Francisco gathered outside on the corner of Taylor and California Streets and laid a cornerstone. That cornerstone was a time capsule filled with so-called trinkets that spoke of that era: that day's local newspaper, the statutes of this cathedral, a prayer book. One can only imagine all that is in there and wonder about the time when it will be reopened.

We did a similar activity this weekend for the Quest pilgrimage. We focused on the life and works of Hildegard of Bingen, a twelfth-century woman who was born in 1098 and died in 1179, and in doing so we opened up a time capsule that has been sealed for more than eight hundred years. It was sealed because of the tenor of the times, yet guarded and kept by the love and loyalty of the sisters of the Benedictine Order in which Hildegard served.

We learned that Hildegard was bursting with creativity. She wrote ten books and seventy poems. We have over one hundred of her letters to popes, emperors, and others who were well known at the time. We have her recipes for herbal cures, we have seventy-two songs (including a morality play set to music that is considered to be the first opera ever written), and we have her visions. She was a determined and creative woman well known in her day yet silenced over the centuries because of her gender. Now, in the late twentieth century, we are translating her letters and books, putting her cures under the cold, hard eye of science, and singing her music in the wellsprings of our hearts.

Matthew Fox, in his book *The Illuminations of Hildegard of Bingen*, describes the times during which Hildegard lived:

> Chartres Cathedral rose from the grain fields of France with its delicious stained glass and its inimitable sculpture; Eleanor of Aquitaine and Thomas à Becket strode the political stage; Frederick Barbarossa frightened peasant and pope alike—and Hildegard dressed him down; Bernard of Clairvaux both reformed monastic life and launched the Second Crusade; the Cathedral School of Paris was evolving into the University of Paris—and its faculty approved of Hildegard's writings after she traveled there in her mid-seventies with her books under her arm; Heloise and Abelard fell in love and left their tragic story for the generations to ponder.[1]

Hildegard was born the tenth child in a well-to-do merchant family. It was custom in those days to tithe a child, especially a tenth child, to the Church. Consequently, at the tender age of eight she was cloistered in a Benedictine monastery. Later, she would become the abbess of a large monastery.

One of the most interesting aspects of Hildegard's life, and one of the reasons why so many women in our times identify with her, is that her creativity did not come forth until she was forty-two years old, when she became very ill, depressed, and near death. What brought those gifts to the forefront of her life was a spiritual awakening. She described it:

> When I was 42 years and 7 months old, a burning light of tremendous brightness coming from Heaven poured into my entire mind. Like a flame that does not burn but enkindles, it inflamed my entire heart and my entire breast, just like the sun that warms an object with its rays. All of a sudden, I was able to taste of the understanding of the narration of books. I saw the psalter clearly and the Evangelists and other catholic books of the old and new testaments.[2]

The divine world opened to her. She began to receive visions while awake, with her eyes open. (That is why, technically, Hildegard is not a mystic but a visionary. Mystics are usually in an altered state to receive clarity about God. Hildegard was wide-open, wide-eyed, and wide-awake.) While seeing colorful and intricate pictures she heard a feminine voice, which she began to call the voice of wisdom or the voice of the living light, and it directed her to write. "Put your pen to paper and write what you see, write what you are hearing, and write what you are being told." But in order to do this, Hildegard needed to overcome her fear of being misunderstood, of hubris, and of other people's judgment. As soon as she did what she was instructed, she became well.

This difficult spiritual passage to allow her creativity into the world is something that many of us—especially women—experience today. Once we realize that something is trying to find its birth through the finitude of our lives we get frightened, sometimes even to the point of becoming ill. What is stopping you from awakening? What fears do you have to confront in order to claim your birthright to living a creative life?

Hildegard's central message to us is to wake up to the creativity in the cosmos. Wake up to Christ working in our lives! She explains that the gift of life is to be useful; however, we cannot be useful until we awaken. We are to awaken to our gifts, and, out of love of creation and love for one another, we are to use them in service to the world.

THIS power that each of us possesses to create in the world around us is what Hildegard defines as virtue. Boy, is that a different spin on it! Virtue is the power that each of us possesses? (I never liked the word *virtue*, and I don't think I ever used it in my lifetime. Do you like the word *virtue*? To me it meant "Be virtuous," which had a strong moral or Pollyannaish overtone.) Let's start by reflecting on the power of patience. My patience with you may make a difference to you. I know yours certainly does to me! The power of your forgiveness, the power of honesty, the power of faithfulness. Using these creative forces to help one another is good use of our power as individuals and as persons standing within the broader collective we sometimes call community.

Hildegard knew what it meant to be interrelated, to be connected. She saw the Holy Spirit bringing that interconnection, and she described it as the web of creation. Now, talk about interconnection is popular these days, but few of us really know what it means. (We've heard of the butterfly effect: a butterfly waving its wings down in Hawaii affects us right here. Does that touch your lives? It doesn't mine, partly because we are so used to the butterfly waving its wings that we get numb.)

Hildegard's theology embraces a cosmic, planetary vision. Her way of describing the Holy Spirit, the source of the living God, is "the greening power of God." The greening power of God! Isn't that a wonderful redefinition of the Divine working in our everyday lives? If you want to experience God, watch your rose garden grow. Through these simple activities we can discover the mystery woven into our lives here on planet Earth. For the most part, however, Christianity has missed this spirit-filled connection to the cosmos. We have become focused on a Christ who is a policeman over "little" sins instead of a Christ who is universal and loving to all. Hildegard knew that the Church was making poor decisions back in her day. She stated that the Church's task was to empower us. It was not about rules, or watch-dogging morals, it was—and is—about birthing creativity.

The Christian tradition divides sins into two categories, warm sins and cold sins. We pay a great deal of attention to warm sins, sins of the flesh, and we ignore the cold sins, sins of the hardened heart. We covet our excessive resources, greedy and without care for those who have no food or shelter. We ignore that we are in a major crisis. Ecocide (the killing of the planet) and genocide (the killing of one another) continue as a matter of course. I heard something three times this week, and the repetition drew my attention. Three different people mentioned that we probably have about ten years left on this planet as we know it. Now, I do not want to be a prophet of doom and gloom, but frankly, ten years is scary. We ignore that we have hardened hearts. We ignore the injustice that surrounds us and are numb to it. If we are closed and frozen, rather than warm and moist, then the greening power of God cannot penetrate us.

We are called to live creative and flowing lives in service to the Divine Good. Hildegard was always pushing herself; always writing, composing, and articulating the movement of the Spirit. She lived on this creative edge until she was eighty-two years old. She outlived twelve popes! Trusting the creative spirit as if she were a feather on the breath of God. And we, too, are called to live on the edge.

Now there are three ways we can handle this message from Hildegard. First, and most common, we can run from the edge.

We can hide out of the sheer weight of being put to the test. Be at my creative edge? Are you kidding me? Do you know how scary that is? To be flowing is frightening, so we hide. We freeze. We become hardened, wrapped up in the security of habits until we are like robots. Waking up in the morning, brushing our teeth, and going on automatic for the rest of the day. Hildegard said that the true nature of sin is drying up. Drying up! With the greening power of God as the Spirit, it makes sense that the ultimate sin is to run from the creative forces in our lives. Ask yourself where your soul is this day . . .

The second response to living on the edge is to be over the edge. Many of us experience this. We are overwhelmed and addicted to behaviors that don't help us. We are like squirrels caught in a cage. We act out, spin out, and push ourselves mercilessly. For the first group—those of us who are sleepy and numb—the message is to wake up. But to those who are over the edge, the message is to become grounded in the beautiful earth. Breathe in the air, plant your feet firmly on the ground, and look at the glory of nature. Let yourself come into your own presence.

The third response is to truly be on the creative edge. And at this edge there is a balance between push and force. We need to push ourselves at certain times in the birth process, but we cannot force birth, because it does not work. If you are pushing and begin to move into force, the greening power of God evaporates. In order to stay at the creative edge, we are usually birthing something until we come to blockage. The flow stops and things do not feel so good. It is painful, but it is only temporary. Then the process continues into breakthrough, where things begin to flow again. It's the wonderful, mysterious, God-given process of the Holy Spirit. Martha Graham said,

> There is a vitality, a life force, an energy, a quickening, that is translated through you into action, and because there is only one of you in all time, this

expression is unique. And if you block it, it will never exist through any other medium and will be lost.[3]

Stephen Nachmanovitch, in his book *Free Play,* put it a little differently when he wrote,

> . . . the creative process is a spiritual path. This adventure is about us, about the deep self, the composer in all of us, about originality, meaning not that which is all new, but that which is fully and originally ourselves.[4]

Our fingerprint. Our originality. We are called to birth our originality, not to create something new. We are to take our thumb and press it into the meaning of life, to allow it to flow and to flower. We need to trust in the greening power of God to do that.

Hildegard is being released from the time capsule for many reasons. Her understanding of the whole cosmos as the creative expression of the Divine is foremost. She alerted us, in a vision, that there would be a time when we would have fish dying in our rivers and seas. She alerted us that there would be a time when we would have what she called "dense and heavy black fog" that would cover our cities. Do you realize that the children of Los Angeles cannot go out and play in their playgrounds on the days when the air is especially heavy with smog?

We are called to help heal the created order. We are called out of ourselves, to forget our fears or move through them. Each of us is called upon to birth ourselves into the fullness of our being. Each of us is to discover why we are on this planet at this particular moment and bring that realization forward as a gift to our times. We are given the help of the Holy Spirit, the Greening Power of God, to dig our roots deep into the soil, to green, and to burst into flower on behalf of the creative and loving God. **AMEN.**

THE REVEREND CANON DR. LAUREN ARTRESS *is a canon at Grace Cathedral in San Francisco and author of* Walking a Sacred Path: Rediscovering the Labyrinth as a Spiritual Tool. *In 1986, she became Canon Pastor for Grace Cathedral and, in 1992, Canon for Special Ministries. She created Quest, Grace Cathedral Center for Spiritual Wholeness. She is the originator of the Labyrinth Project, which is reintroducing the walking meditation into the Christian tradition. Nationally and internationally, she offers workshops and lectures on the Labyrinth and Hildegard of Bingen, and creates large group events such as the Theater of Enlightenment. Lauren holds a B.A. in Special Education from Ohio State University and a M.A. in Education from Princeton Theological Seminary. Her D.Min. was granted in 1986 by Andover Newton Theological School, in Boston, Massachusetts, in Pastoral Psychology. An Episcopal priest, she is also a licensed psychotherapist and maintains a practice in San Francisco, where she resides.*

THE REVEREND DR. DOROTHY AUSTIN

The Motherhood of God

On Images of God

REVELATIONS 21:1–3

GREETINGS to all of you and Happy Mother's Day!

It is a great pleasure and no small challenge to be the guest preacher on Mother's Day. One of my colleagues, a veteran Methodist preacher, said to me: "I hear you're preaching on Mother's Day in an Episcopal church. Can I give you some advice?"

"Please," I said, "go ahead."

"Keep it short," he said, "and keep it sweet. Sweet because you've got all those mothers out there, and short because it's Episcopalians. Just remember," he said, "good Episcopalians are basically Methodists who can read. They have a high-church, high-falutin appreciation of the spoken word. They're happy to be instructed and inspired by the preacher, but they expect you to do the job faster than it takes to pass the collection plate."

I think Mother's Day should be a feast day of the Church. Contrary to popular belief, Mother's Day was not conceived by Hallmark Cards. Nor was it thought up—as I heard it rumored— by the American Association of Florists. In actual fact, as I learned recently from my colleague, Leigh Schmidt,[1] the American historian, Mother's Day was conceived *in church,* around 1907, by a Methodist woman named Miss Anna Jarvis.

As Leigh tells it, Miss Jarvis was a radical suffragist, a Sunday School teacher, and an advocate of temperance who hailed from the hills of West Virginia. Keen to honor the life and influence of her *own* mother, Miss Jarvis encouraged the members of her Sunday school class to honor *their* mothers in some special way, by visiting with them or by writing them a letter. It wasn't too long before the World Sunday School Association picked up on Miss Jarvis's idea and Mother's Day went international. By 1914, Woodrow Wilson had declared Mother's Day to be a national holiday, to be celebrated on the second Sunday of May.

So on this day, in church, we honor our mothers, our grandmothers, our foremothers, our ancestors, those women who blazed the trail and charted the course before us: pioneers, settlers, immigrants, and natives; hardworking women who labored to bring us, and subsequent generations, into this world. We honor all mothers: living and dead; strong and vulnerable; simple and complex; rich and poor; broken and heroic; mothers who have loved and labored for us, on our behalf, as best they could.

The other day, I asked a five-year-old boy what he thought I should tell people on Mother's Day, in church. "Tell them," he said, "that boys need chocolate cake! My mom is always on a diet. She thinks chocolate cake is bad. I think chocolate cake is good." He was grinning, obviously relishing this chance to set the world straight on such important matters.

"I've got it," I assured him. "What else? Anything else you'd like me to say? Anything about church or about God?"

He smiled, kind of a wry little smile—the sort of smile a small boy can get when he's fastened onto a good idea and knows perfectly well that he's got a grown-up hooked and waiting, all ears, for what he's got to say. "Tell them," he said, "that up in heaven, God makes chocolate cakes, and God eats them!"

If ever we were to doubt that we were made in the image of God or, more to the point, whether God, in turn, is fashioned in our image, our man-made, woman-made, girl- or boy-made image, then perhaps this story of a cake-making God may give us some insight into the nature of our complex human ways of imaging God, whether we think of God as Father or Mother or Ground of Being; as Creator, Redeemer, or Maker of Chocolate Cakes.

This matter of imaging God is a struggle of enormous importance in our devotional lives and in the life of the Christian Church. The way we image and imagine God, the person of God, the gender of God, has everything to do with how we imagine ourselves, one another, and the world. I'm speaking now of the imaginative power we humans have to conceive of God. We know that whoever has the power to name God is likely to have power and dominion over all the earth, and over the people and animals who dwell upon it. As women and men struggle in the Church to find new ways to work together to bring forth a new heaven and a new earth, the Motherhood of God, the conception of God, is of paramount importance to us.

When I asked a young man, an undergraduate religion major and political activist, what he thought I should say in church on Mother's Day, he said to me, "Talk about the role of women in the peace movement; talk about Mothers Against Drunk Driving; talk about the ways that women hold the world together; talk about the ways they network and all that stuff. My mother likes to say that the personal is political. My mother's a feminist. My father says my mother should run for the Senate. I think he's right. My mother's a lawyer."

"Anything else I should say?" I asked him.

"Yes!" he said. "Tell those people in church that men can be feminists. I'm a feminist," he said. "So's my father. You should see the bumper sticker my mother gave my father for Father's Day. It says, 'Real Men Don't Support Patriarchy.' My father loves it. As soon as my mother gave it to him, he went right out and put it on his car. When people pass him, they honk and give him thumbs up."

"Anything *else* I should say?" I asked.

"Yes, one last thing," he said. "Tell them God is black; she doesn't like being 'dissed.' So we humans better get it together."

I thanked him. "I'll be sure to tell them," I said.

I liked what this young man had to say. I found him thoughtful, a new breed. I would like to have met his mother and his father and some of his friends. When I asked him whether he attended church, he said he had been part of an active youth group when he was in high school. Now that he's in college, he works in a soup kitchen at a local church. Recently they asked him if he would help lead the junior high school youth group. He said he thought he would.

When I questioned him further about the role of women in the Church, he said: "In the Episcopal church I go to, there's a woman priest; she really has raised my consciousness. She's terrific. It makes a tremendous difference having her there. Better say that, too," he said. "It's really important: having women priests."

Are we beginning to see a new heaven and a new earth? It's no secret that the Christian Church has had a complicated relationship to women and to motherhood, including the Motherhood of God. More than twenty-five years ago, in 1973, in her ground-breaking book, *Beyond God the Father*, feminist theologian Mary Daly reminded us that the Ancient Fathers of the Church were not all that favorable toward women: It was Tertullian, for example, who said to women, "You are the devil's gateway." St. Augustine was of the opinion that "women are not made in the image of God." Thomas Aquinas spoke of women as "misbegotten males"; and the great Protestant reformer Martin Luther said that "God created Adam lord over all living creatures but Eve spoiled it all." The great Calvinist John Knox composed a piece called a "First Blast of the Trumpet against the Monstrous Regiment of Women."[2]

On a more contemporary note, one of our own flock, Episcopal Bishop C. Kilmer Myers, wrestled with the question of women's ordination. Myers claimed that

> the overwhelming majority of Christians cannot tolerate the idea of the ordination of women to the priesthood . . . A priest is a God-symbol whether he likes it or not . . . In the imagery of both the Old and New Testaments God is represented in masculine imagery. The Father begets the Son. This is essential to . . . the Christian Faith, and to tamper with this imagery is to change that Faith into something else.[3]

We know this battle—the role of women, the status and meaning of motherhood (and fatherhood), the way we think and speak of God—is far from being won. Should women be priests? Some say "Yes," and some say "No."

Even as I speak today, I am remembering a recent storm of alleged heresy in the Christian Church being brought on by a group of women, lay and ordained, who dare to claim that Sophia, that ancient female figure of Wisdom in the Hebrew scriptures, might well serve as an ancient and contemporary way of imaging, and imagining, God. Such a devout conceiving of God not only as our Father but as our Mother as well seems to some to be so threatening to the authoritative teachings of the Church that it warrants theological censure.

I must say, I find the heresy charge theologically regrettable. It makes the Church look foolish, misogynist, imaginatively constricted, unappreciative of mothers, and historically uninformed.

Meister Eckhart, one of the great Christian mystics of the Church, born in the thirteenth century, once wrote that "we are all meant to be mothers of God, for God is always needing to be born."

Obviously, "motherhood" takes many different forms. Motherhood is not solely a biological event; it is also a spiritual expression of the feminine. And it's to be found in women and men alike. Motherhood is the spiritual capacity to nurture, care, and suffer for the offspring of this world—in body, mind, and spirit.

It is no coincidence, no accident, that a central image of our faith is that of Mother and Child. The coming of God as the holy infant breaks open our hearts to the unconditional love of mother and child. When a child is born, our eyes are opened to the profound mystery of human life—our appearance in this world, our vulnerability, our suffering, our finitude, our divinely human capacity to be all that we are meant to be—in this human birth, this human life of ours, this moment of incarnation.

When I asked a seventeen-year-old mother, whose child was three months old, what she thought I should say about Mother's Day in church, she said, "Tell them I love my baby. I mean," she said, "I can't believe how much I love my child. Nothing's so important to me as this child. I mean, I'm in school and everything, but it's because I need to be everything I can possibly be, now that I have this child."

"Anything I should say about church?" I asked her.

"Yeah," she said. "People who say they're religious should be more understanding. You know, my pastor wouldn't marry me and my boyfriend when I got pregnant, even though Jimmy and I knew we wanted to get married. Our families even gave us permission. But our pastor said we were 'outside the church,' that's what he said. He said we had 'sinned.' Finally, Jimmy said to him, 'Look, man, give me a break. We're still having this baby whether you marry us or not.' We were unbelievably disappointed. We wanted the baby to be baptized and everything, but the pastor said, 'No way,' we were 'sinners.' "

We've all heard these kinds of stories. We hear them every day. But they're not going to stop us. The tide is turning and the clock has moved ahead. There is a march to freedom and inclusiveness in the Christian Church that cannot and will not be stopped. There are life-giving partnerships between women and men that will give birth to a new generation of authentic, practicing Christians, worldwide. There will be a new heaven and a new earth. And we desperately need it.

I'll close with one last story. When I asked one young woman what she would say in church on Mother's Day, she surprised me.

"I don't know what I'd say," she said hesitating. "My mother used to lock me in the closet when she got mad at me. She drank too much. To tell you the truth, she was a mess. But still, she was the only mother I had. When she died last year from cirrhosis of the liver, I couldn't stand it. I miss her terribly. I don't miss the torment, but I miss the mother who was trapped inside my mother's life."

We spoke at length about her mother. Finally, I asked her, "What about church? Anything to say about church?"

"Oh, I don't know, not really. It would be wonderful, of course," she said, pausing, "if the Church were really the great Mother we'd like her to be. You know, the all-embracing Mother who just opens her arms to everybody and says, 'Come home. Whatever you've done, wherever you've been, come home, there's a place here for you.' I think that would have mattered to my mother," she said, "if somebody had said that to her. My mother felt really bad about herself. If somebody from the Church had reached out to my mother, it might have made a difference. Maybe it could have saved her life. She really was isolated and lost."

If it is true, as it says in today's text, in the book of Revelation that "the home of God is among mortals," then let it be said—on Mother's Day—that God's hospitality is truly in our hands.

It is up to us to practice the hospitality of God. This is "motherhood." You and I are the household of God, the ones who have to spread the table; call in the hungry; put food in people's bellies; give sustenance to hungry souls; get the homeless off the streets; find the lost and the lonely and talk to them, listen to them; give some comfort to the miserable, to those who have all but given up; make a life-giving connection to those who have lost a spouse, a lover, a friend, a parent, a daughter, a son, a child. Grief can kill us when we feel we're alone. We've all been there, we know what this is about. What do we have in common? The labor of suffering, and the miraculous relief we feel when someone reaches out to touch us, to mother us in a way that really matters. Suffering is the gateway to compassion if it will open our hearts. May God bring the truth home to us: "We are all meant to be mothers of God, for God is always needing to be born." **AMEN.**

THE REVEREND DR. DOROTHY AUSTIN *is an ordained priest in the Episcopal Church. A professor of psychology and religion, she holds a joint appointment in the Graduate and Theological schools of Drew University. She has also served as lecturer in psychology and founding director of the Clinical Program in Psychology and Religion at Harvard Medical School's Cambridge Hospital. For many years she served as the director of the Erik H. and Joan M. Erikson Center, where she initiated the Carriage House Project, apprenticing minority youth to retired members of the Carpenters Union in order to transform an old carriage house into a day center for elders, affordable housing for teen mothers, and exhibition space for community artists. Dr. Austin has also developed an around-the-clock home care program for elders, which includes a creative arts program, staffed by community artists, for people with Alzheimer's disease. She and her partner, Diana Eck, were recently appointed the Masters of Lowell House at Harvard University, in Cambridge, Massachusetts.*

THE REVEREND HOLLY VINCENT BEAN

If You Speak:
Burden or Blessing

On Language

GENESIS 32:22–31

ONE of the regrets emerging from the pace and demand of my daily life is the scarcity of free-flowing conversation with my friends and family. Too often the need to attend to practical concerns, the business of living, precludes the opportunity to listen without time pressures to the views of others and have my own thoughts expressed and tested. I find that this regret is becoming all too familiar; conversation—the kind that is satisfying in its unmediated honesty and completeness—is rare these days.

I am fascinated by words themselves, though I tend to think that actions speak louder and more accurately. Despite tendencies to be either charmed by or skeptical of language, I am convinced that simple conversation is deeply important to me, not because it gives me answers or brings me closer to my goals, or even because

it makes me happy, though it may provide all these. It is important to me—and, I believe, to others—because it provides a precious opportunity, free from many formal constraints, for language
to flow like water, to shape itself into the form of a relationship
and eventually yield up reliable bits of truth. This will happen
mainly when the people conversing trust the process and each
other, and are willing to join the conversation directly and without guile. The result is a kind of matrix of meaning from which
each one can better understand experience and belief and, eventually, decide on appropriate actions.

Without this matrix, the articulation of experience and belief
resembles a shattered mirror. Our perceptions of what is happening around us, to us, and to others in the world remain undigested,
unintegrated, in pieces that distort rather than illumine reality.

Now, there are times when I am tempted to dismiss these un-
fettered conversations as so much hot air. Being a practical person,
I put my trust in getting things done—feeding the children is more
effective than talking about it. Obviously, language can be used to
procrastinate and avoid truth as much as it can be used to search
for it. But I find more and more that what one says is a form of
what one does, and words can often feed the children in essential
ways as well.

If you suffer the same conversation deficit as I do, you may resort to talking to yourself, but we know that this has its problems.
Annie Dillard states it well in *An American Childhood*. She writes:

> The interior life is often stupid. Its egoism blinds
> it and deafens it; its imagination spins out ignorant
> tales, fascinated. It fancies that the western wind
> blows on the Self, and leaves fall at the feet of the
> Self for a reason, and people are watching . . . The
> trick of reason is to get the imagination to seize the
> actual world—if only from time to time.[1]

In addition to reason and imagination, we need one another and the language we share to help us "seize the actual world." Language has the strange power not only to describe but also to heal and to hurt, to build up and to destroy. In all forms and levels of significance, our words provide a way to transcend ourselves and find life-giving meaning in and through our relationships—the good ones and, even, the bad ones. And language is almost all we have to evoke and invoke God.

If human conversation is on the endangered list, conversation with and about God seems almost extinct. In churches where the line dividing sacred from secular is very thin, a lot of traditional religious language sounds quaint or empty, hard to take seriously. There is a danger, however, in the implied assumption that if the language does not fit, the reality does not exist.

Sallie McFague's *Models of God*[2] provides some help. She urges us to understand language itself as flexible, not identified with the reality it seeks to represent. She makes a strong case for using metaphors to talk about God—metaphorical theology—in order to maintain continuously new interpretations of God and the world. As Jacob the patriarch, the carrier of the blessing of the Hebrews, was renamed in his nightlong struggle with the unknown man, our faith tradition and experience can be renamed, and should be, if we do not wish to lose touch with religious truth in our time. We need to apprehend the power we in the Church have in language to "seize the actual world" and our need to "get real" in using it.

Language has the power to name, a power with awesome implications for issues as diverse as nurture and authority.

Many people who have been abused, physically or psychologically, have found genuine healing in the opportunity to articulate their experiences. "Telling our stories" is familiar and foundational to the women's movement. It has led a great many women out of undifferentiated, voiceless existence into clarity and self-definition. It has enabled them to emerge as unique individuals from lives that would deny them that. Most of us would affirm the amazing power of the "talking cure"—therapies from psychoanalysis to twelve-step programs that rely on the power of language. Many people are now adapting this form to meet their need for conversation about religious issues and the life of faith, to spiritual direction.

It might seem to some that these forms of healing are primarily forms of introspection and could be perceived as self-indulgent. But language used in these methods also requires listeners, often more than one, often people who may be quiet but are hardly intended to be passive. This healing power of language does not come from just talking to oneself. It comes from conversation, specifically structured and directed in the service of personal recovery.

Even if recovery is not at issue, even when one is feeling fine, language is still a primary means for the growth of the human spirit. When I recall certain formative statements my parents made to me, I shudder to think of the effect my words might have had on my children. It seems plain that we shape not only our own perceptions with our words but also the perceptions of others, consciously or not. Indeed, messages are received all the time.

We need helpful language, images and phrases that can carry us along paths of righteousness, beside the still waters of sensitivity, and restore our souls and those around us. And we need to use those wonderful words with care. Language used artfully and responsibly could be said to bring a blessing—a divine gift, a sign of God's love—into the lives of those who use and hear it.

Blessing is one of those words that is often misused and probably overused but I like it and I use it because it signifies an experience of grace, a glimpse of truth that does not seem to calcify into doctrine or dogma too quickly. A friend of mine once shared with me over the phone these lines from *The Song of the Bird* by Anthony de Mello:

*The devil once went for a walk with a friend. They saw a man
ahead of them stoop down and pick up something from the
ground.*

*   "What did that man find?" asked the friend.*

*   "A piece of truth," said the devil.*

*   "Doesn't that disturb you?" asked the friend.*

*   "No," said the devil, "I shall let him make a belief out of it."*

*   A religious belief is a signpost pointing the way to truth. When
you cling to the signpost you are prevented from moving toward the
truth because you think you have it already.*[3]

In the days of the Hebrew patriarchs, before the giving of the
Law on Mount Sinai, a blessing had a slightly different meaning,
though it still signified divine favor, and, though not a belief, it still
pointed to truth. In those days a blessing also meant an inheritance
and was a means for naming a primary heir. Blessing implied destiny. Once given, it could not be revoked.

The scripture reading concerning Jacob's blessing needs to be
seen in context. Before this incident, through cunning and collu-
sion with his mother, Rebekah, Jacob had deceived his father,
Isaac, into granting him the crucial blessing intended for Esau, his
brother. Jacob knew that Esau was so angry he wanted to kill him,
and so he went away to live with his mother's tribe in the land of
Haran. After twenty years, during which time he had gained wives
and children and flocks, all symbols of wealth in those days, Jacob
prepared to return to his home. Not knowing what Esau would
do, Jacob sent large numbers of his flocks and his servants ahead
of him, apparently to appease his brother. When his servants told
him that Esau was coming to meet him, Jacob became fearful, and,
on the night before they were to meet, he sent all the wives and
children and servants and animals who were with him to camp
across the river.

He remained alone, stripped of all the symbols of his sojourn in Haran, and he wrestled all night with a mysterious stranger. In this struggle, Jacob asked for a blessing, insisted on it, really, and would not let the stranger go until he had received it. Though this unknown man could not overcome Jacob, he did wound him, leaving him with a permanent limp. The stranger granted the blessing, renaming Jacob Israel. This man, Jacob, who had taken a blessing unfairly before, was transformed through honest struggle with the divine messenger and was granted a blessing for which he was finally worthy.

This story illustrates vividly not only the power of claiming a blessing—of naming, the gift of God—even in another culture and time, but also the corruption of it. Jacob had acquired the first blessing through deceit. Though it did not seem to really fit him, this blessing, by its nature, carried a certain status and authority, partly because of the custom of the time, and partly because Jacob was a descendant of Abraham. His blessing was, by implication, a blessing for all the Hebrews. The second blessing, which he also claimed, legitimated his status and authority.

This language of ours gives us not only the power of naming but also of pronouncing what is good and granting authority to it. We can choose which words to pay attention to and we can choose who will speak for us.

Several new books on the market analyze speech patterns between men and women. Some of the writing on this subject has been very helpful in identifying characteristic ways that men's and women's conversation patterns undercut their communication. In such a realm, questions of authority abound. What prior assumptions do we bring to a conversation? What blessings may need to be legitimated?

Certainly we have a lot to learn about the behavior of talk and how it validates some and invalidates others. Certainly we need to learn how to remove barriers to good listening and clear speech. Perhaps we can come to understand why someone with perfectly sound, well-stated ideas may be dismissed in favor of someone whose charisma or status inflates the modest value of what he or she says. This happens all the time.

Here the issue is, again, how to get at the truth, too often obscured rather than revealed by those in authority. Within the Church, the ancient authority on religious truth, many find themselves withholding trust, even when we know the difference between believing in the Church and believing in God. I have observed that many thoughtful churchgoers are taking a kind of "show me" attitude toward the Church's claims on religious truth. And who could blame them? In the eyes of so many people—many women and other people from marginalized cultures—the Church's witness in the world appears as two thousand years of articulated negativity. But, if the Christian Church, like Jacob, has an ill-gotten status and authority through the misuse of its earlier blessing, it might also be transformed through honest struggle into a legitimate agent for God's grace.

This is why the struggle for inclusive language should not be abandoned and should not just focus on pronouns. This is why the feminist and womanist biblical research can be powerful, when informed by the need to update and restate the foundations of the faith tradition. This is why we need to be able to bring all that we are—humor, passion, and anger as well as reason and memory—to bear on our words about and to God. This is why we need to be in conversation, listening and speaking in mutual trust.

May the words you find and the words that find you be sparks to ignite your imagination and your passion to "seize the actual world" and work for its transformation.

THE REVEREND HOLLY VINCENT BEAN *is an ordained minister in the American Baptist Church. She serves on the Ministers' and Missionaries' Benefit Board of the American Baptist Churches as Coordinator of Member Education. A thirty-year membership of Judson Memorial Church in Greenwich Village in New York City has deepened her love of pastoral and prophetic preaching. She has served Judson in a variety of capacities including moderator of the Congregation. She is a graduate of Mount Holyoke and holds the M.Div. degree from Union Theological Seminary. Inspirations in her life have come not only from her friends and family—her beloved husband, who is an actor, and her college-age son and daughter, as well as a large extended family—but also from the women and men who labor in ministry and dare to speak the truth. Raised in Illinois, she now lives in Montclair, New Jersey.*

BARBARA BEDWAY

Bridges to God

On Dual Religious Traditions

THE night before our mother's surgery we laid out for her, my two sisters and I, the things we thought she would need. On the bed beside her suitcase there were nightgowns that tied in the front, slippers without backs, bottles of lotion with vitamin E and aloe. There was also one guardian angel pin; one heart locket that had accompanied my sister's friend into a dangerous but successful surgery; a sealed, square-inch packet containing "Material touched to the body of Saint Therese of the Child Jesus, Carmelite of Lisieux"; and a miniature basket with six Guatemalan "trouble dolls" inside.

It was easy for us to make light of the dolls, in whom you are supposed to confide your troubles, and who, when you sleep, will solve them. But the other items—talismans, charms, and relics, solid clusters of a kind of faith you can hold in your hand—these we could not quite laugh about. My sister, the clinical nurse specialist, the levelheaded, clear-eyed one who looks after the patients with the bleakest prognoses—she proffered the heart locket. The angel pin I had found only days before my arrival in Florida, but the packet I had kept since childhood and had never parted with, until now.

"Whatever a man prays for," Turgenev wrote, "he prays for a miracle. Every prayer reduces itself to this: 'Great God, grant that twice two be not four.' " In this world below heaven, whenever I faced a crisis, my prayers tended to take the form of research. And so I called breast cancer hot lines, spent evenings in bookstores and libraries ferreting out the experts. Then I called them, trying to tally Turgenev's sum. My mother's lump was very large, but had not shown up on the mammogram she'd had only three months earlier. Medical oncologists explained to me "infiltrated lobular carcinoma," and asked about the "aggregate tumor size." Their tally came to this: "total mastectomy and axillary node dissection."

"I'm not ready to die, you know," my mother said that evening, sitting on the bed.

"Well, you're not going to," I answered, too swiftly. "You've got estrogen receptors on your cancer cells. The doctors say that's a good sign. And you've got her," I added, holding out the guardian angel pin with a chip of my mother's birthstone as the angel's heart.

"I almost got you one of those pins once." She laughed ruefully, fingering it in her palm. "But then I thought if you ever lost it, you'd feel just terrible."

She knew my sisters and I were the sort of children who took faith very seriously, perhaps because we'd not been raised in one of our own. The marriage in 1947 of our Lebanese Catholic father to our Scotch-Irish Presbyterian mother had caused such pain to their deeply religious families that our parents thought it best not to raise us in either religion, but to let us attend both churches and then choose for ourselves when we "came of age."

But we worried we were always "coming of age," or that we

might have passed through it—even missed it entirely, perhaps—
the age when God is made clear and the path you should take is
revealed to you. That was the way it had happened to Saint
Bernadette, in the movie my sisters and I had seen and loved.

"God has chosen you," the nuns told the future saint in *The
Song of Bernadette,* a girl barely older than ourselves. "Now you
must choose God."

My sisters and I had chosen God, but we did not know what
to do about it. Not wanting to offend either side of the family
with an outright preference, we'd begun making up a religion of
our own, an odd hybrid of Catholic mysteries and Protestant facts.

Our Lebanese grandmother had come from a country where
graves of saints dotted the hillsides, and shrines containing a sacred relic were as much a part of the natural landscape as the cedars
of Lebanon that had lived for two thousand years. For those who
believed, Heaven joined Earth in these holy places. For those who
believed, their prayers of intercession were heard by the martyrs
within, and delivered straight to the ear of God.

That was the faith our grandmother brought, and why her
home was filled with religious statues and pictures of Christ, God
multiplied in things you could touch. Even the food we ate there
was laced with holy mysteries. On Good Friday she made a bean-
and-lentil soup with tiny dumplings of bulgur wheat. Those
dumplings, she told us, were the Blessed Mother's tears, shed for
her suffering son. And the "tears" were indeed salty, and were the
color of rain; to us, the Good Friday soup was a far more appealing
and believable story than what we had been told about communion wafers, and wine, and the body and blood of Christ.

For a while, my sisters and I tried to believe that you could
build a sort of bridge to God out of the holy specimens we found
in our grandmother's house. We collected enough once to build an
altar in our bedroom made out of vials of holy water from the
River Jordan; long, yellow fronds from a Palm Sunday past; the
packet of holy material I'd begged from Aunt Phoebe; and the nun

doll our father had won at the Saint Casimir's Festival in Adena, Ohio.

We had then the complete faith of children, a kind of open, earnest expectancy that soon, because of our particular prayers and rituals, a sign would come to prove we were part of something larger than ourselves. And hadn't we actually witnessed how pardon and protection could be granted through such faith as our grandmother displayed? Hadn't she prayed at her doorway every Sunday as our family pulled away in the car, and weren't we delivered home safely every trip? Hadn't we been told, over and over, how she had crawled on her knees down the block to St. Casimir's, to fulfill her promise to Saint Anthony, who had brought our father home alive from the war in 1945? And hadn't she offered, when our Aunt Phoebe persisted with *"When will your first communion be?"* this pardon for the grandchildren who would never see a catechism class: *There are many paths to God.*

Our other path led across railroad tracks and up a hill—Church Hill—to where our other grandmother lived. If we wearied of incense and celestial mysteries, our Presbyterian grandmother would bring us back to earth. She was a master gardener who believed that the very existence of flowers was evidence of God's great feelings for us growing in the world. We loved her profuse garden, especially the tall sunflowers that seemed to look down at us with a kindly aspect as human as ourselves. When we heard her play the organ in church on Sundays, the only place where she allowed her feelings their full expression through the sacred music, we imagined we were hearing something like the voice of God.

Every evening she read from the Bible, and altered her habits not a bit when my sisters and I were visiting. We sat on two ottomans at her feet, fresh from a bath with Dove soap and shining with Jergen's hand lotion that we rubbed into every pore for the rich, sweet scent of it. We listened with a passionate attentiveness to the unfamiliar words, quietly happy so long as listening was all she required. We did envy her, serene in her reading of the Psalms, at home in the wisdom of Ecclesiastes.

But some nights, she read only a few proverbs, or a little of the prophets, then closed her Bible expectantly.

"Tell me, Andrea," she asked my oldest sister one evening, "who is your favorite saint?" I thought we at last might please her with an answer that was correct. She had taken us to Sunday school earlier in the summer, where we had been welcomed into a class that was busy coloring a picture of Joseph's coat. Though my sister Marcia was clearly too old for coloring books, she chose the kelly green crayon and turned that coat into a solid mass of waxy splendor. The teacher, who was our grandmother's oldest friend, held up the drawing to the class and said, not without pity, "Children, tell our visitors why this cannot be Joseph's coat."

"Don't you have a favorite saint?" she asked again, and Andrea answered, "Bernadette," just as I knew she would. The three of us smiled at one another in anticipation of some praise. But our grandmother remained silent as she looked searchingly at us, one by one, then opened her Bible again.

"There are only four saints, you know. Matthew, Mark, Luke, and John. Only four. They're right here in the Bible. Not made up afterward."

My sisters and I were silent then, caught in the circle of buttery light from the lamp, exposed again for our ignorance. *Matthew, Mark, Luke, and John.*

"You know, girls," she said, at last looking up and fixing on us the complete wisdom of her blue-green eyes, "we all have to face our Creator alone. There are no . . . intermediaries, no person, living or dead, no special 'thing' that can 'help you out' but your own selves. Do you understand?"

What we understood was that she expected us to reach God on our own, no interceding by the human saints, no token presence of the Divine cloaked in a blessed piece of cloth from the recognizable world. *Matthew, Mark, Luke, and John.* Was there only

God, and Christ, and the shivering faithful? The image terrified us, and, secretly, we hoped the Catholics were right.

Yet in that moment, we could not help looking on our grand-mother as brave beyond all measure, brave enough to choose sun-flowers and music as her only protection before God.

WE didn't talk about God with our mother, not when we were children, and not now, as she gracefully accepted all our tangibles of love and luck and faith that we placed in the corners of her suitcase. I don't know what she made of that packet, but she has always been respectful of her daughters' need for solace and mysteries.

As fear chilled us all that hot Florida night, and faith seemed most of all a kind of courage we had no choice but to profess, I could see why we children had hoarded all these years our inventory of the holy. Blessed cloth and images of the Virgin had once brought the sacred within reach of our human hands. Who would not want to cut down that wide space between us and the infinite, and put at least a shred of the dear familiar on the abstract face of God?

Hours and hours after our mother was taken for the mastec-tomy, her surgeon came into the waiting room to give out the news. No, the cancer had not spread. If she wished, our mother could choose to be treated with hormonal therapy alone. For now, twice two would not be yielding four. Our father kissed the sur-geon's hands.

But my sisters and I, stunned, relieved, and grateful, could not credit the doctor's skills first. Our mother is, after all, a Presby-terian, and even though she doesn't go to church, isn't she her mother's daughter? Doesn't she play the piano and grow flowers of her own? I imagine she would agree with that other great gar-dener, Sido, who laughed when her young daughter Colette brought home a "blessed posy" from the Virgin Mary celebration: "D'you suppose," she asked, "it wasn't already blessed?"

BARBARA BEDWAY *is a writer whose essays and fiction have appeared in* The New York Times, Child, *and the* Iowa Review, *and in the children's anthology* On the Wings of Peace. *She lives in Nyack, New York, with her husband and son. She was very surprised to find her work selected for an anthology of sermons by women, but as her grandmother told her, "There are many paths to God."*

Rabbi Donna Berman

Through a Keen Lens of Empathy

On the Holocaust

ONIGHT we break the silence. *Va-yi-dome Aharon.* And Aaron was silent. That was what we were told five weeks ago when we read of the tragic deaths of Aaron's sons, Nadav and Avihu. You might remember them. They were the two sons who, the Torah tells us, "each took his fire pan, put fire in it, and laid incense on it, and then offered before God *aysh zarah,* alien fire which God had not enjoined upon them. And fire came forth from God and consumed them and they died before God." Then Moses said to Aaron, "This is what God meant when God said: Through those near to Me I show Myself holy, and assert My authority before all the people." "And Aaron," the Torah concludes, "was silent."

Since that story was related five weeks ago, there has been no mention of the tragedy. There were laws about cleanliness, disease, and purification, and then there were two portions read in honor of Pesach, which interrupted the flow of the Torah narrative. And now we return, five weeks of silence later, to a Torah portion called *Acharei Mot,* "After Death," which begins, "God spoke to Moses after the death of the two sons of Aaron who died when they drew too close to the presence of God."

Rabbi Yitz Greenberg has suggested that the ultimate litmus test for a theological viewpoint after the Holocaust is this: that one's theological claims must make sense in the presence of burning children.[1] This jarring hermeneutic, this jarring lens through which to view theological ruminations after the Holocaust, shocks us into remembering that theology cannot afford to be merely theoretical. It must make sense in the context of real life. It must make sense in the context of real pain. This kind of test keeps the theologian grounded and keeps the theological enterprise legitimate. I believe Yitz Greenberg's approach is vital if we are to speak meaningfully after the Holocaust, and I propose that this week's Torah portion can be instructive as we struggle to answer the silence. It is, after all, called *Acharei Mot,* "After Death"—that is, after the burning death of Aaron's two sons, Nadav and Avihu.

Let me begin by briefly reviewing for you some of the questions that have haunted theologians in the wake of the devastation of the Holocaust.

The most shattering theological problem posed after the Holocaust is, of course, How does one make sense of the world after the destruction of eleven million people? How does one make sense of God's role in a world where such things are possible? If God is good and all powerful, how could God have allowed such evil to occur? (This question—known as theodicy, the problem of evil—has been paramount in the minds of many of us during the past ten days as we search for explanations through the physical and emotional debris left by the Oklahoma City bombing.)

The world, simply put, is imperfect. And that, theologians have suggested, forces us to consider several basic, unpleasant alternatives in terms of our belief systems. The first alternative is to assume that there is no God. The second alternative is to assume that there is a God, but that this God is either all powerful but not good, or good, but not all powerful. How could a good God who is all powerful not intervene to stop the destruction of God's own creatures? Since it is untenable for most Jewish theologians to postulate that there is no God or, for that matter, that God is not good, most theological discussion after the Holocaust has been about the limits of God's power, since an acceptance of the lack of God's omnipotence seemed the least disruptive to a Jewish worldview constructed over centuries. For example, a theologian by the name of Hans Jonas suggested that after God created the world, there was a self-forfeiture on the part of God, what Jonas calls an effacing of God.[2] In other words, God pulled back to make room for creation. Notice that Jonas is telling us that God chooses to limit God's own power; it's not that God is innately lacking omnipotence. Martin Buber spoke of the Holocaust as the eclipse of God.[3] Richard Rubinstein speaks of God as creator, but as One who has no power to intervene in history.[4]

Beyond all these considerations lies an issue probably most problematic for the Jew, which is, How do we make sense of the covenant after the Holocaust? Covenant means to us that we have entered into partnership with God and that God has agreed, if we remain loyal covenant partners, to sustain the life of our people. In light of the Holocaust, then, does it not seem that God has defaulted on God's part of the agreement?

Covenant is so basic to Jewish self-understanding that to lose faith in it is potentially as traumatic to Jewish life as was the destruction of the temple in Jerusalem. Such a loss of faith would demand a whole new way of thinking about the world. S. Daniel Breslauer writes:

> As long as covenantal thinking prevailed the Jew
> could cope with challenges to faith. Disaster could

be understood as punishment, personal failure as a
training ground for independent moral decision-
making, martyrdom as a willing acceptance of tribulations of love. Both historical and natural disasters
could be interpreted as means by which a personal
relationship with the deity was strengthened, maintained, and affirmed.[5]

Covenant, in other words, makes the world make sense. The
converse is also true: without covenant the world, to the Jew, does
not make sense. So another thrust of recent theological discourse
has been to redefine covenant so that it need not be abandoned,
so that it continues to be a viable concept for Jews to claim as part
of their religious identity. Eliezer Berkovits, for example, points to
the dignity and nobility of the behavior displayed by Jews in concentration camps as the essence of the covenant. "The Jews were
victims but," he contends, "they were also the point for the crys-
tallization of moral direction in history. That is the ultimate significance of being the chosen people of God."[6]

S. Daniel Breslauer suggests that "the covenant significance of
being a Jew is that of pointing out the moral state of the world."[7]
Breslauer views the Jewish people as a barometer of the battle between the forces of good and evil. Emil Fackenheim states that,
after the Holocaust, survival of the Jewish people is an additional
mitzvah.[8] Eugene Borowitz, among others, points to the creation
of the State of Israel (and the miraculous Israeli victory in the
1967 Six-Day War) as proof that God did intervene in history
and that the Jewish people were not abandoned, but ultimately
saved, that God's part of the covenant was not, in the final analysis, broken.[9]

It is these last two suggestions, that Jewish survival is now an
additional or, some would say, our tantamount *mitzvah* (commandment) and the suggestion that Israel represents the fulfillment of
the covenant, which have settled in as normative belief in the past

twenty-five years but which recently have begun to be critiqued by Jewish thinkers.

The problems/questions, as espoused by leaders of our community as varied in perspective as Jacob Neusner,[10] Marc Ellis,[11] and Larry Hoffman[12] are these: Has an exclusive focus on Jewish survival made us less sensitive to the needs of others? Has it made us myopic, able to see only our own oppression, unable to see past our own victimization, dampening our fervor for social justice? Has seeing Israel as a religious category in and of itself led us to redefine commitment to Judaism as unquestioning financial, emotional, and spiritual support for the land of Israel to the point where critique is seen as heresy? Is a kind of bureaucratized, organizational, institutional Judaism, designed to empower and protect us, now draining the lifeblood from our community? Has all of this created a spiritual vacuum for us that ultimately threatens the healthy survival of our people? The questions these thinkers ask are not so much about where God is or who God is, but rather about where we are and who we are.

But we have strayed from our original course. Our task this evening is to break the silence, to respond to the senseless deaths of Nadav and Avihu, of our children, of all children. Our task is, as Yitz Greenberg reminds us, to create a matrix of values that will not sustain another attempt at genocide.[13] Our task tonight is to do theological work that makes sense in the presence of burning children.

The Holocaust forces us to evolve theologically. It forces us to make a paradigm shift, to see God differently, to see ourselves differently. We cannot look such evil in the eye and not have our vision of the world be drastically altered. In a way the Holocaust compels us to grow up theologically, to—some would say—abandon the kind of images of God that people like Sigmund Freud declared to be unhealthy: a bigger-than-life version of our own parent, our own father perhaps, who would punish us and judge us and ultimately protect us.[14] The first response of Jewish theologians, understandably, was to attempt to protect the integrity of God and of the theological conceptions of the past. The physical devastation of the Holocaust was enough. How could our people survive the decimation of the concepts they had held dear? And so theologians attempted to keep everything intact. God exists and God is good and God is even omnipotent, they assured us, but God decided to give up some of that omnipotence to make room for human freedom. And, as for the covenant, God didn't desert us. God enabled us to found and successfully defend the State of Israel. But I would argue that this kind of theologizing, however understandable it may be, no longer serves our people well. It has given us pat answers to complex questions. It has, to a large extent, stifled self-critique. It has tended to numb us to issues that do not directly involve our own survival, and it is time for us to move on theologically.

The other night I watched a rebroadcast of the memorial service that was held for the victims of the Oklahoma City bombing. The Reverend Billy Graham spoke, and he voiced the question that so many people asked him: How could God have allowed this to happen? In response to this question he suggested that there was meaning in what happened, but that only God could understand it. I resented his saying this. I resented his saying this to people who had lost their loved ones. In the presence of such profound grief and despair, platitudes are not called for. *Va-yi-dome Aharon,* and Aaron was silent. Aaron had the right idea. He knew there was nothing to say into the abyss of senseless death.

In the most recent volume of the yearbook of the Central Conference of American Rabbis, Rabbi Sheldon Harr candidly shares his thoughts on the third anniversary of his daughter's tragic death in an automobile accident. He writes:

> Very many of the theologies, for me, espoused in
> much of our liturgy are difficult to accept. The

transcendent, omnipotent, omniscient God, who seemed quite capable of conquering the Egyptians and saving the Hebrews, couldn't this God have conquered the moment and saved one more life? Does God's loving spirit really hover over all the world, and to what effect? . . . I think a true faith and a true movement . . . will know that so many of our people, deeply hurting in their own lives, need and, in fact, crave honesty in theology . . .[15]

And so tonight we break the silence. We could do what Moses did, which is very similar to what some theologians have done. We could attempt an explanation. We could attempt to protect God. After the death of Nadav and Avihu, Moses says to Aaron, "This is what God meant when God said, 'Through those near to Me I show Myself holy, and assert My authority before all people.' " No wonder Aaron was silent. No doubt he was silent in the face of his tremendous loss, but I'm sure Moses' attempt at an explanation contributed to Aaron's speechlessness. I think that Aaron was dumbfounded by his brother's words. The truth is, we don't know much about God. Certainly for us as modern Jews most of our preconceptions about God have been shattered by the Holocaust.

But there are certain things that we do know. We know how it feels to be oppressed. We were slaves in Egypt. We know how it feels to be hated, to be persecuted. We were almost destroyed by Hitler. Those memories are seared, both literally and figuratively, into our people's flesh, into our people's soul. We do know, empirically—all we have to do is look around us—that a matrix of values does exist that could, and in many parts of the world does, sustain other attempts, some subtle, others more blatant, at genocide, even as we speak. And we, as Jews, are obligated by knowledge of these things to take action and to identify with those who are oppressed. We are obligated to raise our voices in protest in the face of injustice and to speak for the forgotten, the ignored, the voiceless.

As Michael Lerner puts it, "Judaism emerged as the first historical liberation movement by challenging the necessity and the inevitability of systems of oppression." Lerner points out that thirty-six times in the Torah it says, with some variation but with the same basic message, "Do not oppress the stranger, for you were strangers in the land of Egypt. You shall love the stranger as you love yourself." No other injunction, Lerner reminds us, is reiterated as many times as this one. It is repeated thirty-six times.[16] Even those of us who are not usually seduced by *gamatria* (the Jewish equivalent of numerology) must be tempted to succumb. As we all know, thirty-six is a significant number in Judaism. It's "double chai." Some say the Torah contains secret messages hidden away for those who seek them. Is the message here that kindness to the stranger, to the one who is different, the one on the margin, is a pathway to "double chai," to fuller life?

We must not lose sight of the fact that we who have been marginalized have a unique perspective that those in the center do not have. Being on the margin allows one a breadth of vision. We see possibilities where others often only see inevitability; we see new and better worlds where others, more centrally located, often only see what is. We need to take advantage of our placement as Jews on the margin and we need to, in Adrienne Rich's magnificent words, "turn Otherness into a keen lens of empathy."[17]

But what about God in all of this? What about covenant? I believe, along with liberation theologians, that the Bible teaches us that God is on the side of the oppressed. I draw from this that every act of liberation on our part is a Godly act.

We don't have to be Moses. We don't have to lead an entire people out of slavery. Our contribution to liberation might be as simple as a phone call or letter to a politician telling him or her that we do not want our tax cut to be at the expense of the poor, the sick, the elderly, the young. It could be contributing time or money to organizations that feed the hungry. It could be speaking out the next time and every time we hear someone say something hateful or bigoted. If the Holocaust has taught us anything, it has taught us that injustice and hatred are extremely resilient and will take root wherever they are allowed to go unchecked. We must be vigilant and never underestimate the power of even the smallest act of decency.

I believe that sometime in the not-so-distant future our people will look back at the Holocaust as marking the beginning of a new covenant between God and the Jewish people. To the covenant with Noah, to the covenant with Abraham, to the covenant sealed at Sinai will be added this new covenant which is unique in that it has been initiated, not by God, as the others were, but by us. We who have remained Jewish after such tragedy, we who continue to be Jewish despite the risks involved, are covenant makers simply by virtue of our continued adherence to a faith for which millions were murdered. We are covenant makers by virtue of our adherence to a faith that enjoins us to be *Or l'Goyim*, a light to the nations. We are covenant makers by virtue of our adherence to a faith that has at its heart a commitment to create a better world for our children and for all children. This covenant is not undermined by the Holocaust. It is underscored by the Holocaust. Out of the experience of our own suffering, we have been given a mandate to alleviate suffering and to bring healing to the world. In what better way can we honor the lives of those we have lost?

I remember as a child sitting in Mrs. Millstein's Sunday school class. It was there that I learned about "Prophetic Judaism" which was how the Reform movement defined itself in the early sixties. Prophetic Judaism was about changing the world, working for peace and freedom, standing up for justice. Together, in class with Mrs. Millstein, we would read the words of the Prophets. From Micah: "It has been told you what is good and what God requires of you: to do justly and love mercy and walk humbly with your God" (Micah 6:8). I would sit mesmerized by the words. Sometimes I was moved to tears. My vision of the world and of Judaism was formed in that classroom and was reinforced in my home. I can still hear Mrs. Millstein reading these verses from Isaiah:

Is not this the task I have chosen: To loose the bonds of wickedness, to undo the heavy burdens, to let the oppressed go free, and that you break every yoke? Is it not to share your bread with the hungry, and that you bring to your house the poor who are cast out . . . (Isaiah 58:6-7)[18]

And her voice would come alive with emotion as she read the conclusion:

Then your light shall break forth like the morning, your healing shall spring forth speedily, And your righteousness shall go before you: The glory of God shall be your rear guard. Then you shall call, and God will answer; you shall cry, and God will say, Here I am. (Isaiah 58:8-9)[19]

This, to me, is what theology after the Holocaust must be about. It is the only theology that makes sense to me in the presence of burning children. It must be about breaking the silence by saying to those who are oppressed, to those who are in pain, what Moses should have said to Aaron. It's about saying, *"Hineni.* Here I am." It is about hearing God answer back, *"Hineni.* Here, and in every act of liberation and compassion, I am too."

RABBI DONNA BERMAN *is a Reform rabbi currently serving as the Jewish chaplain at Mount Holyoke College in South Hadley, Massachusetts. She is the Rabbi Emerita of the Port Washington Jewish Center in Port Washington, New York, and the founder of the South Bronx–Port Washington Community Partnership. Berman graduated from Hebrew Union College in New York City with an M.A. in Hebrew Literature and holds an M.A. in Sacred Theology from Yale Divinity School. Having returned to her undergraduate institution, she is completing her Ph.D. in Religion and Social Ethics at Drew University. A writer and activist theologian, she is editor of* Wisdom, You Are My Sister: 25 Years of Women in the Rabbinate, *published by the Central Conference of American Rabbis. She has written various articles about Jewish feminist ethics. A native of Long Island, New York, she resides in West Hartford, Connecticut.*

THE REVEREND DR. SHARON V. BETCHER

Resurrecting Mortal Life

On Resurrection

H E and I had nothing in common, except my ritual bagel and coffee on the way to the library. We had nothing between us, until that day three weeks ago, when the weather was miserable and those wanting to comfort themselves were many. I tumbled to the back of a discombobulated line; with the rush of customers, the owner came forward to assist. We could not exchange my travel mug across the cooler, so he in his hurry told me to "just get up to the counter." Taking more body space with my cane than others would, I could find no way to wend my way through the crowd, and shrugged. He, irritated, yells, "Just get up here!" I, hurt, yell, "I am trying, sir!" The crowd parts and I—now a spectacle—limp my way forward. He reddens and, cringing, says, "I didn't know, I couldn't see. I mean, if I had known . . . I hope you don't think that I usually treat people like this. I just . . . ." The apologies gush endlessly, while he pours the coffee, gathers the bagel, pleads with me to take them for free, and follows me to the door. I get in the car, then drop my shoulders, and let my chin sag. During the ensuing week, I stew.

In religious vocabulary, he needs and desires forgiveness. He landed his frustration precisely where he shouldn't have, and it had hurt. We knew that between us. I resolved to reset my shoulders and go back, as was my habit, just to show him (and myself) that we could withstand a little hurt.

Unbelievable! We both know that there was some slight hope I would never show my face there again. I can tell by his quick turn to the wall to compose himself that neither of us would ever have chosen to deal with each other again. But we are forced, by the happenstance of the numerical lineup, into an intimacy that even I hadn't quite planned on. When we get to the cash register, he leans forward and says, "I hope you still don't hold that against me." I retort, "I'm here, aren't I? Let it go. Most don't even try to apologize." Again I return to my car, drop my shoulders, and let my chin sag.

Unbelievable! Even with the best of intentions I could not muster, in this slight infraction against my dignity, the simple gesture by which we redeem the hope of human community. Well aware of the gesture that could heal, I nevertheless deliver a backbite of cynicism. I too had needed a way beyond my own hurt and, instead, wound the story around my own wound. I gathered my identity, as so many of us do, from the lot of inhumanity practiced against me. From refusing communion over bagels and coffee to the intolerance of human foibles, we are cloistering ourselves in a deep cynicism of human community.

Lawsuits pile up as we indict each other for the risk of the mortal condition. Doctors, with the best of training and integrity, fail to foresee every potential complication and we rush to sue them for their lack of more than human knowledge. Legal railroads of vengeance seem the quickest way to deal with the loss of a loved one. Sometimes these are no small hurts: lives are irredeemably lost, unjustly and tragically injured. And there are clear cases of negligence, especially among people of color, women, and gays, to whom forgiveness is peddled as a legitimization of ongoing injury and postponement of justice. There are legitimate reasons why we have had to learn in recent decades to draw the line; to retain sins, as John puts it in his gospel, in order to insist on dignity in and from the human community. But what does it mean when the hurt and pain boil into vengeance, into unremitting pyres of fury? When we become slaves of our own hurt, caught up in reactive chains of unending denouncements and condemnations? We are eager to let the fist fly, to loft the chin in cynicism or to drop it in despair, but we are unable to recall the redemptive gesture of human community. We are falling out of love with the mortal life.

Turn on the news and watch the dramatic interplay of the human community around our hurts. A police officer in New York City is killed. In the wee hours after a suspect is arrested, the district attorney refuses to invoke the death penalty on the grounds that there simply has not been time to review the evidence. He has gone on record as being conscientiously concerned about the way in which more people of color are executed than whites. The governor, within two days, removes the D.A. from the case for failing to execute the will of the people, for failing to abide that sickening cry that boils up in the immediacy of hurt and irredeemable loss. It is a drama uncomfortably familiar, if slightly more righteously refined and encoded in the privacy of our own souls: hurt wanting someplace to land itself; hurt stuck in a reactive cycle, no one daring to disarm him- or herself.

Even in the best of Christian communities today, do we not individually sequester ourselves by wrapping our identities around our hurts or by holding our breath in fear of finding ourselves in the posture of the bagel baker? Are we not also dying of mortal embarrassment in each other's presence? In a conversation with Bishop Will Herzfeld of the African Evangelical Lutheran Church, an African-American, I unthinkingly used the term "black sheep in the family" when referring to myself and my cousin (his friend), both of us Caucasian. And while I'm sure I will never do that again, in my embarrassment, have I withdrawn my breath completely, afraid that I cannot offer myself the gesture that comes with great difficulty to the human community: forgiveness? If we try to deepen the dialogue on gender, heterosexism, ableism, we will need rituals of forgiveness, or we will end up sequestering our souls by trying to do it righteously, exchanging the promise of solidarity for mere cordiality. In human community, we will be hurt; we unknowingly and unwittingly will hurt others. What we seem unable to remember is how to heal. We seem unable to remember how to create breathing room for the contours of mortal life, for the likes of us humans. The Orthodox Easter liturgy opens like this: "For the resurrection's sake we will forgive one another everything . . ." Easter as a day of jubilee? It might be easier to part with our possessions than our hurts and our fears.

In those brief hours after horror and hope washed together, Jesus' friends locked themselves up in self-righteous indignation that one so just should be so unmercifully murdered. He had embodied a living, realistic hope for the liberation of peoples from crushing political power. However, if it's true that they were together trying to grieve this irredeemable loss, then it's equally true that they secluded themselves for reasons of their own feelings of guilt and complicity. Can't you imagine them rehearsing each of their own gestures, ever wondering if some one of their actions could have forestalled tragedy? Locked up in fear and guilt, all stewing together, they slammed the doors on life. Perhaps it was with good reason. Nonetheless, they were caught withdrawing their breath, holding back on their passion for life, and withholding their bodies from communion with all beings.

Unbelievable! In these wee hours after horror, there appears one further holy terror. By dynamics they never would have chosen, these friends of Jesus are going to have to deal with their martyred brother face-to-face. Now if it were not horror enough to recognize one's own complicity in putting the Spirit of Life to death, they are haunted by the presence of Him who they had ever so slightly hoped would not show His face around there again, Him in whose presence they were mortally embarrassed. Unbelievable, almost.

The ecstatic Presence of Spirit. There, in its embrace, they are held in that moment of self-incrimination, in that moment before the soul moves to despair or to vengeance. There, in those horrendous contradictions, the countenance of God countenances humanity and breathes peace without a backbite of cynicism. There and then, Spirit breathes in them, inspires them, folds them back into the flesh, and holds out to them a hope fit for the living. Mind you: It's not a hope fit to the grand schemes of the mind (which sees so omnipotently in hindsight and with such idealistic foresight). No, this is a living hope all the more powerful because it is fit for the flesh, contoured to the corporeal. Enfolded in compassionate presence, in full accountability for the wounds against the Spirit of Life, they are kissed with peace, embraced until they feel again the quickening of that passion for life deep in their bones. Their flesh now feels all new, and, encouraged, they are able to work the redemptive gestures of binding themselves together across the realities of fear and hurt. The All-Embracing Presence of Spirit provided the sanctuary in which they could rehabituate themselves into human community. Then, as surely as Israel had been led on an exodus from slavery by Shekinah-Spirit's protective presence, the disciples, overshadowed by the palpable nearness of the Divine, are led from their seclusion into the Pentecostal community of the nations.

In this Easter kiss of peace and forgiveness, Divine Spirit renews its passion for mortal life. We are invited to fall in love with the mortal frame, and invited to renew our worldly compassion. Here in the ecstatic embrace and simple kiss of peace, the power of spirit encourages flesh to do what was unthinkable: to open out life beyond the reality of fear and tragedy and hurt. Resurrection: the present and communal exodus of God's people. Coming out of seclusion, we are given only one key to retain community with each other: the forgiveness of sins, which makes mortal life possible because it gives us breathing room.

I asked my eight-year-old philosopher what difference forgiveness made, a ritual now so regular between us, it seems to me, that it has grown perfunctory. She, dressed down with the attitude of an eight-year-old, hits me with profound simplicity: "Duh! If we didn't forgive, we'd be separate; and you would not feel like lying down beside me at night while I fell asleep." Could it be that the keys to the communion of being are anything so simpleminded as forgiveness, which packs no deterrent force and has no hard posture of resistance?

Today we stand in the midst of God's wounded body, the earth. It does not take any stretch of the imagination to touch the wounds. The fact of our power over the ecosystem is Good Friday horror; we can kill the spirit of life. Truly we prefer the untrammeled wilderness. The haunting on this second Sunday of Easter rather suggests that the All-Embracing Nearness of God persists even here at these wounded sites. Dare we wait beside these ecological graves, where we must come face-to-face with the scars of our entanglement?

Soon after I became disabled three years ago, I began to visit the Raptor Center, sanctuaried on the edges of Jersey's Great Swamp. Birds injured in their encounters with the human community—pesticides, oil spills, electrical wires—recuperate here. I greet them. "Teach me," I say. "We are all winged here. Teach me the resurrection of the body, the love of life." Admittedly I had not expected any great reply; they had no reason to countenance one of the human race. Nevertheless I moved around to admire them: the incredible six-foot wingspan of the golden eagle, spinning its feathers in the sunlight; the white puff of a snowy owl, now vesting with its summer herringbone suit. Amazingly it has resurrected enough love of life to foster-parent two orphans. Then I move on to the barred owl, whose divergent eyes gaze past me, seemingly oblivious to my presence. I scrutinize its eyelids, which fall like exaggerated monastic hoods, then move on. Something eerily follows me; I turn back. The owl stares straight ahead, its hoods rhythmically failing and being pushed back from its full moons. *Hmm.* I again turn to move on, only this time in a game of peek-a-boo I catch those arched eyebrows craning around the wind shelter. Its body leaning forward, it peers after me. I've been hoodwinked! "Hey, Jeff," I call to my partner, moving my discomfort with the real presence of this life to mine, into discomfort in the philosophical abstract, "Do you think nature is interested in us?"

In our time of ecological crisis, when the spirit of life of these little ones has been injured by our human community, I take that act of curiosity as a "kiss of peace." Hoodwinked by the Spirit of Life, I find my own flesh exhilarated. The mercy of mutual attention, the key for entering back into communion. The key to the resurrection of life.

Yes, "for the resurrection's sake, let us forgive one another everything."

THE REVEREND DR. SHARON V. BETCHER *is an ordained pastor of the Evangelical Lutheran Church in America and an adjunct professor in the area of ecotheology at the Theological School of Drew University. She received her Ph.D. from Drew with a dissertation entitled* Getting Grounded: Spirit Incarnate and the Kindling of Livelihood, *an attempt to voice a feminist and ecological pneumatology. She is affiliated with the Church of the Redeemer in Morristown, New Jersey, where she lives with her husband and their adopted Korean daughter.*

JEAN SHINODA BOLEN, M.D.

Mother Wisdom, Mother Earth, Mother God

On the Divine Feminine

I AM privileged and awed by the opportunity to speak from the pulpit of this great cathedral, which has been my home church since I was a medical student and came to pray in the tiny wooden chapel on California Street that was wedged between the sidewalk and the cathedral wall. Here in the main sanctuary, I was married. Here my two children, Melody and Andre, were baptized. And here, today, on this Mother's Day, I invoke thoughts about Our Mother who art the Earth.

On Mother's Day, it is fitting to recall the maternal aspect of divinity, the feminine face of God, that has been missing, especially from our Protestant experience. It is fitting to wonder if we are in a liminal or threshold time, when the archetype of the sacred Mother, the Sophia of the Gnostic Christians, is returning in a new form.

On Mother's Day, it is fitting to think of how being pregnant and giving birth to a child is a transformative experience at the body and soul level. It was a profound initiation that I shared with every woman through time who has ever birthed a child. In the experience I, as an individual, was irrelevant as a vessel for new life. I was an extension of the fertility of Mother Earth, through which every living thing is born. I was unprepared to find that it was a mystical experience, a means through which I would be initiated into the mystery of the mother goddess, who comes, especially to women, through embodied sacred experiences. Mother wisdom comes through the surrender that pregnancy, labor, and delivery requires. It is a wisdom that teaches us to cooperate with Nature to seek to know her, rather than oppose or attempt to control her. It is a wisdom that accepts that there are seasons and cycles. It is a wisdom about time, that is so well expressed in Ecclesiastes.

Everyone incarnates through the body of a personal mother. As spiritual beings on a human path, we begin life this way. In the uterus, we were attached to her through a placenta that fed us, so every pregnant mother enacts the communion words "Take, eat, this is my body; drink, this is my blood" as literal truth. If we were nursed, this continued into infancy, for breast milk is made out of the body and blood of the mother. We have an inchoate memory, an imprint, of when we were one with our mother. Just as Mother existed before we had words, and the memory of her becomes part of the forgotten past of our first years of existence, so has the presence of a divine Mother been a lost part of prehistoric human memory.

As we approach a new millennium, this feminine aspect of divinity is emerging once more into awareness. Goddess archetypes have come into psychology, goddess sites have become unearthed in archeology, and the gender of God is a theological issue. Images of a divine feminine are emerging in the dreams of ordinary people, and in the creative expression of artists, especially women. It would seem that the goddess—as the sacred feminine—is coming into human consciousness now, through the embodied and subjective experience of individual men and women.

As we approach a new millennium, science and technology have given us the means to destroy life on the planet through the use of nuclear warheads. But through the Apollo space mission and the Russian equivalent, science and technology have also provided the means to see planet Earth from outer space. We have secular knowledge and power that humans never grasped before.

The photograph of the Earth taken from outer space may be the most significant image in the evolution of human consciousness in the twentieth century. Through the vision of the Apollo astronauts, we saw the Earth as a breathtakingly beautiful sphere contrasted against a sea of blackness: a sunlit ocean-blue globe with swirls of white clouds and glimpses of continents. This is our Mother the Earth who nourishes and sustains us from her body, and holds us to her with gravity. We breathe her, we eat her, we drink her, and we become part of her when we die. Several astronauts, on seeing the Earth from outer space, were spiritually transformed as they looked upon the Earth. Awe and beauty and grace came together in a moment of gnosis. This image of the Earth touched the heart; we saw our Mother for the first time, and she was gorgeous. There she was, full of life, in the midst of the lonely void of space, with nuclear weapons of destruction in the hands of her irresponsible human children. It was this image that initiated us into planetary consciousness and, I believe, made it possible for nations with nuclear weapons to begin to behave like responsible adults.

This new awareness of Mother Earth parallels shifts in awareness of our personal mother. Until we gain some distance from our own mother, we cannot see her at all. For the infant, mother is food, warmth, and comfort or the absence of it. She is the environment. The child and the adolescent see the personal mother more distinctly than the infant does, but not by much. She is still experienced in relationship to our needs, which become more psy-

chological as we grow older. This remains so for adults who continue to see and react to their mothers from the child-places in
their psyches.

We respond as an adult only when we can see our mother as
she is, separate from us, and separated from our needs and expectations of her. We love her with an adult heart only when we accept who she is, appreciate her as she is, and love her regardless
of her flaws. To be an adult is not a matter of chronological age,
not a matter of being eighteen, or twenty-one, or forty. It requires
spiritual growth to be an adult: the development of compassion;
the capacity to forgive; the knowledge of gratitude, remorse, and
humility; the awareness of our own imperfections as well as those
of others. It also requires psychological growth to be an adult: accepting responsibilities, developing social and moral consciousness,
and taking a stand where it matters.

Not until we saw the image of Earth from outer space was it
possible for humankind to have an adult response to Mother Earth.
Until then, she was a taken-for-granted environment, a Mother toward whom we had no ties of responsibility. With planetary consciousness came awareness of the devastating ecological consequences
of our technology and competitiveness and of our aggression and
misuse of nuclear energy. Ecology has as its root *eco,* or home; *ecology* means understanding home. Earth is both Home and Mother.
If humanity enters adulthood, might there be hope for a convenant
between humankind and Earth, to care for each other? Might we
come to appreciate the sacredness of the Earth, and might this prevent the Earth from becoming a wasteland? This is a hope.

The Grail legend tells us of the wounded Fisher King whose
kingdom is a wasteland. Nothing grows in the wasteland; there is
no greenness, no creativity, no sensuality, no new life, no joy. It is
a spiritual metaphor and a potential planetary reality. The wounded
king can be a personal symbol for men and women who seek
power and prestige and who live in an emotional wasteland of depression, addictions, anger, or meaninglessness. The wounded king

is also a patriarchal symbol related to the acquisition of power and domination of others.

In the legend, only the Grail can heal the wounded king, and only if his wound is healed will the wasteland be restored. For this to happen, an innocent or a fool must enter the castle, see the wounded king and the Grail, and ask two questions. In the first and most famous version of the story, the innocent knight is Perceval, who saw the wound and the Grail but who, because he feared to appear ignorant, didn't ask the questions which would have healed the king and restored the wasteland.

When he saw the wounded king, Perceval failed to ask "What ails thee?" Before healing of any kind can take place, the problem and pain need to be acknowledged. Whether the story applies to our personal lives or to the culture in which we live, we need to ask and find the answer to the question "What is the matter?" or, restated, "What is it that makes our internal landscape or the external world a wasteland?"

When he saw the Grail, Perceval failed to ask the second question: "Whom does the Grail serve?" Most of us at one time or another have had a Grail experience—a numinous, awesome, or wondrous moment of connection or communion—which can transform us, but only if we seek to know "What is the meaning of this sacred experience?" or "How will this change me?"

When we feel one with nature and know we have a place in the universe, or when we participate in the sacrament of communion and are filled with grace, it is a Grail experience. When we have a mystical or sacramental moment that heals us and we are no longer cut off from the divinity within us and the divinity that exists around us, it is a Grail experience.

The Grail that could heal the king and restore the wasteland is often thought of as the chalice that was filled with wine and used by Jesus at the Last Supper, over which he said, "This is my blood." The Grail in this context is a symbol of Christ. But, a chalice or vessel is a feminine symbol, and in every version of the

Grail legend, it is always carried by a woman. Might this symbol of the sacred feminine or goddess be the Grail that needs to return to the culture for the wounded patriarchy to be healed?

On Mother's Day, it is good to remember the many forms and embodiments of the sacred feminine: our personal mothers, surrogate mothers, Mother Church, Mother Nature, and Mother Earth. It is good to recall the individuals who, for a time, mothered us, nourished our bodies, fed our souls, and loved us—and the environment that grounds us and gives us our home. And it is with reverence and appreciation that on this Mother's Day, in Grace Cathedral, I speak from the pulpit about feminine divinity, about Mother God.

JEAN SHINODA BOLEN, M.D., *is an internationally known Jungian analyst and author of* Goddesses in Everywoman *and* Gods in Everyman. *She has also authored* The Tao of Psychology, Ring of Power, Crossing to Avalon *and* Close to the Bone: Life-Threatening Illness and the Search for Meaning. *She is a clinical professor of psychiatry at the University of California Medical Center in San Francisco and a fellow of the American Psychiatric Association and the American Academy of Psychoanalysis. She is currently at work on* Goddesses in Older Women *and* The Millionth Circle: How to Change Ourselves and the World. *She lives in the San Francisco Bay area.*

THE REVEREND MARIAH BRITTON

Making a Wise Investment

On Values

ECCLESIASTES 1:2, 12–14; 2:18–21, 23; LUKE 12:13–21

THE Ecclesiastical writer, known as the Qoheleth or the Preacher, is rooted in the wisdom tradition of ancient Israel. The sages of the past looked at people, watched what happened in human interaction, and tried to draw some conclusions, solid truths about human existence. You know, if you stick around long enough, most things in human exchange that go around, come around. What's true in human deportment for today might not be true tomorrow. But the wise teacher was duty bound to make the call, to tell it like it is, so to speak. The Ecclesiastical writer attempts to share observations from life experiences that offer practical knowledge of laws concerning the world; he endeavors to master reality for the sake of human survival and well-being. He presents words that help the listener to cope with the inconsistencies of life, and he offers sug-

gestions for a right word or a right action for the present condition.

If you read through Ecclesiastes, you will find some startling
and unsettling observations about life. The writer repeatedly suggests that life is vanity. All is vanity. Vanity, in the context of
Ecclesiastes, means something that lacks substance or longevity;
something that is so flimsy it disappears, much like the breath that
leaves your body and disappears into thin air. In fact, some trans-
lations say, "Vapors! All is Vapors." It suggests you can't hold on
to anything because nothing endures.

The writer observes there was nothing he could do in life that
would leave a definite mark, a residue, the slightest suggestions that
his life had lasting value. Nothing in the brief life of humans—not
accumulation of wealth, not fame—lasted beyond that life. All that
you acquire will be left for someone else to enjoy or to squander
foolishly while you get nothing for all your toil and labor. All your
days are full of pain. Even at night you do not rest. It is an unhappy business that God has given human beings to be busy with.
All is Vanity, a chasing after wind.

The writer would say to you today that your house is vanity,
your education is vanity, your car is vanity, your art collection is
vanity, your artistic endeavors are vanity. All is vanity, vapors,
empty, puffs of smoke.

The writer has some serious blues. You think some of the rap-
pers of this day paint a bleak picture of the world? Read
Ecclesiastes; it really gives you cause to shake your head and moan.
I hear his words like a Mississippi blues man on the docks of a
mud-slung river.

> *I searched for wisdom but the girl done showed up wrong*
> *Said I searched for wisdom, but the girl done showed up wrong*
> *She give me mighty fearful contusions*
> *Make me toss all night long.*

I mean, at first glimpse this stuff is bleak, makes you wanna holler, throw up both your hands, pack it in and give it up. If you want to get some hint of who this writer is, you've got to read between the lines. Perhaps the writer was an older person, disillusioned by the accomplishments of his (it was a male) life, because he spoke often about enjoying youth. Or maybe the writer had amassed great wealth but it was an empty accomplishment for it gave him no peace. Maybe the writer was unsuccessful in romance because bitter remarks about women reflect that he may have had some unfortunate experiences with them. Or maybe the writer was disappointed in his relationship with God, for there seems to be little said about the sovereignty of a God who is faithful, a God who will redeem humanity.

The writer says, "Vanity, all is vanity!"

The Ecclesiastical writer's life seems to lurk at the edges of the light—you know, the places where shadow begins to creep in the divide creating lacy fringes of despair and hope. A time to be born and a time to die; a time to love and a time to hate; a time to kill and a time to heal; a time to weep and a time to laugh; a time to mourn and a time to dance; a time to embrace and a time to refrain from embracing. You've heard the wisdom of one who has observed much in human history. The writer rummages in the room of the questions that will not keep still or silent, questions that persist even in the sweetest kiss (will he love me tomorrow?) or in the moment of victory (who will best me?) or when you make an A on the exam (will I be able to do it again?). The writer takes residence in that twilight zone of human existence.

But all is not unstable or bleak, for the writer does eventually suggest a few things that offer some comfort. He says, There is nothing better for mortals to do than to eat, drink, and find enjoyment in their toil, for tomorrow is not promised. He recommends that humans live fully in the moment because now is all you really can enjoy.

There is some wisdom in the writer's observations, but thanks be to God that the Ecclesiastical writer does not have the final say. For there was a man from Galilee who was full of wisdom and grace, who opened a wide realm of possibility. There was one who went to the dark regions of the soul and brought back a light of faith.

You've heard the story of the rich fool. He thought he had it all—enough to fill many new barns—and he looked forward to a life of considerable ease. But his life was cut short.

It may seem that God was unjust to demand the rich man's life at precisely the moment when he was achieving his life's ambition. Such an unfortunate event brings to mind the very question the Ecclesiastical writer raises—What good is toil and gaining wealth when it's the people who survive you who enjoy it?

But if we examine the text, we learn that it was the land of the rich man that gave abundantly. He had a bumper crop that year; he had a great reaping, which was not all his doing. The earth is the Lord's and the fullness thereof, so some recognition of the gift of God was in order.

The rich man is often characterized as one with lustful ambition seeking only to provide for himself. It seems he neglected to recognize the needs of others. Rather than sharing his abundance, he chose to build bigger barns for himself so he could rest at ease. He chose to believe his wealth would bring his soul peace.

The rich man's problem was greed, plain and simple, and Jesus used this parable to teach us not to be rich in things but to be rich in God.

Investment advice in the parable is to recognize that the things of God are more important than material wealth. Investment advice in Ecclesiastes is to enjoy the life you have and to enjoy your work. What do you trust in? That's the question wisdom asks. In what do you place your confidence? What's reliable? What can stand the test of time? In what is your life vested?

Maybe you buy lottery tickets. I'm not sure about you, but I know there were a few times this week when I wished I could make my way to get one of those Power Ball tickets. The possibility of instant wealth, or even gradual wealth, is an attractive prospect. The seduction of winning is quite alluring when a quarter of a billion dollars is the prize, even at odds of 80 million to one. Given the combination of the average American salary and a maddening culture of blistering consumerism, investment in a lottery ticket seems wise.

You might invest in the stock market, which has enjoyed an unusually long run of growth and increase. But the experts look at the Dow Jones, NASDAQ, and the unsettled dust of the economic problems in Asia and they declare that the market may be at the last stages of a bull market and they may be heading toward a bear market. Do you maintain? Do you sell or do you buy? The slightest thing can cause a ripple among investors. And the irony is that it's all so mercurial; the more we invest, the more anxious we can become.

In the midst of such uncertainty, what can you trust that will hold out through generations? Jesus gives us a hint: Don't be a fool. You know what a fool is? One who does not learn from life, one who does not learn from experience, one who denies God's activity in the world.

Seek wisdom but do not be so earthbound in wisdom as to miss the transcendence of life. The Ecclesiastical writer did not understand that all we do is moving toward something other than ourselves—our life's work is connected to what has been before us just as the work of our children will be related to what we have done in this age.

Each generation tests truths acquired by previous ones, discarding whatever contradicts present experience. And each generation's heart works are nurtured by the society who cared for them—for good or for bad.

And so it would seem that the true investment, the wise investment in life, is not in our labor for bread, shelter, and clothes—

the wise investment is in building honest, loving relationships with one another. These are the riches of God. Yeah, it's that love thing.

I learned this again last Wednesday when I sat listening to the many people who spoke at the memorial service for Dr. Carl Fields, a distinguished member of this congregation. What people remembered was that he cared about them; he took time to be of assistance; he had an incomparable will to help people identify their life goals and to move toward them. To me, those are the riches in God that Jesus talked about. Not anything you own now—or will ever own—will make any difference in life if it is only with yourself and your clan that you share it.

A wise investment is characterized by what you do in light of the teachings of Christ. A songwriter put it this way—Only what you do for Christ will last.

You've got to take a hard look in the mirror and ask yourself, "Is there any more I could be doing to strengthen the love in my life?" I don't mean just your lover or spouse or children or kin but neighbor and stranger as well.

When you are besieged by the encroaching shadows of doubt about the value of your life, let me give you this insider tip: *Invest considerable portions of the wealth of your time toward building loving relationships with others.*

The bit of wisdom the Ecclesiastical writer missed is that the life lived sharing the riches of God's love moves ceaselessly through all generations.

> I am a witness, the strength of my life flowed
> through my parents' parents.
> The strength of my life is encouraged by my sib-
> lings.
> The strength of my life is encouraged by relatives
> and friends.

The strength of my life is encouraged by co-workers
and colleagues.
And because I know I am lifted by their love I can
take time to share with someone else who might
make the day easier for another.

There's only one reason that this New York project kid is here
before you today. Somebody invested time and care in me; invested
time and care to listen and respond. And when my eyes close
never to open again, I trust—in the one who holds all life, all time,
all things—that my living shall not have been in vain.

So I say to you, my sisters, my brothers, my family in Christ:
Gain all the wisdom you can, but in life make a wise investment.

THE REVEREND MARIAH BAPTIST BRITTON *is an or-
dained minister serving as Associate Minister to Youth at the Riverside
Church in New York City. A writer and poet, she served as Writer-in-
Residence at Adam Clayton Powell, Jr., Junior High School in Harlem. Her
work has appeared in* Essence *magazine,* New City Voices, Earthwise,
and other publications. Editor in chief of the anthology Long Journey
Home, *she was selected to attend the International Poetry Festival in Acieali,
Italy. She received her M.Div. from Union Theological Seminary and an
M.A. in Creative Writing from the City College of New York. Britton is
pursuing a Ph.D. in Marriage, Family, and Human Sexuality at New York
University.*

Going Fishing

On Community

LUKE 5:1–11

S a longtime subscriber to *The New Yorker* magazine, I thought my name and address had already been given to every mail-order business in God's creation, but a recent change of address assures me this was not the case. Along with other new catalogs our household inherited from the previous residents is one on fly fishing. Curiosity may have killed the cat, but it is a virtue in a preacher, so I opened the pages to explore the unfamiliar world of fly fishing. Our British friends call it angling. It was amazing to discover the specialization of the items offered for sale. There were lines of particular weights and colors depending on what species you were angling for. And there were hundreds of flies. For those of you who need plain speaking in this area, as I do, flies are fake bait used to attract the fish. It was hard for me to see the difference between many of them, but apparently the fish can, and again one uses different kinds of flies depending on whether one is out to catch bass or salmon or trout. It seemed clear from this catalog that in fly fishing one does not just go out willy-nilly to catch any old fish, but to catch a particular type of fish.

By now, you may be wondering what on earth fly fishing has to do with the gospel. And the answer is, absolutely nothing at all. Because Jesus' example of fishing is the absolute opposite of angling for one kind of fish. Jesus uses a net, and a net catches a little bit of everything. It is a messy business. These days we worry about the dolphins among our tuna fish, because there is some evidence that dolphins are smarter than we are, but other fish get netted with the tuna, too. In our gospel story this morning, Jews cast their net in the lake of Genesaret, another name for the Sea of Galilee, and there they would have caught, among the other fish, catfish and eels, which their culture taught were unclean. What a mess the abundance of Jesus' miracle made! The nets so . . . undiscriminating, full of clean and unclean, smelling more than a little fishy, and so full that they threatened to sink the boats.

The Church has sometimes tried to ignore or even censor the diversity in Christ's net. You may have been astonished to hear in this morning's epistle, for example, that when Paul recites the story of the appearances of the Risen Christ, passing the story along as he says it was told to him, there is no mention of the appearance to Mary Magdalene and the women! Paul's account begins with the appearance to Cephas, or Peter.

Despite such censorship, the evidence for diversity is never far from us. If you don't believe that Jesus fishes with a net and not a rod and reel, just look in the pews around you. At least a few of us in the congregation are small fry, caught in the middle of the net surrounded by larger fish. Some of us are flying fish, flashy performers who show God's glory for all to see. Some of us are very old and gray and have swum the great depths that life has to offer. Some of us are catfish, scavenging for God's realm, and helping to keep the waters clear. Some are eels who dart through a few times a year, afraid to stay here for long. Some are kind and gentle dolphins, playful companions. Some are sardines wondering how to commit ourselves to Christ's work when we labor so hard just to avoid being eaten. Some of us don't even feel alive enough to qualify as fish right now, more like seaweed thrown in for flavor. There are turtles who are shy and slow, but determined. And yes, a few of us are sharks, darting around scaring the others. The community will have to decide whether to throw us out or cherish us as an endangered species that adds a certain excitement to the mix. Yes, fishing with a net makes for a wonderful mess.

By now, it is only fair to confess to you that this sermon is about evangelism and discipleship. I have waited as long as I could, because even in this decade of evangelism, we Episcopalians are put off by that word. It smacks of doorbells interrupting a leisurely Saturday breakfast. Well, I think the gospel tells us evangelism done with the inclusive net of Jesus does indeed interrupt the status quo. You end up with this mess of fish, you have no idea what you will do with all of them, there is not enough help to bring them in, and the boats are in danger of sinking. I read last week that one local high school has identified students from sixty-five countries in its student body. That is just one kind of diversity we risk by net-fishing in these parts. We Anglicans are often more comfortable with angling. In searching for a ministry I saw statements from one church after another that wanted a priest who would help them attract more young couples with families and more young professionals. As it happens, we are a church in the inner city without children living in the neighborhood, and so it is appropriate for us to be concerned about how to be hospitable to children if we are to be the "mixed catch" that the Body of Christ is intended to be. But surely that cannot be the case in every church in the country. Where, in the want ads of our churches, are the ones who want a priest who can help attract more wise elders to the congregation, or more single parents, or more people who have been alienated from church? Where are the churches that simply want to attract more sinners into the waters of baptism and the net of Christ's redeeming grace and love?

Now I have said that this sermon was also about discipleship, and that is because Luke's story of Jesus and the nets shows that the disciples are caught in the net, too. The fact that they are caught on the holding end of the net is beside the point. They are just as caught in Christ's net as the fish are. Jesus calls them the way God has called people throughout history—at their daily life and work. In today's three readings, God called Gideon threshing wheat, God called Paul through Paul's work of persecuting Christians under the Jewish law, and God calls Peter, James, and John as they are cleaning and mending nets after an unsuccessful night of fishing. What does Peter have that God can use? A boat to teach from. Some nets for a miracle. The discipline of hard work. A habit of hopefulness gained from fishing, a work where there are good days and bad days, and it is not always skill that makes the difference. All those things from Peter's daily life became important to his following Christ. "Do not be afraid," Jesus tells him. From now on, you work for me.

Our daily lives can flow into our discipleship, too. One morning I arrived at five-thirty at National Airport weary and filled with dread at the beginning of a long business trip. When the parking shuttle bus was loaded, the driver's mellow, joyful voice came over the loudspeaker. "Welcome to the sunrise special," she said. "It will be my privilege to drive you safety to your airline destination, and I hope you will enjoy seeing dawn at the water's edge along the way."

That woman's greeting to a group of strangers changed my whole week. As I noticed the cross around her neck, I thought, "I get it. She is not just working for the airport. She works for the building up of the community of God. So do I."

And so do you. With such a great catch of fish, all hands are needed. The disciples must be as diverse as the catch. Each one of us has something God wants to use. If not a boat or a bus, then

maybe it is a computer or an oven, a drafting table or a bank account, a wrench or a broom, a paintbrush or a musical instrument.
Or perhaps God most needs the attitudes and habits we have cul-
tivated through our daily life and work: our quality of patience, or
cunning, or compassion, or tolerance for noise, or the ability to do
many things at once. This very week, God will interrupt our
daily routine to call us again to discipleship. Let us not be afraid.
From now on, we work for the one who cast a wide net, and has
caught us all.

*THE REVEREND ELIZABETH CARL is an Episcopal priest in
Washington, D.C. Her early interest in sermons arose from sitting in the children's choir behind the pulpit and watching the preacher's knees knock. She
emerged as a preacher through training with the Reverend Dr. James A.
Forbes, Jr., the Reverend Barbara Lundblad, and classmates at Union
Theological Seminary in New York City. She continues to be formed by reflection with those to whom she preaches. She is a member of the Associate
Faculty of the College of Preachers, D.C. Habitat for Humanity, Integrity,
and the Board of Directors of Union Theological Seminary.*

I am indebted to the Reverend Katharine Rhodes Henderson's sermon "Bound Up Together
in a Call of Love," preached April 4, 1990, for the image of a congregation as different
kinds of fish.

THE REVEREND MARY LYNNETTE DELBRIDGE

She's in My Face

On Advocacy

MATTHEW 15:21-28

T HE story we just read about Jesus and the Canaanite woman in Matthew 15 certainly isn't on my list of top-ten gospel favorites. It's an unabashedly "in-your-face" story. I'm uncomfortable with the picture it gives us of Jesus calling that Canaanite woman a dog. At best, he comes across as a man caught off guard, as a man struggling to figure out whether his ministry is large enough to include non-Jews. At worst, he comes across as an insulting bigot.

I'm also uncomfortable when I hear or read this story because whether the real, historical Jesus insulted the woman or not, the insult reflects something very true about the people of the early Jesus movement, people who are my spiritual forebears. I'm not very proud of what I see, either. Loving Jesus did not immunize his followers against feelings of mistrust, against ethnic prejudice, or against the desire to exclude others. The story of the Canaanite woman gives me a glimpse of the struggle that went on in the early church. I can see the stonewalling. I can hear the whispering, the nasty words that must have been flung back and forth as Jesus' original followers came to grips with the persistent Gentiles in their midst. I can almost smell their discomfort as they struggled with the implications of God's all-embracing love.

But finally, and most important for me, I am uncomfortable with this story not because of Jesus' behavior or the behavior of his disciples in the early Jesus movement. I'm uncomfortable with the Canaanite woman. You see, I've been trained since way back when in Baptist Sunday school to look for the hero in a Bible story. And once that hero is found, well, I'm supposed to go and do likewise: like the Good Samaritan who cared for the wounded traveler; like Paul who kept preaching the gospel even when he got beaten or thrown into prison; like Lydia who welcomed, fed, and housed traveling apostles.

And who's the hero in this story that I'm supposed to emulate? Well, it's not Jesus. And it's certainly not the disciples! The hero in this story is the Canaanite woman, and she won't get out of my face any more than she would get out of Jesus' face. You see, she is an advocate to beat all advocates. And it's her persistent advocacy on behalf of her daughter that makes me uncomfortable.

She persists when Jesus stonewalls her and ignores her cry, "Lord, Son of David, have mercy on me. My daughter has a demon."

She persists when the embarrassed disciples make it abundantly clear that she is not welcome and they try to get rid of her.

She persists when Jesus tells the disciples, perhaps just loudly enough for her to overhear, that he has only come for the lost sheep of Israel.

She persists when Jesus insults her to her face, when he calls her a dog.

She persists until her persistence and her words shake Jesus, until they shame Jesus into claiming the best part of himself and the best he knows of God. She persists until Jesus changes his mind. She persists until she gets what she wants, health and wholeness for the daughter she loves.

And so I wonder. Can I, can we, go and do likewise? I listen to her loud, insistent cries. She is hardly the polite southern lady I've been socialized to be. I watch her falling down before Jesus, and I cringe to think of myself shamelessly kneeling to beg at the feet of some man. I hear her quick retort that moves Jesus to re-think, to face and then let go of his prejudice. (Introvert that I am, I never think of the right thing to say until the words of a heated exchange have long settled into silence.)

No, I think sadly; I feel defeated by this woman who stays in my face with her example. I could never throw myself with such abandon at the feet of a Mayor Giuliani or a Governor Pataki. I would hate groveling before some powerful doctor or school offi-cial. And I really can't imagine myself falling at the feet of an itin-erant evangelist traveling through town just because he has a reputation for healing miracles. I would hate letting people like that insult me. I would do any and everything within my own power to help someone else first before begging a more powerful person to do the job for me.

I am ready to walk away from this Canaanite woman, but she persists even now. She is in my face. "No," she sternly says, "come back here. I'm not going to let you off so easily. I'm no un-approachable hero. I'm going to stay in your face until you stop making excuses for yourself, until you begin to look beyond dra-matic miracles for all the ways God does bless the advocacy that takes place around you. It's not impossible."

"Okay, okay," I say, "I'm listening."

"Well, let's start off with your sister, Catherine, and your niece, Elizabeth. Elizabeth has a brain that almost travels faster

than the speed of light, way, way faster than most other brains living in seventh-grade bodies. When she gets bored in class, she either withdraws in depression or she acts out and makes sarcastic
remarks to the other students. The other students start thinking
she is strange and different. Elizabeth starts feeling strange and different. So what does your sister, her mother, do? She takes on the
teacher, the principal, and the superintendent of the county school
system to get Elizabeth into a higher math class. And when no one
will listen because moving her up would cause too many schedul-
ing problems, because it might give other gifted children and their
parents uppity ideas, what does your sister do? She keeps on
going. She goes to the local community college where she is told
that they never make exceptions; they never take students under
age fifteen. Does that stop your sister? No, she goes on to the city
schools and finally finds a principal and a superintendent with the
power and the will to help Elizabeth. Elizabeth switches schools.
She is still in the seventh grade, but she goes over to the high
school every day for math. She likes herself. The other students
like her, too."

"Okay," I say, "so my sister advocates for her daughter. But
she's supposed to . . ."

"I'm not finished yet," the Canaanite woman breaks in. "Think
about the people who use the Hundred Twenty-fifth Street subway station. Remember the escalator that didn't work for years and
how old people and people with babies and just plain old tired-
out-from-work people had to climb up all those steps to get to the
train? So what did Betty Bolden and the Harlem Initiatives
Together Chapter here at Union do? They found out who at the
Transit Authority was responsible for the escalator. They made
phone calls; they wrote letters; they persisted until no one was left
at the Transit Authority to pass the buck. Finally, they demon-
strated. They took a Union Chapel service down to the subway
station. They had Jim Forbes preach and pray over those subway
steps, and lo and behold, the next day the escalator was working.

The people who had power at the Transit Authority were finally shamed into remembering that customers in Harlem deserve decent subway service, too."

"Okay, okay, I get the picture," I say. "We all get the picture. Every now and then we manage to advocate for others and miraculously it makes a difference, but . . ."

"But what?"

"But what happens when we can't figure out who has the power to change things and we go shouting after all the wrong people? What happens when we persist, when we research and write letters, when we make phone calls and sign petitions, when we join demonstrations and raise hell and still nothing seems to make a difference? What happens when we just can't seem to find the right words?"

"Now look," the Canaanite woman says, "I never said being an advocate for another person would be an easy job or that you would always have the satisfaction of seeing obvious results. Just ask Melissa: 'Is it easy to advocate for students at Union?' Ask Edwina: 'Is it easy to advocate for the health of this institution by working insistently to get a new academic dean?' Ask Ruth and Paul: 'Is it easy to advocate for gays and lesbians who want to be ordained?' Ask Jill and Anthony: 'Is it easy to help your children grow up in this strange and complex world, to see that they have what they need to be whole and healthy?'

"Nobody says it's easy. Nobody promises that you will always have the wisdom to know who has the power to help you. Nobody promises that you won't get insulted, that you won't get a reputation for being a troublemaker. Nobody promises that you will always have the perfect words to shake and shame the powerful into changing their minds and offering their help."

"So," I say, "if it's not easy, then how did you find the wisdom, the thick skin, the eloquent words? How did you do it? How are we supposed to do it?"

"It really wasn't great wisdom or a thick skin or eloquent

words that made me an effective advocate for my daughter. It was love. I loved my daughter. I loved her desperately. I could feel her pain in my very bones. Love made me into a persistent advocate. Love made me go tearing down the road from Tyre and Sidon to find this Jewish miracle worker I had heard about. Love made me keep on even when Jesus was silent and the disciples wanted to get rid of me. Love made me care enough that Jesus' insult slid right off my back and passionate words came pouring out of my mouth.

"It's love, the same love that made Jesus an advocate for all those tax collectors and sinners. It's the same love that made him heal people on the Sabbath and got him into trouble for it. It's the same love that made Jesus accept ridicule on the cross. It's God-given love that makes you care enough to go and shake the very gates of heaven and hell for someone else. It's love so strong that you know the God who filled you up with it is the same God who will do anything to bring all children health and wholeness. Love, yes, it is God's boundless, powerful love which grants our deepest wishes."

And then this Canaanite woman takes one more parting shot before she temporarily gets out of my face. "Go ahead, my sister," she says. "Pray if you want to for wisdom, so you will know who has the necessary power to help you. Pray for a skin thick enough to deflect the inevitable insults. Go ahead, pray for words fast enough and eloquent enough to shame people out of their preju- dices. But most of all, yes, most of all and always, pray to be filled with God's love."

THE REVEREND MARY LYNNETTE DELBRIDGE *is an ordained minister in the Moravian Church in America and assistant professor of New Testament at the America Baptist Seminary of the West in Berkeley, California. She is currently completing her Ph.D. at Union Theological Seminary where she served as a teaching assistant in New Testament and Homiletics. Her current research focuses upon the relationship between early Christianity and the Greco-Roman household, especially as it is portrayed in the Pastoral Epistles. Her passions include music, worship, and advocacy for children. A native of North Carolina, she is married to a Moravian minister. They make their home in Oakland, California.*

TERESA DELGADO

Calling All Wild Women

On Wilderness

LUKE 4:1–15

I FIRST want to express my gratitude to the women being commissioned this evening for giving me the honor of sharing this ritual event with you. It hasn't been an easy journey to this point; as one who has traveled this path, I know it is fraught with fear, anxiety, and apprehension, even amidst the anticipation of what lies ahead. With hopes of easing some of that anxiety, I invited the women we are honoring today to meet at my home a few weeks ago to share our feelings about this moment of transition in our lives; the sense of utter uncertainty, of awesome responsibility, and even of deep solitude. And when, during our time together, I asked these women to think of a text that embodied their feelings, without exception each woman was led to the gospel text we had just heard: "Jesus in the wilderness," sometimes referred to as "Jesus' temptation in the desert."

As I was privileged with the awesome task of preparing a homily on this text, I thought about it, I read about it, and perhaps since I am no biblical scholar nor versed in homiletic technique, my mind kept going back to an old story told to me by one of the women in my family. It was a story about a woman, in Puerto Rico, who during the Lenten season would go "on strike." She did the bare minimum to maintain the well-being of her five children, but no more. Most days, the folks would see her in her garden working or just sitting, her children fluttering around her in their own world, her husband in front of the TV with a beer and leftovers, wondering whether forty days could be accelerated this year for his benefit. And every Easter Sunday, she emerged from her annual ritual different somehow, or so the story goes. I remember the storyteller saying that this woman acted as if she had come out of a trance but was still very aware of herself and everything around her.

Putting aside all the criticism accompanying the story—how could a mother do that to her children, a wife to her husband, a Latina no less—I remember admiring that woman. I understood her even more when I was pregnant with my two daughters, Francesca and Celeste: the hunger, heartburn, nausea, and fatigue. I understood these physical conditions as a cleansing taking place by the fact that I was now set apart and marked by the role to come. In preparation for my calling as a mother, not knowing how that role would take shape or if I really wanted to go through with it at times, I would often retreat into myself for a blessing, an affirmation that what I was doing—what my body was doing—was my most true self in action.

So, what does this have to do with Jesus in the wilderness, of all places? What could a story about a weird woman's Lenten ritual, or my pregnancies for that matter, have to say about commissioning, about sending forth into ministry? Let me ask you to indulge me in an exercise. If you like, I ask that you close your eyes for a moment and see what comes to mind when you think of the wilderness. What specific images does that word convey? Notice the terrain, the physical environment, the sounds, and the degrees of light and dark. But also be aware of how this space/place in your mind's eye makes you feel in your body. Does it frighten you, the way a child is frightened when awakened in the middle of the night to complete darkness? Does it put you on the defensive, ready to go on the attack? Does it put you at ease, at peace with yourself?

And as you open your eyes, I ask that you keep this image with you. For me, the reason I go back to the story of the woman on strike, and even to my pregnancies, is that these are wilderness experiences not unlike the story of Jesus in the wilderness. His story, and mine, is about what happens in the wilderness places of our lives, places where we are called to be "wild." I do not understand "wild" in the pejorative sense that we have become accustomed to associate with this word, but as a natural place where we can live in a close-to-natural state; free from fear, anxiety, and apprehension, as well as free to be creative, at peace, strong willed, transformed. I know that this is the wilderness to which Jesus was led, and it is where the Spirit leads us. I believe that the wilderness is a good place because I cannot believe in a God who would lead me to a place of brokenness, pain, and fear. The Spirit of God in whom I believe leads me to places of healing, as my pregnancies and the miraculous children who emerged have been for me, as these stories (like the one I referred to earlier) have been in Puerto Rican culture. And we are led into the wilderness by the Spirit to be healed and to be prepared to take on our role as agents of healing in the world.

The wilderness, then, is a place of becoming whole; of becoming conscious of who we are, even if we are unsure of how we should live out our truest self day to day. The wilderness, then, is anything but frightening, because it is where we can be transformed into the conscious agents God intends us to be.

For the women who are being sent forth into their respective ministries, this biblical text can draw many poignant parallels.

These forty days in the desert were the transition toward Jesus' public ministry, and in many ways Union Theological Seminary, has been a desert for Roman Catholic women in a predominantly Protestant environment. Like Jesus, you have been tempted to forgo your ministry in exchange for greater wealth . . . God knows you won't get rich in this business! You have been tempted to jump the Roman Catholic ship to be "rescued" by the more modern, more inclusive, more ordaining Protestants . . . and with more opportunities to preach, at the very least!

Jesus' experience in preparation for ministry as teacher, preacher, and prophet is one that is shared by you in the broadest sense. But Jesus' story is your story, shared by the fact that, despite official declarations to the contrary, you are his direct apostles in ministry. I challenge you, as his apostles, in this: to welcome the Spirit to lead you to the wilderness experience over and over again in your vocational lives. You see, the wilderness is not Union per se, or the church, or even the world out there into which you are commissioned forth, although it can feel that way when the wilderness is understood as a Godforsaken place. Yet, the wilderness is anything but Godforsaken. The wilderness is the core of your self—your soul—and you are called to be wilderness dwellers— wild women—because God has commissioned you to be your most natural self: the whole you, the unbroken you, the fearless you, the you who is bold enough to claim Jesus' experience as your own, the you who is courageous enough to speak Jesus' words against the tempters and around the communion table as your words. The wilderness will re-create you and transform you because it is God given and Spirit blessed. It is yours.

A word of caution: The devil will seek you out in the wilderness without fail. You will be stalked, lured, attracted, and even seduced into doubting your own worth as a minister called by God. But you need not fear being lost forever. Because from this day forward, as from the day you were born, as from the day you were baptized, you are wrapped in the warmth of God's wilderness, with Her ground to sustain you and Her sky to watch over you. And as long as you seek out the wilderness places and give yourself the time to take in their breath, you shall be blessed.

May God bless you now and always. **AMEN.**

TERESA DELGADO, *currently a candidate for a Ph.D. at Union Theological Seminary, was born and raised in New York City. She graduated magna cum laude from Colgate University in 1988 and received her M.A. from Union in May of 1993. In September of that year, she began her Ph.D. and in December gave birth to her first child, Francesca. She and her husband, Pascal Kabemba, have also been blessed with Celeste and Josiah. Despite the demands of family life and graduate studies, Teresa remains committed to seeking justice for people of color, in general, and Latinos, in particular, through her involvement with numerous organizations, including Harlem Initiatives Together and more recently as a board member of the Center for Community Leadership. She has facilitated courses and workshops at Union and Auburn seminaries on the emerging theological voices of Latinos in America. Her graduate work is focused on the relationship between Latina culture and theology/spirituality. Her family, however, is the creative work-in-progress of which she is most proud. They make their home in New Rochelle, New York.*

THE REVEREND DR. REBECCA EDMISTON-LANGE

Hemerocallus: Eternity in a Day

On Dying

> The mind wants to live forever, or learn a very good reason
> why not. The mind wants to know all eternity and God.
> The mind's sidekick, however, will settle for two eggs over
> easy.
>
> —*Annie Dillard*[1]

THE day promises to be one of those July days—
hazy, hot, and humid—so the morning hours are the
best time for outdoor work. But it's not only for this
reason that I'm out so early.

My mother is still sleeping and I want her to sleep. Outside
I won't disturb her. I heard her in the middle of the night, walking slowly from her bedroom to the kitchen, pushing her walker
in front of her. Startled awake, I thought at first that someone was

moving furniture. I fell asleep again soon after, so I don't know how long she was awake. But she has told me that she is often awake for hours in the middle of the night. And so I am determined to let her sleep—through the morning if she can.

I'm also determined to rid this flower bed of weeds. There are parts of my mother's garden that are overrun with weeds. Even the huge expanses of daylilies show the effects of my mother's diminishing powers. It is a red-letter day now when my mother can come outside simply to sit and observe her flowers. Working in the garden, especially in the heat and humidity of July, is not a possibility for her. And yet, I know that she feels the weeds as a reproach. Even if she cannot see them, she knows they are there. In the few days I am visiting her I can't eliminate all the weeds, but perhaps I can eradicate them from the two borders closest to the house and still do the other things I want to do for her while I am here.

My mother's time is running out. Oh, it's possible that she might live a few more years. But it seems equally possible that she might die in a few months' time. She is eighty-five years old, eighty-six in November. Congestive heart failure, failing kidneys, and chronic bronchitis plague her movements, sap her strength, and swell the extremities of her body. She's been in the hospital several times over the last year. She almost died last winter of pneumonia until an effective antibiotic was found. But she is still here, living in her house alone, where she wants to remain as long as possible. A nurse comes twice a week to check her vital signs, a nurse's aide once a week. My two sisters and my brother, who all live nearby, visit her on the other days, perform her routine errands. I know all this, have visited when I can through the year, have had long conversations with my sisters about her health and her doctors and treatments. And still, when I arrived yesterday I was shocked again by how old and worn she looks, by the number of prescription bottles that litter her kitchen table. I know she has to die, that she cannot live forever, and nearly eighty-six years is quite a span of days. And yet my heart rebels. Why can't the people we love go on and on? As Annie Dillard says, "The mind wants to live forever, or learn a very good reason why not."

I am up to my armpits in daylilies. The petals of the ones that will bloom today are just beginning to crack open. As the sun moves higher in the sky, the swollen tapers of blossom will spread wide in their classic six-petaled shape, three petals below topped by three above. The petals of yellow and gold and red and purple and lavender and pink and salmon and rose, and even white—and a hundred subtle variations of color in between—will spread wide to reveal the throat of the bloom and the arching stamens. The throats and the stamens also vary in color. This one has a lemon-yellow throat, this one a lime-green, and this a corona of perfect peach. My mother has nearly a thousand daylilies of several hundred varieties. Who knew there were so many daylilies?

As I stoop to my work, I develop a rhythm of pull and gather. This particular border is overrun with a grass that seems uniquely suited to be the bane of a daylily enthusiast. Its sawlike fronds grow in fans, as do the daylilies. The fans of the grass have become interlaced with the daylily foliage, obscuring its roots. I separate the daylily fans with one hand and pull with the other, transfer the pulled weed to the other hand and separate again. When my separating hand grows too full, I stand and toss the weeds to the side of the border. Is this your particular ecological niche, weed, I wonder, to grow among daylilies?

As I work and my movements become routinized, my mind is free to wander or to focus. And I begin to think about the nature of grieving. For I know I am grieving, anticipating my mother's death. I feel I have little time left to be with her, to do for her. But still I want to imagine that she can go on and on. Oh, I know I will survive her death. The patterns of my life have for some time incorporated my mother's absence. I know she will never see my new church building, for example, even though she has followed its progress from blueprint to reality in our conversations.

She will never see the place in which I have lived for the last nine years and which is now my own. She will never get to know my stepchildren. Life must come to her now and has had to for some time. And when I am honest with myself I know that there are things I do not tell her as her energy for conversation diminishes, as her sense of hearing grows fainter. Some things just require too much effort on both our parts. And yet, to imagine the future without her is to invite a yawning emptiness. For being with her is still a blessing. And doing small things for her, bringing her what pleasure I can, is still my way of staving off that inevitable day.

There is a Middle Eastern legend about a spindly little sparrow who was lying on her back in the middle of the road. A horseman came by, dismounted, and asked the sparrow what on earth she was doing lying there in the middle of the road with her feet up in the air. "I heard that the heavens were going to fall today," said the sparrow. "Oh," said the horseman, "I suppose you think that your puny legs can hold up the heavens?" "One does what one can," said the sparrow. "One does what one can." And so I weed.

I am here with her now and I want to do what I can for her while here. I fix her special meals, things she thinks she will enjoy though food has lost some of its flavor, and eating is sometimes a chore. I suggest menus and watch her reaction. "Steamed shrimp for tomorrow night when Margaret comes?" "Yes, shrimp would be nice." "Chicken breasts sautéed with shallots, mushrooms, and white wine when Steve is here?" "Yes, that sounds good—whatever you fix is always good, honey." "Scallops?" "Oh, yes"—and a big grin spreads over her face—"I've been looking forward to having scallops while you were here—that way you have of fixing them."

And so I shop and mince and cook and take delight when she cleans her plate with obvious relish. Old-fashioned southern potato salad made with sweet pickles; baked rice; bacon, lettuce, and tomato sandwiches; and, oh yes, the scallops are obvious hits.

I cook and my mother naps and we eat. And in the evenings we watch taped episodes of *Mystery* and *Masterpiece Theater* and maybe Mother stays awake, maybe she hears enough to follow the plots. And when she has the energy, we talk—mostly about family and flowers, always flowers. My mother, the eternal optimist, is planning what she will plant next spring.

I cook and I weed. The sun has grown in ferocity and sweat pours out of me, soaking my clothes, running into my eyes. The daylilies are fully open now, achingly beautiful in their embrace of the light. What is it about this flower, whose blossom lasts only a day, whose blooming season is only a few weeks, that has so enraptured my mother? She has other flowers, but daylilies are her passion. One of my self-appointed tasks for this visit is to choose and mark specific daylilies that I will transplant to my garden in the fall. I've intended to do this for some time, but the task has taken on a new urgency now. It is not just that I want to have daylilies in my garden. I can buy daylilies whenever I want. No, I want daylilies from my mother's garden, and I want to learn their names from her mouth while there is still time. By transplanting daylilies from my mother's garden I am preserving a piece of her, hoarding some of her loveliness against that emptiness that will result from her passing.

And yet how to choose? In my tiny town-house garden I have, at best, room for ten or eleven daylilies. And my mother has hundreds of varieties. Taking a break from my weeding, I walk and look and compare. This one or that one? Is this one different from that over there? Back and forth, I walk. I know very few of them by name. And I fear that if the weather follows the forecast—hot and humid all week—my mother will not be able to come outside even to sit and instruct. How will I choose what of my mother's garden to preserve in my own?

A few I know I must have. "Becky Lynn," for example, which graces the edge of this bed I weed. Partly for its name, perhaps. But more for its coloration—a rose blend with a greenish-yellow throat. Each time I straighten from my chore, I am arrested by its sight. It is so beautiful, I can hardly stand it and I, more than once, in a gesture I echo from my mother, cup the blossom in my hand and exclaim, "Oh, you are so lovely!" And I think again of the appeal of this flower.

My brother's daughter Kathryn came to visit yesterday. She, too, delighted in the huge expanses of daylily blooms until she discovered the reason for their name. "Why are they called daylilies?" she asks. "Because the bloom lasts only a day," I explain. "What a stupid flower! Why would you want them?" she bemoans. And I wonder, How can one explain to a nine-year-old perfection in a day?

"The mind wants to live forever," writes Annie Dillard. It hungers for eternity. Perhaps. But, barring that, when it comes to facing the death of those we love, we more likely want to know how much time we have left. We want assurances about when the end will come. Or so it seems to me as I anticipate my mother's death. It's the uncertainty that tears at you. More than once during the last year I have asked myself, in facing choices about how to spend my time, "If I knew she would die next week, what would I do?" But, despite the pundits, it is impossible to live each day as if tomorrow is the end. The mind, whether curse or no, will project into the future.

And while those who are left behind may want to prepare themselves, protect themselves, by knowing exactly when the moment will arrive, those who are facing death may have very different reactions. I've seen people who think they have lived *too* long, surviving their friends and family and interests, for whom death comes as a release. And I've seen people whose lives were tragically cut short. And I've watched people fight long and hard against painful, debilitating illnesses and imagined that if I were they I would have long since given up the struggle. But I've also wondered how and when one knows that that moment to yield has come. It is easy to say, from the standpoint of observation, that one wouldn't want to live once there is no pleasure left in living. But how to measure pleasure? Perhaps the mind's sidekick will settle for something like two eggs over easy or the pressure of a loved one's hand while lying in bed. I think of a colleague of mine who, living with AIDS, reacted to what he called the "premature assurances of his demise" by having a T-shirt made that read "NDY—Not Dead Yet."

Do we want to live forever or do we want to know the precise moment of our death? And if we knew the measure of our days—if we could anticipate, as with the daylily, the exact extent of our life span—how would that inform our living? Would we be happier knowing? Would we live more fully and well? I know the answer that suggests itself, have heard it, said it myself that the trick to living well is to live as if each day is a precious gift of borrowed time. To not defer one's living until—until the kids are grown, or until retirement, until whatever. To give oneself to life. To enter into the moment. That life is too short for resentment or bitterness or regrets. And certainly there is wisdom in this approach, for, in the context of the infinite, our life span, whatever the sum of the days, is, like the daylily's, only the blink of an eye.

And yet, isn't it the projection into the future that the mind cannot, will not, resist, that gives us hope? Maybe planning what she will plant next spring is what is keeping my mother alive. And are there not times and situations when one cannot live fully in the present moment? There are times, it seems, when one has to wait, for strength to return, for example, or for clarity. Times when one has to garner one's resources, marshal one's strength, bide one's time for the good talk or the walk outside. Sometimes, as with my mother, life is more a matter of pacing oneself. But, then, pacing oneself implies one knows the extent of the journey.

I weed and I ponder. Brushing up against the blossoms, my

arms and legs and my face, too, I suspect, have become streaked with daylily dust. The reds, yellows, purples, and pinks adorn my body like sacred paint in some shamanistic rite. This is ritual, this weeding. And ridding this flower bed of unwanted plants is linked with mystery. For I know I am recapitulating the actions of thousands of adult children of aging parents. Doing for my mother what she no longer can do for herself. Trying to find the ways to express the love I feel for her and the gratitude for all she has given me. Trying to stave off the inevitable while preparing myself to accept it at the same time.

Finally, the sun drives me inside. Mama is up, eating her breakfast. She frowns at my wet clothes, sweaty arms and brow. "Honey, don't overdo. I don't want you to work all the time you're here." "No, Mama, it's okay." And I try to explain. "Weeding is good. It helps me think. It's kind of like prayer." And she nods and says, "Yes, I've felt that way. In fact, there have been times when I didn't know what else to do but weed and somehow weeding helped."

Yes, weeding helps. And the next day dawns cool and clear, an unexpected respite from the July torpor. In the afternoon Mama is able, with my assistance, to come outside. She has several plastic molded chairs scattered throughout the lawn. We maneuver to the nearest one and she sits. She sits and feasts her eyes on her daylilies. And when she is rested enough to move again we navigate to the next chair. And so it goes. I ask her the names of specific daylilies I particularly admire. When she cannot tell one from where she is sitting, she instructs me to break off a blossom and bring it to her for a closer look. I hesitate to do such violence. But she shakes off my reluctance—a few blooms more or less won't hurt. And in the context of all that are in bloom she is right. And so some of the blossoms are sacrificed to my need for continuance and a mother's bequest. With my mother's help, I make my choices, mark their spots for my return in the fall.

Enraptured by the beauty of the day and the glory of the flowers, we stay outside too long. As we make our slow progress back to the house, I can tell my mother is overtired. She will pay for this outing tomorrow. But I know she would not have it any other way. For it is not just being outside and seeing her flowers and sharing her knowledge that has transpired here. It has been transcendent time. And it is not merely daylilies that have absorbed our interest. Those flowers—those flowers whose bloom lasts only a day—have been the currency of love.

Mother is not dead yet. No, she is very much alive. And, in spite of her limitations, she still has pleasure in living. As I help her up the stairs into the house, I note that though she looks tired, her appearance has changed to me in the time I have been here. She no longer looks so pale, so shockingly worn. Her countenance is, again, that of my beautiful, beloved mother. Time may be running out for her. But here she is and here I am and time with her is precious and full and blessed. And the pleasure I take in being with her cannot be compared.

The mind does hunger for eternity. But perhaps the mistake we make is thinking that eternity means time going on forever. Perhaps eternity is more like apprehending the eternal—the timeless in the now. Something like the beauty of the daylily and the constancy of love.

My mother, Mary Edmiston, died surrounded by her loving family March 2, 1999.

Ordained in 1986, THE REVEREND DR. REBECCA EDMISTON-LANGE *has served for thirteen years as the minister of Accotink Unitarian Universalist Church in Burke, Virginia. A native of Virginia, she received her M.Div. from Union Theological Seminary in 1978 and also completed a Ph.D. in counseling from Catholic University in 1990. In August 1999, she will begin serving the Emerson Unitarian Church in Houston, Texas, as co-minister with her husband, Mark Edmiston-Lange.*

THE REVEREND LAURIE J. FERGUSON

Jesus: Not a Victim for Our Sins

On Transformation

MARK 11:1–11; 14:1–9

P ALM Sunday, Passion Sunday. The lectionary and the liturgy present us with an either-or. We can celebrate one way with palms and hosannas and happiness or we can observe a day that begins the sober and painful Holy Week. The truth in Jesus' life, as well as ours, is that they were not separate or compartmentalized. As he moved into Jerusalem that day, going through the portals toward betrayal, suffering, and death, there was excitement, joy, and anticipation. What kind of strange combination was that? How do we begin to understand this movement toward his death that combined palms with passion?

If we read the words to Palm Sunday hymns, those definers of popular theology, the language is about sacrifice. Jesus is moving to be sacrificed, and the joy is interpreted as rejoicing in the salvation that comes through Jesus' death.

This interpretation of palms and sacrifice takes us in a dangerous direction. What is communicated to us is that Jesus was a sacrifice, echoing from the Old Testament the practice of sacrificing the perfect, unblemished lamb or goat, the unfinished sacrifice of Isaac by Abraham. Jesus is the sacrificial offering, the victim who goes innocently and quietly to the slaughter. *Victim* is the defining word. Jesus submits to this horror. He endures it for our sake, but he didn't choose it.

Two problems emerge from this understanding of Palm Sunday and the road into Holy Week. The first has to do with the image of God. We are presented with a picture of a God who demands victims, sacrifice, and death; and preferably (or only) good people should sign up to submit and endure. That's the other problem. If Jesus acted this way in the face of evil and injustice, if it was not only okay but right that Jesus should be a victim, then so should we. When we face injustice at the hands of a person or a system or an institution, we should bow our heads, meekly expose our necks to the blade, and submit, endure. If we can't bear that, if we refuse to be victims ourselves, then the only alternative given to us is to swing to the other pole, to fight back, to rage, to beat our heads against the powers that dominate and destroy.

Victim or aggressor, what other role is there?

It is imperative for our own spiritual health, and for the sake of the communities and systems in which we live, that we take another deep look at this story of Jesus and begin to understand another way for ourselves as we understand his way. It is clear from the story we heard this morning about Jesus' entry into Jerusalem that he went of his own choice. He was not dragged into Jerusalem; he was not programmed like a cyborg to go on no matter what the danger. He was a full human being who knew this was the next step for him—to talk to the religious authorities in Jerusalem and to teach and heal there. Something had to change in this religious system. Something had to change their idea of

God's law and demand because the way they were teaching cut the people off from truth or hope.

Jesus knew his work was to hold to the vision of God. He had to teach this vision, not compromise it. He knew there was confrontation and danger in Jerusalem, but he also felt the joy and hope of new life and freedom the people got from him as they made way for him entering into the city. Transformation brings with it joy and celebration.

It also brings great cost. For someone to be transformed personally, there is great risk and great sacrifice of what has been. Eda LeShan wrote about this in her book *Grandparenting in a Changing World*:

> At a dinner party many years ago, I sat next to a man who was an oceanographer. At one point he asked me if I had ever wondered why lobsters could weigh one pound, three pounds, even ten pounds. When they had such a hard shell how could they grow? I had to tell him this was a problem that was not very high on my list of priorities. He smiled and proceeded to tell me that when a lobster becomes crowded in its shell and can't grow anymore, by instinct it travels out to some place in the sea, hoping for relative safety, and begins to shed its shell. It is a terribly dangerous process—the lobster has to risk its life, because once it becomes naked, vulnerable, it can be dashed against a reef or eaten by another lobster or fish. But that is the only way it can grow.[1]

To be willing to be transformed, changed, sacrificed on behalf of someone else is just as costly and even more complex. Jesus went into the heart of the religion in Jerusalem knowing something big was going to happen. He knew there was anger, hatred, and jealousy from the institution, which did not understand and was inflexible. But he could not compromise what he knew to be true.

He wasn't going to shave the edges, bend a little here and there so they could all coexist. He was not victimized by their hatred. He did not endure it, try to grit his teeth and get through it. He did not bow his head and submit.

Jesus surrendered himself with full understanding. He saw what his choices were and what the consequences were. He could choose to be quiet, to give up what he knew, to shut up the fire in his bones and try to defend and appease them. Or he could allow the process to go on and not let go of his truth and what he knew, even though it would put him directly in the path of destruction. He did not swerve. He surrendered to sacrifice. He was open and allowed the forces of destruction to use him.

There is deep trust in that act. Trust that God is stronger than evil. Trust that life and goodness will prevail over hatred and all that seeks to box in love and control it. Jesus may have felt the metaphor for this possibility, this understanding of sacrifice the night the unnamed woman broke a flask of ointment and poured it over him. She gave up the precious, costly stuff in one burst of love and joy and sensuous gratitude. She didn't quibble about waste—as the disciples did—so much at once! "Why the whole jar? Why not just put a dab on his head and then maybe his feet? Why such a waste of a resource? It could have been bartered for money and done some good. Why pour out something as useless as perfume on one person?" Was it waste or holy sacrifice? Maybe that was Jesus' internal debate about his own life and actions. "Where would I do the most good? Pour it all out at once? Waste my life in sacrifice when I could be doing practical healing and teaching each day? What is my call? What must I do?"

However we begin to understand the passion for our own faith, with its layers of meaning, Jesus was not a passive victim of

God or of fate, and neither are we. In each of our lives our call is to listen as intently to the Spirit as Jesus did and to wrestle with the questions raised on our journey to faith and life. Our decisions to follow may not be costly in the same way Jesus' were, but we can be assured they will be no less difficult or demanding. We will be asked the same question about our decisions—waste or holy sacrifice?

When we are acting and believing as Jesus was, with our full weight of integrity and courage, we can also be assured our work and our lives will be transforming. Change and new life will spring out of our surrender, our gift of ourselves. In that understanding, the palms this morning are not ludicrous or even ironic. They speak of this joyful truth.

In a recent interview, Alice Walker spoke about her conviction regarding how one can deal with the injustice and pain of the world: "My way of fighting back is to understand [injustice] and then to create a work that expresses what I understand." Walker believes that creative expression is a useful alternative to "throwing a rock or a bomb" because creating something not only provides healing for the artist but also responds to whatever outrage has been encountered.[2]

What might be our creation? Your creative act?

Palm Sunday invites us on a way that has neither victims nor aggressors. It is a way of surrender, of transforming sacrifice, a way of creating something from our souls. It is the way of Jesus. **AMEN.**

THE REVEREND LAURIE J. FERGUSON *was the pastor of the Palisades Presbyterian Church in Palisades, New York, for fifteen years. She received degrees from Smith College and Princeton Seminary, and is currently studying for a Ph.D. in Clinical Psychology at the Derner Psychoanalytic Institute of Adelphi University. She is also a consultant to the Board of Pensions of the Presbyterian Church. A native of Ohio and a fourth-generation Presbyterian minister, she lives beside the Hudson River with her three children.*

DR. MARY FOULKE

Living with Betrayal

On Evil

MARK 14:12-25

TONIGHT we are talking about betrayal. I want to reflect upon both sides of the human experience of betrayal: the experience many of us can identify of having been betrayed (though perhaps not to the extent that Jesus was betrayed), and the experience many of us do not identify, but which is just as common, of having betrayed another or having betrayed ourselves.

To say it another way, I would suggest that this biblical story offers a reflection of how to live in the midst of evil—both the evil that we do and the evil that we encounter in the world. In this text from Mark there are two examples of how to handle betrayal: The disciples offer one response; Jesus offers another.

The disciples' response is denial. "Surely not I," says my translation, and we can imagine "*Mm-nmm*, not me, I would never, what a terrible thing to say, no way . . ." and so on. This denial of the presence of evil and the accompanying denial of personal responsibility is a common theme among human beings today. Surely none of us wishes for evil, nor should we want to see it in our midst, and in our denial we are not intending any harm.

What we want is to manage and control the world so that no suffering can occur, no evil can be present. But this is impossible. When we try to control the world we can bring about evil as profound as any we seek to avoid. Such efforts to master evil stem from goodwill and a sense of responsibility on our part, but when the truth is discovered that we cannot prevent or escape evil, we retreat into denial. We either go into a survivalist mode (I and mine against the world) or into an escapist mode (seeking only our own pleasure and ignoring the rest of the world). Either way we turn away from God, away from Jesus who is betrayed tonight, and away from all people.

The desire to deny evil, whether in ourselves or others, is incredibly strong. When I led a support group on the Upper East Side of New York City for women in abusive family situations, I listened as one seemingly perfect woman told us about her husband repeatedly punching her in the stomach (so no bruises would show) and then holding a pillow over her face until she passed out. As she told this story, she was smiling, denying her feelings, doing her best to deny the terror and evil of that situation. Then she talked about the good times. In her own attempt to manage or control a very out-of-control situation, she betrayed herself. She tried to escape. I know. I have been there.

When I was in college, my popular, all-American, charming boyfriend put a knife to my throat and asked, "Do you trust me?" Of course I said, "Yes." Later he would ask the question again, this time with a gun to my head. He told me that he would kill me if I ever went against him or tried to break up with him, and he told me exactly how. I told myself that he was insecure, that he had had a troubled childhood, that he was a good person deep down.

All those things might have been true, but I denied the presence of evil in the threat of violence, and I betrayed myself. I told no one and put forth a sunny disposition. I was embarrassed, scared, and determined that I could manage the situation and control the violence. I went into a survival mode—no one was trustworthy, no one could help. All I could do was to try to protect myself.

How did Jesus respond to betrayal? What lessons can we learn from Jesus about how to deal with evil in our midst? To begin with, he identified it, named it, and so confronted Judas in the midst of friends. Jesus did not try to control evil. Knowing that he would be betrayed, he did not throw out all the disciples and eat alone, nor did he pretend that nothing was wrong just so the dinner party wouldn't be ruined. Jesus was neither a survivalist nor an escapist. He did not turn away from God or God's people; he continued to love and care for all of them.

Jesus left the control of evil and his own survival up to God. He named the evil and then broke bread with his disciples, offering them in the signs of bread and wine strength and comfort, and the grace of God for all to receive. It was a proclamation of hope in the midst of evil. Communion is not a reward for the innocent and good, nor is it a protection from evil; communion is the proclamation of God's goodwill for the world, the celebration that even in the midst of evil, God will keep the divine promise that the world will be saved and evil will be vanquished. Betrayers, deserters, deniers, abusers, controllers, all of us share in the bread of heaven, the cup of salvation, to proclaim the reign of God until God comes.

"How can *you* say *that?*" some of my friends have asked me. "Are you just a victim? Are we supposed to accept evil? What about justice?"

The trouble is that in leaving our own survival and the control of evil up to God, there is no assurance that this will work any better than striving for full mastery of the universe. I cannot pretend that Good Friday did not happen. Jesus broke bread with his betrayers and friends, and the next day he was killed.

The difference is that the noncontrolling behaviors (like those of Jesus) are much less dangerous to people and to the world. Danger and continuing evil come from those seeking mastery of others, those who will destroy in the name of protection and safety. I think of most of the countries in this world, piling up more and more dangerous weapons in the name of security for their citizens. Or, I think of my own situation. I was always fear-ful of the outsider, and yet it was someone close who was the at-tacker. In my own situation, I did not act as Jesus did. I tried to control the situation through denial, thereby cooperating with evil. In my attempts, I became a victim. I was trying to protect myself. By going along with evil, I thought I might not be hurt as much.

But one night, by a power I name as the Holy Spirit, I was strengthened to confront the situation after a particularly violent episode. It was getting worse, and I think I did not see any other option. I named the evil. He denied it. I named it again, feeling more scared and more vulnerable than I had ever been, but strangely no longer a victim. He said that he didn't want to hurt me. I maintained that he had. I put my life into God's hands alone. We talked. He left. I was told by friends of mine that he joined the Navy the next day. I never saw him again. I told no one of my experience for at least five years, and this sermon is the first time I have spoken of it in public.

I do not use this example to show that if you put your life in God's hands, it will all be okay. Certainly everything was not okay, nor would it be for a long time. I do use this example to say that the identification of evil, and leaving it up to God, sometimes can place us in greater danger and subject us to even greater evil, and sometimes it can save us. There is no guarantee. What is guaran-teed is that when we trust in God, God will be with us. God has never meant for us to be alone, ever. God will be with us in the worst as in the best of times; and even through death, God promises to meet us on the other side. We are called to trust in

God and to love God and in doing so to love and care for all of creation, even ourselves.

With God life remains hopeful, open to possibility, to renewal and restoration, even open to freedom. God is the source of our very being, the mystery that creates life, sustains and transforms life, and that constantly breaks apart our efforts to control, limit, close off, and contain the boundaries of life and love. God will break through all evil—this is the comfort in the presence of the betrayer at the table. If God welcomes Judas, surely God will welcome us. Even with our deepest secrets and denial, even with our most glaring faults, we are loved and invited to share bread and wine and a vision of God's freedom for all people.

In the breaking of bread and the sharing of the cup, we celebrate this mystery. We celebrate the breaking in of new possibilities to transform our lives and our world into the kingdom of God. During this week, the evil that humanity is capable of, and indeed our own participation in evil, should be all too evident. At this table, we share with others the covenant to love and care for all of God's creation, to identify and name evil and to proclaim God's good news for all. Let us recognize evil and betrayal, even here in our midst, and let us come to God's table in hope, looking for the vision of renewal, restoration, and freedom. **AMEN.**

DR. MARY FOULKE *is the Senior Associate for Children and Family Ministries for All Saints Episcopal Church in Pasadena, California. She was an ordained minister in the Presbyterian Church, US, for nine years and holds an E.D.D. in Religion and Education from Teachers College, Columbia, University. Formerly the Protestant chaplain at Wellesley College, she was also on the staff of the Brick Presbyterian Church in New York City as Associate Minister for Education and Christian Discipleship. An antiracism and antioppression consultant, she makes her home in Pasadena, California, with her partner and their daughter.*

Not Like Us

On Homosexuality

MARK 12:28–31; ROMANS 12:1–5

I MAGINE you live on a planet where there is no longer gender, male or female. Imagine our species has evolved to the point where these distinctions are considered a lower evolutionary form, disgusting and backward. Everyone you know considers himself or herself genderless, at least publicly. Those who indicate any leaning toward male or female are institutionalized in retraining programs designed to teach that these categories are against nature. People who secretly possess this old identification, being man *or* woman, don't know how to find one another and risk their freedom and job security if they hint about it to the wrong person. There is an underground network of people who claim to be male and female, some of them in couples, some alone, and they offer one another limited support. Yet public day-to-day life is never secure because every conversation, every interaction, every allusion to sexuality or your social life is open to speculation.

I saw this scenario hauntingly portrayed in a television episode last year, and I haven't forgotten the pain of the characters. The genius of the program was that it used an element common to everyone, gender, in order to make the point of what it feels like to be different and without power. Many of us have known what it feels like to have someone say "You are not like us," and there-fore be set apart. It might be our color, our gender, our way of dressing, our religion, our economic class, or our opinions. Not like us. And the door shuts in our faces.

Today I want to focus on a particular exclusion that has been so much a part of our national debate recently: the issue of ho-mosexuality. I know that some of you may be thinking, "Why do we have to talk about this in church?" "Why can't people keep their sexual orientation to themselves and not put it in my face?" I believe the answer lies in how this has become in our time a re-ligious issue, in our time a civil rights issue, and in our time an issue of how we treat our neighbors. I just don't think we can turn the public religious debate over to the far right when so much is at stake in terms of human lives. I am doing this to open dialogue about one of the central debates of our times, and I genuinely in-vite discussion. I want to hear your opinions, because I am going to share mine.

One reason this is an issue for us is that the Bible, the central document in our own faith, is used as ammunition by many who oppose homosexuality. There is no ambiguity here: Leviticus, Romans, and Timothy are absolutely clear in their statements that homosexual practice is sinful and wrong. Yet it is also clear that many who point to these passages do not follow the dietary re-strictions considered mandatory by the Hebrew scripture, do not believe women should be silent in church, and do not think Abraham actually lived one hundred and seventy years. We all pick and choose, fundamentalists included. But these passages on moral behavior carry special weight.

I think it is important to understand that the Hebrew scriptures were written in an age of embattled tribal survival. And the New Testament was written in a time when the notion of being gay, lesbian, or bisexual didn't exist. There was homosexual practice, but homosexuality as a statement of essential identity and orientation was not imagined.

It is equally important to compare these anti-homosexual morality statements with other biblical teachings about moral behavior. Jesus had something to say about how we treat people who are "not like us." The second great commandment: You shall love your neighbor as yourself. Neighbor to Jesus certainly did not mean only people just like me. And Paul, who was clearly against homosexual practice, also writes, "So we, who are many, are one body in Christ, and individually we are members one of another." In our times, the body of Christ is full of people who are gay, lesbian, and bisexual; some we know, and many others we will never know. So how shall we treat our neighbors, some of whom are in the pew next to us? How shall we treat the body of Christ?

As Christians, we believe in principle that we should be nice to people we think are not like us. But is this the final matter for us as people of faith? This is simply not the end of the discussion in terms of the realities of our times, because a more complex debate is emerging. And it can't be the end of our moral decision-making because of this fact: Gays, lesbians, and bisexual people are being dehumanized, beaten, and murdered for who they are.

Bishop Desmond Tutu spoke these words to the All-Africa Church Conference:

> When two persons are engaged in a conflict and one of them is considerably stronger than the other, to be neutral is not just and fair and impartisan, be-

cause to be neutral is in fact to side with the powerful.[1]

Neutrality is an illusion. Not to stand with those who are persecuted is in fact to stand with those who perpetrate violence
against them. Being nice to people we see as not like us may not
be enough. We may need to say that hatred, bigotry, and malice
toward our neighbors is wrong.

The United Church of Christ at the national level has taken
just such a stand, as have some UCC conferences and associations,
one of them being the Metro Boston Association. So have about
eighty-five churches across the nation, five of them in our area.
These bodies have designated themselves "Open and Affirming"
after a process of internal education and dialogue. This context of
"Open and Affirming" is based on two understandings of sexuality that are not from a context of tribal survival, or a context where
sexual orientation was not yet considered, or a context in which
women and children were considered property in a male-run economic system. Rather, the context assumed is one of love and
choice in human relationships, for men and women.

The first understanding is this: People meet, are attracted, fall
in love, make commitments, plan lives together, dream of families,
have children, and grieve separation, loss, and death. They may be
male and female. They may be two men. They may be two
women. Homosexuality isn't any more or less about how people
have sex than heterosexuality is. It may be about love, respect, and
mutual commitment, or it may not. Just as in heterosexual relationships, some are working and some aren't. So who is "us"?
Who is "not like us"? We are all human beings, created by God,
searching for affirmation and connection.

The second understanding is as follows: Sexual morality is not
based on gender; it is based on the appropriate use of power and
the justness of behavior. Is a man raping a woman acceptable be-

cause this is a heterosexual act? Is a woman sexually harassing her co-worker acceptable if he is a man? Is it okay for an adult to have sex with a child if they are of different genders, but not okay if they are both male? Do we affirm a relationship where one party is beaten and abused by the other because it is heterosexual? Is a minister seducing her grieving parishioner appropriate if he is a man? Of course not. Ethics around sexuality have everything to do with behavior and choice and are not based inherently on orientation.

Now we all know that, given the congregational system, any of the national bodies of the UCC, or any association or conference, can declare themselves "Open and Affirming." And we, or any other church within the UCC, can do as we please. We are free to articulate opposing positions, or we can ignore it all. But what are the consequences of neutrality in this matter?

Gays, lesbians, and bisexual men or women, even those in heterosexual relationships, turn on the radio daily and hear their deepest self and those they love vilified. They walk down the street and experience verbal harassment and physical violence, which is rapidly on the upswing in all major cities that track hate crimes. They remain silent in conversations where they are assumed not to be present. They experience pain and division within their families, who may reject them; with their heterosexual friends, who may drop them; and with their bosses and co-workers, who may fire them. And day to day they live with the constant hiding, fear, and potential self-loathing that takes an incredible emotional toll.

Remember the planet of no gender? What would it be like to pretend you did not know you were male or female? To hide your gut feeling about your attractions, perception, and experience? To never, at any time, relax the vigilance of pretending you were just like everybody else? Just like them.

In this season of Lent, in this time of preparation and looking within, let us examine who we have claimed are "not like us."

When we say "not like us," we create divisions that cause real human beings, like us, enormous pain. When we say "not like us," we deny God's creation.

In our current climate of hatred and violence based on race, based on gender, based on religion, based on whom we say we love, there is no neutrality possible. When we are silent, we are supporting the suffering and death. When we are silent, we are failing to love our neighbor as our self. When we are silent, we are breaking the body of Christ. And I think God grieves for all our loss. **AMEN.**

THE REVEREND LOUISE GREEN *is a United Church of Christ minister who has served Memorial Congregational Church in Sudbury, Massachusetts, and Judson Memorial Church in New York City. She has been involved in various arts ministries as a dancer and performer, including five years with the Just Peace Players in Boston. Currently Louise works as a community organizer with member congregations and schools of the Metro Industrial Areas Foundation, focusing on public school issues in New York City. A Texan, she makes her home in New York City.*

THE REVEREND ANN HALLSTEIN

Simple Things

On Experience

I JOHN 5:10–12

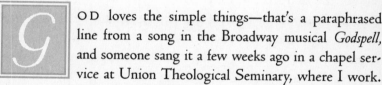OD loves the simple things—that's a paraphrased line from a song in the Broadway musical *Godspell*, and someone sang it a few weeks ago in a chapel service at Union Theological Seminary, where I work. It set me to thinking. God loves the simple things, and yet we work so hard at complicating our lives, our faith, our spiritual journeys! Our culture—our increasingly complex technology, confusing economic models, and proposed health-care systems which few of us can grasp in their entirety—all conspire to make life complicated. And while these intricate theories and convoluted systems are given great weight and value, the simple is made to seem simplistic.

One thing among many that I dearly love about New England is that the true line, the honest effort, the thrifty householder, and the orderly garden and woodpile are all given weight and value.

There's a spareness, an appreciation for the essential, that makes life more livable—it nourishes the place in us that calls out for simplicity and truth. It feeds the soul. I don't intend to equate New Englanders with God's chosen people in America: that's already been done, as I recall! But I do want to say a few words about life in the spirit—spiritual life—and how it can be enormously satisfying, deeply enriching, and yet also quite simple. That's the message of the reading from I John, and it's one that is worth paying attention to, because it can guide and serve us well in our attempts to live lives that are spiritually rich and purposeful.

This letter was written to a particular group of early Christians, sometime in the first century. Apparently the group was veering from what the author considered to be the true faith, and he was trying to outline the basics, to remind them of what it means to follow Christ. In verses 10 through 12, the author writes, "He who believes in the Son of God has the testimony in himself. And this is the testimony, that God gave us eternal life, and this life is in his Son. Whoever has the Son has life, whoever has not the Son has not Life."

The person who believes has the testimony in himself—the writer is explaining that you can depend on your own experience to guide you as far as your belief. Your own experience will show you that if you believe in Christ, you'll have larger life. He's not saying to accept some doctrine about Christ, but to practice believing, and see what happens. John's purpose in this letter is to try to set things straight as far as shaping and maintaining the faith is concerned. He is not as much trying to define how one should believe as he is simply saying that the person who believes in Jesus Christ will have life, and she will know what that means by considering her own experience. She who believes has the testimony in herself. Certainly since John's time the Church has developed doctrines, creeds, and teachings centered on what is required if one is to call oneself a Christian, and we've inherited many of those traditions, even with the changes brought about by the Reformation. But this letter, so simple and straightforward, coming well before the institutionalization of Christianity, gives wise advice. Listen to yourself, and give authority to your own experience.

When it comes down to it, you either experience Christianity as meaningful or you don't. But there may be lots of times when you wonder, Can this be true? Am I a fool to believe in this? That's when you need to turn to your own experience—in times of doubt, in times when belief based on something outside yourself doesn't seem to serve. For instance, we hear and read about love as God's supreme action in the world. But you have to have experienced the force of love to know the truth of such a statement. Maybe you've had to take care of someone who is chronically or terminally ill. You run out of energy, are exhausted, and pray for help, for the strength to do what you need to do. And you're given what you need, out of love for the person you're caring for. It may not make the situation any better, but it does make it possible to carry on. John is saying to consider experience like this: Do you think you got through it on your own, or did you feel God (or love) at work through you? If you have ever sensed God at work in your life, you have your own testimony. If you've experienced it, then that's all you need to know—it's simple. The proof is in the pudding. Or, as the renowned preacher Harry Emerson Fosdick put it:

> Our response to experiences of God's transforming and sustaining grace is the basis of faith. A wise theology clarifies them, reassures our faith in them, deepens our understanding of them, but, as for me, it is the experience itself in which I find my certainty, while my theological interpretations I must, in all humility, hold with tentative confidence.[1]

Attend to your intuition, your common sense, and your life experiences, for that is where God works and speaks to you. You have the authority of your own being, and God is accessible there, through yourself. Turn there—that's a likely spot for God to be revealed. This is not to say that a person is always right in matters of the spirit, and that whatever he or she hears is of God. The community, the Church, and our traditions form a center to help keep us balanced, to offer a collective wisdom that guards against excessive individualism. But in matters of God, it is upon our own hearts where truth is writ, and John is saying to honor that as a source of divine revelation.

We don't generally hear these words spoken in Christian teaching—to trust our own experience. But it's true in most areas of our life, and the life of the spirit can certainly be held to similar standards. We all learn certain things growing up that later, based on our own experience of life, we decide to let go of: It doesn't jibe. At a certain point in life, we turn from what we have learned from others and are more apt to listen to what we have learned through our own lives, our own mistakes, our own successes. Similarly, a point comes when what we learned in Sunday school or from the pulpit no longer works for us. Such departures can cause a crisis of faith, or at least doubt, because we have been taught that veering from the "party line" means we're not the "right" kind of Christian. But Jesus himself departed from the orthodoxies of his day and put his faith in what he knew to be true from deep within. That's the time to turn to our own experience of God, our own conception of Jesus, and heed the testimony that is in our hearts—age eighteen, or age eighty-eight, we all have experience to call upon. It's that simple.

Just because something is *simple* does not mean it's *easy*, however. Indeed, heeding simplicity can require great effort. To listen to the heart, to follow your own experience of God, can be hard. Certainly, our culture doesn't support living this way—it is the opposite of our fast pace, our desire to fit in. Listening to your own experience in matters of God requires time and great patience, because God's time line is not the same as ours. As Swiss physician

Paul Tournier once commented, "We devote years to studying a trade or profession. Ought we to show less perseverance in acquiring the experience of God?"

It also requires going our own way, which may feel like being in the outfield when everyone else is in the infield. Listening to the heart may require life changes we feel we can't make—it may call upon us to take risks. Honoring your own experience or testimony means honoring the very particular self you are, because your experience of God will be particular to you. Most of us are not taught to live like this, in deep conversation with our innermost selves, but it is precisely that self you will come in contact with if you listen. It can throw your life into what feels like chaos because, like God's time, God's priorities are not our priorities. Although this way of approaching God will be direct and simple, it certainly requires much more of us than listening to someone else's testimony, like mine, now. You will leave church today and can leave whatever I have said behind, but it's much harder to ignore your own inner pullings and leanings. I urge you to leave behind everything I have said, and listen to your own heart.

Another caution—simple doesn't necessarily mean clear, nor does it mean without mystery. Heeding our own testimony is a simple approach to God, but it is not simplistic, and the God we try to know in this way is shrouded in sacred mystery that we can finally only accept. Like Job, who after encountering God and hearing God's voice realized finally that he could never understand God, so we too need to accept that the awesome, vast mystery of God and God's presence in our lives are beyond our ken. Our own experience is a starting point in journeying toward God, but it can never be an ending point, because undergirding our own experience is the ungraspable presence that is God. Einstein said it more gracefully than I:

> The most beautiful thing we can experience is the mysterious. It is the source of all true art and sci-

ence. This insight into the mystery of life, coupled though it be with fear, has also given rise to religion. To know that what is impenetrable to us really exists, manifesting itself as the highest wisdom and the most radiant beauty which our dull faculties can comprehend only in their most primitive forms—this knowledge, this feeling, is at the center of true religiousness.[2]

Attempting to live life in the spirit, to have the full life promised by Jesus, seems to be something that requires us always to return, again and again, to simplicity. We need not complicate things for ourselves, but rather heed John's words, that we have in our hearts the proof we need to know Jesus' promises were true. If we can let ourselves do this and connect to what is buried deep in our hearts, then we can indeed have that abundant life that Christianity holds out as its great gift. Listening to God speak through our hearts is not easy, it is risky and mysterious, but it is indeed simple. God loves the simple things. The truth awaits you, simply, in your heart; heed it.

THE REVEREND ANN HALLSTEIN *began her spiritual formation during morning chapels at the Laurel School outside Cleveland, Ohio, where she grew up. This subsequently led to a M.Div. from Union Theological Seminary in New York City and ordination in the United Church of Christ. After several years at the Library of Congress, she moved near Northampton, Massachusetts, where she and her partner make their home. She preaches, writes, and does pastoral counseling both at home and in New Canaan, Connecticut, where she heads Pastoral Ministries for the First Presbyterian Church. Her book,* Everyday Healing: Finding Extraordinary Moments in Ordinary Times, *is scheduled for publication in fall 1999 by Pilgrim Press.*

PEGGY HALSEY

Breaking the Silence

On Domestic Violence

PSALM 32

EING with you on the day of the Nelle Morton Lecture is a high honor. I was with Nelle on a number of occasions in the early seventies; I owe much to her and to her friend Anne Bennett. They took seriously the task of mentoring younger women in the faith, in passing on to us some of their perspectives and insights and, yes, the wisdom (*sophia*) that was theirs. Nelle's notion of "hearing into speech" became almost a mantra for a number of us who were quite young then, and more than ready for a uniquely female approach to ministry. "Hearing into speech" feels to me like a particularly rich way of restating the "breaking the silence" concept that is basic to my approach to ministry with abused women and children and families. Speaking the truth about one's life, those painful truths that have never before been given voice and that all too often no one, least of all religious folk, want to hear, is invariably the first step toward freedom and healing for those who have been hurt and betrayed. Often the betrayal is at the hands of the very people they ought to be able to trust to have their best interests at heart: their parents, their partners, and their pastors. In the words of the Psalm for today, "While I kept silence, my body wasted away . . . my strength was dried up as by the heat of summer."

In truth, though, the two concepts, "breaking the silence" and "hearing into speech," are not the same; one goes far beyond the other. "Breaking the silence" may imply that the responsibility rests on the voiceless one. "Hearing into speech" is inherently interactive. It gives the listener a crucial role and suggests much about the nature of ministry with abused and violated persons.

In the Church, we have not heard about violence against women and children because we have not spoken of it. Frequently, clergy questioned about pastoral contact with victims will say, "No one ever comes to me with this problem." Yet when challenged to use words like *rape, battering,* and *incest* in sermons, pastors invariably report that they are immediately approached by members with stories of current abuse in their lives and the lives of their families. It is clear that church folks are not immune to violence and that indeed many are waiting for a signal that these concerns are appropriate ones to share and struggle with in the faith community.

People who know that for many years my work has been with the Church's response to violence against women and children often ask me if I am hopeful or discouraged about the Church's role. Like my father when he was asked if he wanted pie or cake for dessert, my answer is usually "yes"—I am both hopeful and deeply discouraged. On any given day, I may be ready to throw it all in, sure that the Church is the last place where hurt and vulnerable persons can expect to find safety and healing . . . or I may be particularly sanguine, hoping against hope that the Church may finally be learning to be the Church, taking seriously the mandate to "comfort my people." The difference, perhaps not surprisingly, seems to hinge on the nature of the most recent story I have been told.

Listen to a few comments from a recent survey of the crisis experiences of United Methodists and their perspective on the way their churches responded:

From a woman abused by her spouse: "While our children were still small and I was being battered, I went to our pastor for counseling. He probably meant well, but he laid a heavier burden of guilt on me. His advice was to pray harder, have more faith, and be grateful for your six fine children."

From a clergywoman: "I was sexually abused by a family member from age seven to fourteen, until I became smart and confident enough to threaten to go to the authorities. As an adult, I thought I was handling my past well until I learned about a situation of incest in my parish. Memories swelled over me, and I sought out a pastoral counselor who helped me deal openly with my past, with all its ugliness and pain. Finally, twenty years later, the knot is gone from my stomach."

From a laywoman: "My fiancé forced me to have sex with him the night before our wedding. It was not until twenty-seven years later, when I saw a teenage boy who was a friend of my daughter wearing a button that said 'If she says *no* it's *rape*,' that I was able to deal with my anger and shame and guilt. Why couldn't my church have said it that clearly?"

And another: "A church nursery isn't necessarily a safe place for a child. I was abused as a three-year-old while my parents were in church. Screening volunteers is crucial, even in the Church."

Finally, two hopeful stories:

"The incest and sexual abuse occurred during my childhood and the perpetrator was my father, who was also my pastor. When I first told the secret within the church, I was given a place to live with another family—safety—but no counseling. My abuser was removed from his position, but never brought to justice. That possibility was never mentioned. Only many years later, in my present church, did I again tell my story to my pastor. He was immediately responsive, sensitive to my feelings, and supportive without prying. He contacted a nearby counseling service about establishing a support group for adult survivors, and made space available in the church. Thus I found a safe space to continue my own emotional and spiritual healing, and to be a presence for other women who were just beginning to deal with their pain."

"A combination of factors sent me to my pastor when my husband was at his most abusive. It was the first time in forty years that I had ever asked a pastor for help. If she had said, 'God only gives us what we can handle,' as a friend of mine was told by her pastor, I would probably not be a believer today. Fortunately, she was sympathetic and helpful. She recommended a therapist and made other useful suggestions. She said two things I will never forget: 'God intends us to be whole' and 'You can't make your husband well.' The second was especially poignant since I'd always thought his problems were my fault."

It is stories like these that catapult me between hope and despair. They remind me of the awesome power religious leaders have over the lives and health of those to whom we are called to minister.

When we exhort an adult survivor of child abuse to "forgive and forget," we are part of the problem and not part of the solution.

When we ask a battered wife to examine her behavior for the "triggers" that result in a beating, we are part of the problem and not part of the solution.

When we fail to remind an abused spouse, who is concerned that divorce would be breaking the marriage covenant, that the covenant was already broken by the violence, we are part of the problem and not part of the solution.

When we look the other way when a colleague in ministry

uses the power of his ordination to prey on vulnerable parishioners or counselees, we are part of the problem and not part of the solution.

When we imply in our sermons that suffering is noble or, alternatively, that a pain-free life is the reward for goodness or faithfulness, we are part of the problem and not part of the solution.

When we insist that the issue of inclusive language is a trivial one, ignoring the fact that the image of "father" is that of an abuser to at least several members of any congregation, we are part of the problem and not part of the solution.

When we "heal the wound lightly" by failing to hold abusers accountable for their actions, we are part of the problem and not part of the solution.

So what will it take for our churches and for their leaders, both clergy and lay, to become partners in seeking solutions to the evils of violence against women and children? It will take a clear message that while God does not promise that we will not suffer, God does promise to be present with us when we suffer. The promise to victims is that even though all others abandon them, God will be faithful.

It will require a new look at the meaning of the marriage covenant. In violent homes, divorce is not breaking up families. Violence and abuse are breaking up families. Divorce is often the painful, public acknowledgment of an already accomplished fact.

It will take a reinterpretation of a number of scripture passages that are commonly misused in a way that justifies abuse. A prime example is the "spare the rod and spoil the child" misquote of Proverbs 13:24. The truth is that the Hebrew word used there for rod is the same one used in the Twenty-third Psalm—as in "thy rod and thy staff shall comfort me"—comfort me, not hit me. A good shepherd uses his rod to guide sheep, count sheep, keep sheep from harm—never to beat them.

It will take careful reformulation of the notion of forgiveness.

We will have to teach that forgiveness is the end of a process, a long and arduous one. It is not a quick fix; it doesn't happen because someone tells you it should, or that it is time to forgive. It is based on a set of conditions: First, there must be a conscious choice on the part of the person who has been hurt to let go of the experience of pain and anger. Second, a sense of being in control, of no longer being powerless in the situation (a sense that can only probably come through grace) is required. And finally, there must be an experience of justice being done. For anyone—friends, family, therapist, pastor—to insist on premature forgiveness is to promote cheap grace. It can re-victimize one who has already been hurt and prolong the suffering.

The task of ministry in response to sexual and domestic violence is to provide the resources of faith and of the Church to accomplish three basic goals: protection, accountability, and justice. The first most urgent pastoral response required is to the victim: to provide hospitality and sanctuary and to make certain that there is safety and that the abuse is stopped. The next pastoral response is to the abuser, to hold him accountable, to insist that any repentance involve fundamental change and that the abusive behavior not be repeated. And the final response is both pastoral and prophetic: It is the making of justice and requires both truth-telling and restitution. There can be no healing without justice.

So we've come full circle—we're back at the truth-telling, the silence breaking, the hearing into speech. I choose to honor Nelle Morton's memory today by reminding myself and you that the quality of our hearing matters. I invite all present who are or have been victims or survivors, and all who minister to victims and survivors, to hear again these words from Psalm 32:

> Therefore let all who are faithful offer prayer to
> you; at times of distress, the rush of mighty wa-
> ters shall not reach them.

You are a hiding place for them; you preserve them
   from trouble; you surround them with glad cries
   of deliverance.
AMEN.

PEGGY HALSEY *is Executive Secretary for Ministries with Women,
Children, and Families of the General Board of Global Ministries for the
United Methodist Church. A native of Gainesville, Florida, she holds a
B.A. from Pfeiffer College and a M.R.E. from Union Theological
Seminary in New York City. She has written numerous articles for church
publications and has co-authored several books, including* Women in Crisis:
Stories of Ministry and Empowerment *and* Children and Youth in
Jeopardy: A Mission Concern for United Methodists. *She teaches
frequently and serves on several boards, including the Center for the
Prevention of Sexual and Domestic Violence. She studies watercolor paint-
ing and is a longtime resident of Brooklyn, New York.*

The Grand Puppeteer

On Omnipotence

NUMBER of years ago, I attended the National Meeting of United Presbyterian Women. It was a spectacular event. Five thousand women from Maine to California poured into Purdue University for a week's worth of education, fellowship, and nurture.

All kinds of women were there: Native Americans from the Southwest and points east, Republican housewives, Minneapolis feminists, southern African-American schoolteachers. Just nestling in and among all that flesh was inspiring, for I felt the literal embodiment of the Church Universal.

In this environment, I anticipated a taste of the "best" that the Church has to offer. However, each day, as the grand worship events unfolded, I grew agitated, then disappointed, and finally alienated.

What I found to be most depressing was the theology of the

event. Even though there was a variety of speakers, preachers, and biblical scholars, woven throughout the hymns and prayers was a disturbing theological attitude that is unmistakably Christian. Implicit and explicit in the language of our corporate worship was a blatant denial of reality. The language and the theology of this event on the whole did not relate to the substance of people's lives: the small dramas quietly and daily endured, the suffering so commonplace.

The most disturbing theological theme embedded in the language of the conference was a kind of Christian Triumphalism, the assertion that God is in His heaven and all is right with the world. This theological idea is expressed in the words of the hymn we sang:

> *Each color, gender, skill, and age,*
> *Acts out a part upon life's stage.*
> > *Alleluia! Alleluia!*
> *Our weaknesses reveal Christ's strength.*
> *Christ fills all height and breadth and length!*
> > *Alleluia! Alleluia!*
> > *Alleluia! Alleluia! Alleluia!*
> *So let us celebrate and praise*
> *God, the Redeemer of our days.*
> > *Alleluia! Alleluia!*
> *No pow'r of evil can endure!*
> *God reigns!—of that we can be sure!*
> > *Alleluia! Alleluia!*
> > *Alleluia! Alleluia! Alleluia!*[1]

This language undermines our fundamental trust in our own experience and erodes our ability to make sense out of our lives. It makes us insecure and mistrustful of our perception of reality. Unconsciously, it insists that "wishing will make it so." If we just repeat these beliefs long enough and loudly enough, what we say will become what is!

We live life caught within a contradiction, for our lives challenge the belief that God's in control and all's right with the world. If this theology accurately expresses the content of our faith, then what kind of God are we worshiping? Can we in all honesty affirm that "God reigns!—of that we can be sure"?

The language of triumphalism suppresses the truth of our lives. Can we insist that God—or Christ—has it "all under control"? If that is the case, then it's hard for me to fathom what kind of God is in charge—if things are presumably not out of God's control.

The time-honored doctrine of the omnipotence of God claims that God is all-powerful, a kind of Superman, if you will, able to alter the course of any event at any moment, natural or otherwise. God is the Grand Puppeteer, and we are His puppets, acting out our part in a cosmic drama, while God on the other side of the curtain pulls our strings, visits famines, causes accidents to happen, and teaches us lessons.

When we construct God as the Grand Puppeteer, we are satisfied to read our lines and act out our parts, ever ready to succumb to the signs of "God's will" in our lives, ever obedient, ever compliant, ever willing to accept suffering or tragedy as an indication of God's disfavor with us. All manner of suffering is understood as a sign of God's punishment. If I am unhappy or in pain, God must be punishing me for resenting my partner, or being short with my child, or being gay. But if God is in control, meting out punishments to miserable offenders, then what kind of God is minding the store? What kind of God can tolerate the extermination of Jews, the abandonment of children in garbage heaps of Mexico City, the perpetual penalization of those whom the gospel purportedly addresses, the poor? In this scheme of things, God is sadistic.

In her book, *Suffering,* Dorothee Soelle writes:

> [Theological sadism] schools people in thought pat-
> terns that regard sadistic behavior as normal, in

which one worships, honors, and loves a being whose "radicality," "intentionality," and "greatest sharpness" is that He slays. The ultimate conclusion of theological sadism is worshipping the executioner.[2]

The ultimate abuse of God is to blame our sadism on a God of love.

Yesterday was Rosh Hashanah, the New Year, the beginning of another year in the history of the Jewish people. For many Jews, the Holocaust was the death of God. For anti-Semitic or confused Christians, the doctrine of the omnipotence of God can lead to the grossest kind of anti-Semitism: the belief that God willed this brutality. When we consider our God as a God of perpetual punishment who chastises us for our sins, then our focus is upon a God of punishment and not a God of love, a God of wrath and not of grace, a God of grudges, not of forgiveness.

One consequence of this doctrine is infantilization—a favorite theme of Sigmund Freud. At the mercy of a capricious God, we become passive dependents unable or unwilling to make decisions of significance because whatever we do is God's will. What great comfort there is in knowing that we do not have to take responsibility for our actions, our behavior, our decisions. God is in control, displacing our responsibility for living our lives. Our decisions are inconsequential, for our lives are inconsequential. We plod along, assuming that whatever we do is God's plan. Even our suffering is part of God's plan, for God inflicts suffering upon us, just to remind us that we are, after all, wicked.

If the God of omnipotence is sadistic, then we are, in response, masochistic.[3] We define obedience as submission to the will of God, ever assuming suffering to be God's will, ever ready to engage in self-punishing habits that make us ill. Destroying ourselves then can become theologically sanctioned and thereby a socially legitimated way to practice our faith.

A second consequence of this theology is the emphasis upon radical individualism. We can't see the patterns, the corporate nature of our lives. We become obsessed by the meaning and nature of our individual suffering, ferreting out our sin instead of perceiving our suffering as something shared with and experienced by others. We remain preoccupied by the individual and not the corporate meaning of our suffering.

Psychologists tell us that we project upon God those qualities that we value most highly in our culture. Surely our culture confirms this. The violence in our society reflects our worship of a God of violence. We also project upon God our understanding of power. Our need to control, our obsession with power demands a God of power. If God does not have the capacity to control events and change lives, then what good is He? If God can't do anything for us, if God is impotent by our standards, then God is useless.

The French sociologist Emile Durkheim observed in *The Elementary Forms of Religious Life* that religion is the community reflecting itself back to itself.[4] If this is the case, then God inevitably reveals the culture and its values. In short, God *looks* the same as our culture: violent, greedy, power-hungry, punitive. God is no longer the mysterious other. God is a narcissistic personification of all that we value in this absurd world of ours.

Our belief in a God that expresses power in conventional terms of might or aggression is ultimately self-serving. If we expect God to be all-powerful, then when God does not do anything for us or help us out, God is useless. We are interested in what God can do for us, how God can help us improve our lives, our health, our marriage, our family life. Religion becomes another expression of self-help, a form of self-aggrandizement. For the middle class, used to the privileges of power, religion becomes a convenience item, and "success" the point of it all. I often find myself irritated by the barrage of Christian self-help books. For example, a book by Pat Boone presents Christianity as the key to success. Jesus was hardly a role model for success in any conventional terms. He was, after all, put to death for his actions and behavior.

Recently as I walked past a large, prestigious church on Fifth Avenue I noticed a slick, glossy poster announcing an upcoming Bible study program titled "Kyregma: The Challenge to Grow!" *Kyregma* is the Greek word for preaching or revealed truth. I was annoyed and disturbed by the attempt to attract participants to read the Bible by the lure of self-gain. In our capitalist economy, the Bible becomes yet another thing to consume. The Bible is reduced to a self-help program rather than an invitation to encounter the mystery of the divine transcendent. Let us not be confused here: our faith may indeed be helpful to us, but it is about meaning, not self-improvement. This kind of thinking produces a distorted understanding about the center of one's faith. God—my relation to, my quest for God—not me, lies at the core; not God's service to us, but our service to the world.

Finally, if God is omnipotent, then we can fall easily into victim-blaming, which inevitably leads to abuse. The weak are judged, punished, and sinful. Those who suffer deserve it. On the other hand, the successful and powerful are favored by God. Dorothee Soelle asks, "At Auschwitz, was God with the victims—or the murderers?"[5]

It is not easy to unmask our God from the trappings of omnipotence. Like Dorothy who discovers the Wizard of Oz to be fraudulent, simply a mortal man, we cling fast to our notion of an all-powerful God. We do not want to know otherwise.

When I was critically ill, I examined myself for some sign, some explanation for why I was experiencing such tremendous physical pain. I was compelled to atone for my sins, convinced that pain was indeed punishment for something—I knew not what. It was in that time that my God began to die. No longer could I believe that the tremendous pain I was experiencing was God's will, or that God was punishing me. I began to understand the words of Alfred North Whitehead, who said, "God is the fellow sufferer who understands." God grieved my pain, was present to and in my suffering—sharing it, not willing it. I began to understand the power of the crucified God. God was powerless, subjected to senseless cruelty. In the cross we encounter the God of suffering, not success.

The work is in our hands: we can no longer remain passive, wishing to make it so. Our task is to know the suffering, to be present, to see, to act. It is appropriate, on Rosh Hashanah, that we learn from Jack Reimer. He writes:

> *We cannot merely pray to You, O God, to end war;*
> *For we know that You have made the world in a way*
> *That man must find his own path to peace*
> *Within himself and with his neighbor.*
> *We cannot merely pray to You, O God, to end starvation;*
> *For you have already given us the resources*
> *With which to feed the entire world*
> *If we would only use them wisely.*
> *We cannot merely pray to You, O God,*
> *To root out prejudice,*
> *For You have already given us eyes*
> *With which to see the good in all men*
> *If we would only use them rightly.*
> *We cannot merely pray to You, O God, to end despair,*
> *For You have already given us the power*
> *To clear away slums and to give hope*
> *If we would only use our power justly.*
> *We cannot merely pray to You, O God, to end disease,*
> *For you have already given us great minds with which*
> *To search out cures and healing.*
> *If we would only use them constructively.*

Therefore we pray to You instead, O God,
For strength, determination, and willpower,
To do instead of just to pray,
To become instead of merely to wish.[6]
AMEN.

THE REVEREND E. LEE HANCOCK *is a Presbyterian minister whose preaching career extends over two decades and includes serving as a minister at Judson Memorial Church and as the first seminary pastor of Union Theological Seminary, both in New York City. She has been instrumental in founding a number of grassroots AIDS organizations, including Bailey House in New York City, the first congregate living facility for persons with AIDS in the country. Hancock lectures on healing and health care and is completing her Ph.D. in religion and society at Drew University, where she is an adjunct instructor in the Theological School. A program officer with the Newark Project on Urban Religious Values, she lives with her family in Nyack, New York.*

More Life,
More Life

On Parenting

T HE opportunity to preach on Mother's Day always leaves me with something of a dilemma. I am a mother, and I have a mother, and so there is some temptation to preach about mothers. Or at least to tell you about my three excellent children—Kirsten the Bold, Edmund the Brave, and Amanda the Rockette. These days it is harder to know which are brighter, the colors of the cathedral close or the colors my children are showing. I could tell you about my two hundred and thirty other children, the children of the Cathedral School, who are also brilliant and surprising, headstrong and sometimes very funny.

Or I could talk about the Resurrection.

As if they were different subjects.

They are not.

In this season of blossoming flowers, leafing trees, clearing skies, and singing birds we know that Christ is risen. We may know as a matter of personal faith and acceptance that the man we knew as Jesus, who loved us unspeakably well and then left us for a gruesome death, has returned, and will let us see him, but not own him, as he prepares to ascend into heaven. Christ is risen.

Or, if the traditional lines of Christian dogma leave us feeling squeamish and confused—all that business about bodies rising and scientific laws melting away—if that seems too much like a betrayal of reason, we can simply turn to nature and see spring. When we see spring, we know that the One who was the Creating Word is definitely present—new, fresh, green, brilliant as the daffodils, tender as the dew, unsettling as the bright red cardinal that flut-ters past, is seen, and flits away. We see, we touch, we almost grasp. How hard, how arduous was our winter; how jubilant, if fleeting, is the beauty of our spring. He is risen.

Or, we might bring the matter still closer to our touch and talk of mothers, of babies, of the dew-damp skin of those fresh born from the womb, radiant of eye, tiny of hand, blessed. New life, a chance to begin again, to amend what was broken, to repair in the next generation what was damaged in the last.

Do you remember, fathers and mothers, do you remember those first few days? Do you remember the birth itself? How much it felt like falling, a triumphant, excruciating push from one life to the next? Did you feel yourselves falling out of yourselves, and were you alarmed? I know I was. Not long after the birth of my first child I felt sure I was dying. My mouth was dry, my ap-petite was gone, I wasn't sleeping, and my heart raced like a colt. At the sight of the baby the air closed in around me like dead weight. I longed for the comfort and relative quiet of the hospi-tal—by this I knew something was wrong!—and wept over trivial things. I called the doctor, then went to see him. He asked a lot of questions, then took me gently in hand. "Ms. Harriss," he said, "you're not dying. You're terrified. What you are doing is terrible, in the best sense. Terrible. Terrific. You are terrific. You are terrified."

The women who left the tomb on Easter morning were terrified. They were walking at the edges of life. I went home, that day, terrified, having touched the edges of life. Amazed, I went home and resumed what felt, at the time, like an endless walk of responsibility and challenge. I had fallen into the chasm of adult life; my old self was gone. I had become a mother.

In a funny way, I had died, but it was a death so common as to be unnoticeable, not mentioned in the books. I had begun to lay down my life, of my own free will, though sometimes kicking and screaming as I adjusted to it, I had begun to lay down my life, in increments, for a child. It was a thousand little things. Mainly it meant laying down the book I was reading, or the book I was writing; setting aside a cup of coffee, then the time for the coffee, then the friends I once drank coffee with—all for something new, this new life that was quickly becoming all-absorbing. A friend once said of her relationship with her infant daughter, "I feel like I'm just pouring myself into her."

And so she was.

Jesus laid down his life for his friends. He was not constrained, as mothers are, and fathers are, by necessity or natural law, or any law. He was not constrained to lay aside his life for us, but he did. It was the measure of his love. It became the measure of our love for one another: Will you lay down your life, if it comes to that? Will you set aside your interest for the life of another?

I saw a wonderful T-shirt recently. On the front there is a cartoon by the late Keith Haring; on the back, the words "It is in your self-interest to find a way to become very tender."

It is in your self-interest to find a way to become very tender.

As mothers, as fathers, we have at our disposal a wonderful time of rehearsal. We may set aside our interests time and again; we may practice watching the interests of others. But if that sacrificial love starts with our children, and stops there, we will have lost our opportunity to fulfill Christ's commandment, and so have everything that He has promised. Christ's commandment is that we love, not just our children, but one another!

And what a relief that is! I, for one, would never want to have my life evaluated or measured on the basis of what I have done, or not done, for my children. Motherhood, parenting, is very gratifying, yes, but if that were all there was for me, I would be lost. In fact, I would find such a judgment terrifying: terrifying, because of my inevitable mistakes, and yes, I have made a few. But also terrifying in that if I thought my motherhood were all there was for me, I would never be able to let my children go. What would become of me when they left home? Or sooner, when they declared, as they already do, how different are their passions and interests from what I had in mind? How different they are from me? And what kind of God would do that to me, anyway? What kind of God would assign to a human being a role that only takes part of her life and leaves the rest of her time on earth as a kind of emptiness? Most women do live thirty years or more after their children leave home; I know I hope to. What will be left to do?

Jesus said, "Whoever loses his life, for my sake, will keep it for eternity. Whoever loses her life will gain it." If my sacrifice, and yours, is not so much pointed at personal fulfillment, and not even toward the health and satisfaction of our children, but beyond that, to the love of the world and God's creation, then I have resurrection. Whatever I have lost, I will have gained—not in the faces and adulation of my own children but in the living fabric of the world they inhabit. For God always replenishes the heart that has spent itself in love; what I do for love of God's world I do for my children, for it is the world they inhabit.

This is the best news of all, because, mothers and fathers, when our time has come, when, having fulfilled the duties of our state of life we are free to address ourselves to the needs of the world, when it comes time to love one another as Jesus loved us, we already know how! We have already learned! How to touch, how to feed, how to tend, how to heal, how to care, how to love. But. But it is different with us this time, because we act not out of duty. This time, in addition to knowing how to love, we also know why.

Because He first loved us. Because Christ has risen. Because in addition to being seen, spotted, glimpsed walking on earth, our beloved Christ has begun to dwell within us. Through the gift of Holy Spirit, He will take up residence within us. Do you remember the Stephen Foster song, the one that Gordon Lightfoot used to sing, "Listen to them talking about your love's return"?

Having practiced our scales, played the daily exercises of love for our children, the scales of our belonging, now we come to the concerto. Now the music begins. Having loved our own, we now can love the world. Now we rise to the task for which our parenting prepared us. Because he loved us; because while we lost ourselves, not just in sin but in duty, not just in forgetfulness but in earnestness, in our sincere desire to do what was right for our children, because although we lost ourselves in our mothering, God remembered us, and brought us forward, and made us new.

And here we are. More alive than ever, with the evidence of new life standing all around us, these children, raised up like the tulips, crowding the air like a cloud of witnesses, More life. More life.

Do you know these words from Denise Levertov, a poem called "Stepping Westward"?

> There is no savor more sweet, more salt,
> Than to be what, woman, and who, myself, I am
> If I bear burdens, they begin to be remembered as
>   gifts, goods,
> A basket of bread that hurts my shoulders, but
>   closes me in fragrance. I can eat as I go.[1]

Or these words, from Isaiah:

> But they that wait upon the Lord shall renew their
> strength. They shall mount up with wings as eagles.
> They shall run and not be weary. They shall walk,
> and not faint.

Brothers and sisters, mothers and fathers, let us love one another. For Christ is risen. **AMEN**.

THE REVEREND CANON SUSAN HARRISS *is an Episcopal
priest in New York City. Ordained in 1978, she serves as Canon Pastor and
Vicar to the Congregation at the Cathedral of St. John the Divine. She
harkens back to the sermons of her grandfather, who sang and shouted in the
pulpit as an evangelist in the Salvation Army. She loves preaching, which she
hopes, like tap dancing, will make a great American comeback. Although her
three children think what she does is a little weird, her husband, Ken Ruge,
also a minister, is downright supportive. A poet and writer, she is the author
of* Jamie's Way: Stories for Worship and Devotion *(Cowley Publications, 1991). She is also a contributor to Cowley's publication* Ourselves,
Our Souls and Bodies. *A child of officers in the Salvation Army, she attended Denison University and Union Theological Seminary.*

THE REVEREND DR. JOAN E. HEMENWAY

Beyond Belief

On Spirit

JOHN 3:1–8

I AM delighted to be back in your midst for this special Sunday and to be part of your Bicentennial Celebration. I have watched you from afar and kept you in my heart since 1978 when I left my position as your associate minister in order to become a full-time teaching chaplain in hospitals and, more recently, a pastoral counselor. Yes, I have watched you from afar and kept you in my heart—praying your prayers, reading your sermons, singing your songs, loving you and being proud to be connected with you as you offered sanctuary to people from Guatemala, as you sent beloved members of this congregation to bear witness in Haiti and in South Africa, as you dared to become a Reconciling Congregation, as you continued to work to bring renewal to Germantown, and bring justice to this city. You have been for me a beacon on a hill, leaven in the lump, a light in the darkness, a vibrant splash of color

in an often sterile and dull world . . . and now, like a loving
mother, you welcome the prodigal daughter home. For me it is indeed a joyous homecoming. Thank you. Thank you.

It may come as a surprise to some of you to learn that for most
of my life I have struggled with considerable fear and anxiety.
Whenever I had to catch a plane, or figure out how to make a new
gadget work, deal with the unexpected, or preach a sermon, waves
of uncertainty and fear would wash over me, and a knot would
begin to form in the pit of my stomach.

Now, as a person of faith I am aware that if there is plenty to
be frightened about on a human level, our fears can certainly be
heightened tenfold when it comes to trying to be in relationship
with the Divine. Perhaps it is some consolation to know that we
do stand in good biblical company. Adam and Eve were afraid, so
they covered their nakedness with fig leaves. Moses was afraid and
hid his face. Abraham was afraid as he set out for Mount Moriah
with his son Isaac. The shepherds were afraid as they stood on
that midnight hillside. The man with one talent was afraid and hid
his talent in the ground. The disciples were afraid as their boat
suddenly began to sink out from underneath them. And on that
first Easter morning Mary of Magdala and Martha were afraid as
they saw the stone so unexpectedly rolled away from the tomb.

The very act of worship can be fearful if we think about it for
very long or very deeply. Annie Dillard knows all about these
kinds of fears when she writes:

> Does anyone have the foggiest idea of what sort of
> power (our prayers) so blithely invoke? . . . It is
> madness to wear ladies' . . . hats to church; we
> should all be wearing crash helmets. Ushers should
> issue life preservers and signal flares; they should
> lash us to our pews. For the sleeping god may
> awake someday and take offense, or the waking god
> may draw us out to where we can never return.[1]

I currently work in a place where both life and faith are constantly at risk, where fears of a sleeping god who has taken offense are just as strong as fears of a waking god who will draw us out to someplace from which we can never return. Bridgeport Hospital is a three-hundred-bed general hospital. It is located in a city that is struggling with terrible urban problems, and in a state that does not really care very much about improving the life in its cities. Like any hospital, my place of ministry is filled with people who are frightened, hurt, angry, lost, sad, lonely. Some of the stories are beyond belief. They are just plain awful.

For instance, last week a forty-two-year-old woman tried to commit suicide by putting a gun in her mouth. For some reason, the bullet ripped her tongue apart, but not her brain, and she will go home this week. And whatever despair it was that caused her to try to take her life will go home with her. Up in our pediatric intensive-care unit lies an unresponsive five-month-old baby boy. He needed a simple surgery, but unfortunately his body had an allergic reaction to the anesthesia, a reaction that has essentially now ruined his brain. The doctors prepare to remove the tubes as the parents stand ready to receive the little body and put new clothes on him for burial. Somewhere in the wrench and stench of those moments, I learn that this couple has already lost two babies, and now their four-year-old son at home prays daily to die so that he can become an angel and join his siblings in heaven. Even a crash helmet or a limitless supply of life preservers is insufficient protection from such bizarre horrors, to say nothing of whatever may be the divine presence in this situation.

In addition to doing ministry in this place myself, I also teach others—clergy and laity—how to do it, how to stand it, how to be alert and not just frightened, how to be more curious than helpless, educable rather than paralyzed—in a word, how to be courageous and not run away from it all.

One of my students is a middle-aged woman, an Episcopal

priest. Two years ago her teenaged daughter, the love of her life, died of cancer. In the two years since this terrible tragedy my clergy student lost all meaningful semblance of her life, lost her ministry, and lost her faith. She came into training with me warning me that I could not take her grief from her any more than I could give her ministry or her faith back to her—as hard as I might want to try. As she struggles with her life and with her God, and I look on, she shares with me in weekly written reflections what is going on with her, how she is trying to put it together. Last week she wrote:

> I recently heard a story about a woman who had a major stroke requiring brain surgery. After the surgery, the doctor told her she was going to survive and be just fine, except that her face would always be distorted, and especially her mouth, which was twisted and pushed over to one side. At the news, the woman began to cry and begged the doctor to do something because she felt so ugly and deformed. Just then, her husband, who had been standing there listening, bent over and kissed her lips. As he did this, he positioned his own lips to the same twisted shape as hers so that their lips matched. [A] student [of mine] commented: "The point of the story was that's what God does for us. When we're twisted and deformed by life's horrors, God takes on our twistedness to meet us where we are. I like this image. It means God spends most of God's time being broken and battered and bleeding and writhing and swollen and amputated. Maybe God's even a grieving mom, holding millions of her dead kids in her arms, kissing their twisted bodies with twisted lips to match.[3]

Maybe. Maybe.

In our Gospel lesson for this morning we hear about Nico-demus. He was a Pharisee, an aging Jewish leader, who must have heard that Jesus was preaching about being born again and didn't quite understand what Jesus was talking about. Because of the laws of purity separating Pharisees from the rest of society, Nicodemus had to literally sneak out at night in order to see Jesus at all, much less ask his question: "Rabbi, how is it possible for a man to be born when he is old? Can a man enter his mother's womb for a second time and be born?" What a question! How many of us men and women, especially those of us who are now reaching be-yond our middle years, resonate with Nicodemus! Wouldn't all of us, young or old, like the chance to be born over again, to get a grip, get a life or a new start on life, to do it over now that we know more about how to do it right—or at least how to do it real?

At first glimpse Jesus' answer is perplexing. "In truth I tell you no one can enter the kingdom of God without being born from water and spirit. Flesh can give birth only to flesh; it is spirit that gives birth to spirit. You ought not to be astonished then, when I tell you that you must be born over again. The wind blows where it wills; you hear the sound of it, but you do not know where it comes from, or where it is going. So it is with everyone who is born from the spirit."

In New Testament studies there is a basic distinction drawn be-tween the Christ of faith and the Jesus of history. Throughout this century, biblical scholars have worked with varying degrees of suc-cess to sort out these two strands that run throughout the gospel accounts and the Book of Acts. It is generally accepted that the Jesus of history did not think of himself as someone to be believed in. He did not think of himself as the son of God who was sent into the world to die for the sins of the world that we might be-lieve in him and have everlasting life. These familiar words from the Apostles' Creed are about the Christ of faith. This is how the Apostle Paul and the later church fathers began to understand the meaning of Jesus' life and death. And it is their understandings that are expressed in our Christological doctrines and trinitarian formulas and eucharistic prayers.

The Jesus of history was quite different. He was simply a Jewish teacher of wisdom, a social prophet, and the founder of a movement that shattered the social boundaries of his day. Going more deeply, the Jesus of history was a person who experienced God as a reality, as a force to be reckoned with in his life, as a spirit that animated and penetrated all the layers of existence, as the source of everything that was and is and could be. In short, Jesus was a "spirit person"; that is, he experienced the sacred presence frequently and vividly, and he became a mediator of its power to others. Sharing this spirit-filled, God-filled experience is at the heart of Jesus' life and ministry. So when Jesus tells Nicodemus, and you and me and all those who want new life, to be born again in the spirit, he is asking us not to believe in him, but to reach beyond belief into active relationship with God, similar to the kind of relationship he—Jesus—had with God. Jesus is pushing Nicodemus and us to discover, be open to, and be affected by that of God which is both beyond us and within us.

I am convinced that the author Alice Walker is, like Jesus, a spirit person. In *The Color Purple* we hear about a conversation the protagonist, Celie, had with her friend Shug. The conversation is about God:

> "Here's the thing I believe," says Shug. "God is inside you and inside everybody else. But only those who search for it inside find it. And sometimes it just manifests itself even if you are not looking, or don't know what you are looking for. Trouble does it for most folks, I think. Sorrow, lord. Feeling awful."
>
> "It?" I asked.
>
> "Yes, It. God isn't a he or a she, but an It."

"But what does It look like?" I asked.

"Doesn't look like anything," she said. "It isn't a picture show. It isn't something you can look at apart from anything else, including yourself. I believe God is everything . . . Everything that is or ever was or ever will be. And when you can feel that, and be happy to feel that, you've found it."[4]

Perhaps you have had such experiences of finding It right here in this sanctuary.

In our Gospel lesson for this morning, Jesus is saying to Nicodemus and to you and to me that we can all be spirit people. That we are all yearning to be born again and again and again. We don't know where the spirit comes from or where it's going; like the wind it blows where it will, and yet the spirit is as close as our next breath.

Robert Frost has written a remarkable poem in his own inimitable style about this divine mystery as it interpenetrates our lives and gives way to our birthing process. He writes:

> But God's own descent
> Into flesh was meant
> As a demonstration
> That the supreme merit
> Lay in risking spirit
> In substantiation.
> Spirit enters flesh
> And for all it's worth
> Charges into earth
> In birth after birth
> Ever fresh and fresh.
> We may take the view
> That its derring-do
> Thought of in the large

Is one mighty charge
On our human part
Of the soul's ethereal
Into the material.[5]

Now it is important to note that our experiences of the soul's ethe-real charging into the material and our openness in moving beyond belief into closer proximity to God does not set us apart or make us pure and holy. In fact, quite the opposite. Marcus Borg in his remarkable book entitled *Meeting Jesus Again for the First Time* points out that, for Jesus, God was preeminently a God of compassion. In fact, the phrase from Luke "Be ye perfect as your father in heaven is perfect" is better translated "Be compassionate as God is compassionate." To be in active, close relationship with this God, as Jesus was, is to become like God, that is, to experience compassion toward the world and become involved in the world as God, through Jesus, did. Borg writes: "Whereas purity divides and excludes, compassion unites and includes."[6] Thus, one of the most radical parts of Jesus' ministry was his insistence on chang-ing the predominant social and religious paradigm of his day from being governed by laws of purity and holiness such as Nicodemus lived under to being governed by the law of love and the work of compassion. And so he crossed all sorts of boundaries, touching lepers, eating with tax collectors, welcoming women into his group of itinerant travelers, and witnessing to the Pharisee, Nicodemus.

Being in relationship to God as Jesus was sends us into the world, to feel compassion toward and with the suffering of others and be so moved by this as to enter into it and do something about it. We are to feel as God feels toward the world. We are to be as God is toward the world. Furthermore, compassion at work in the world is not an individual, private religious stance; rather, when taken as seriously as Jesus and God intended, it is a community commitment and a starting point for public policy. So to be born again, as spirit people, to let the spirit blow anew through our lives, is always a supremely political and potentially subversive act in relationship to the conventional laws of society.

It is not surprising to learn that the root of the Hebrew word for compassion means "womb." To say that God is compassionate is to say that God is womblike. "Like a womb, God is the one who gives birth to us . . . As a mother loves the children of her womb . . . so God loves us and feels for us. For Jesus, God was a nourishing, caring, embracing, encompassing mother. And that is what he calls us to be for all the world."[7]

So it is that you and I are born again and live out of secret, and sometimes not so secret, places of fear—where at any moment some sleeping god may awake and take offense or a waking god may draw us to places from which we can never return. So it is that we are born again and live out of places of horror, where human tragedy and loss overwhelm and even destroy faith—at least for a while. So it is that we are born again and live out of places of hope where God twists Her lips to kiss our own contorted faces—in a remarkable demonstration of risking spirit in substantiation. So it is that we are born again and live out of places of compassion, where the old rules and purity laws and boundaries are transgressed and finally destroyed for the sake of bringing God's radical love into a weary, weeping world. So it is that we are born again and live out of places of faith—where God is in and through everything that ever was, is now and ever will be.

And when you can feel that, and be happy to feel that, you've found it.

If you are fans of ice skating, as I am, you will recall the tragic death last November of twenty-nine-year-old Sergei Grinkov. He and his wife, Katya Gordeeva, had skated in the pairs competition and won two Olympic gold medals. They were totally in sync with each other both on and off the ice. This past week Katya made her first appearance since her husband's untimely death. She skated alone to Mahler's Fifth Symphony at the Hartford Civic Center.

According to the newspaper account, she began her piece

under a lone blue spotlight holding an outstretched hand quietly waiting, waiting, waiting for her husband and partner to join her as he had for the fourteen years of their skating career together. She then covered her face as the horrible truth of his absence sank in. She raced around the ice looking for him, eventually dropping to her knees in despair. Slowly she kissed the ice as if it were a grave. After looking to the heavens imploringly, she rose and began to skate again slowly at first, then faster and faster, jumping, spinning, turning, gliding, circling round and round, and even smiling at one point, carrying on as Sergei would have wanted, indeed insisted, celebrating his life and hers and theirs together. At the end of the piece, her eyes awash in tears (along with the eyes of thousands of strangers who witnessed her incredible performance), she skated to the end of the arena and gently took her three-year-old daughter, Daria, in her arms. And then she hugged Sergei's mother and her own coach who had convinced her she could skate again in Sergei's memory.

Afterward, Katya said: "I think everyone has their terrible times in life when you have to find the strength and go through difficult things. But I want everyone to know that life is beautiful and people have to give love to the person they love and continue living."[8] AMEN AND AMEN.

THE REVEREND DR. JOAN E. HEMENWAY *is an ordained minister in the United Methodist Church. She currently serves as Director of Pastoral Care and Clinical Pastoral Education (CPE) at Bridgeport General Hospital, and has also served as the associate pastor at the First United Methodist Church of Germantown in Philadelphia. She is a lecturer in Practical Theology at Yale Divinity School and author of* Inside the Circle: A Historical and Practical Inquiry Concerning Process Groups in Clinical Pastoral Education. *A fellow in the American Association of Pastoral Counselors, she has been a CPE supervisor for more than twenty-five years. She earned her M.Div. from Union Theological Seminary, in New York City, and her D.Min. from Andover-Newton Theological School, in Newton Center, Massachusetts. She makes her home on the Connecticut shore. She says, "Preaching has helped me to be faithful."*

THE REVEREND MARY BYRNE HOFFMANN

Worship: Dreams and Visions

On Heaven

ACTS 2:17–21

SOMETIMES in the midst of my nightly dream time, when the day is done and suddenly there is quiet and space and enough darkness to roam the crevices without seeing the cracks, the voice of my child cuts through the stillness from his recurring nightmare.

"Mommy, come here," he says with a slight anguish. And I go a little begrudgingly but I go quickly because there is something familiar in the tone of his request. I know he's having those thoughts again.

"Mommy, I'm having those thoughts again," he says on cue. "I can't get it out of my head . . . I keep thinking about death. What will it be like? I'm so afraid that I won't ever see you again."

This fear, and the conversation that ensues, has been occurring since my son was about five. He is eight now. I guess by the books it coincided with school and socialization and friends and a confrontation with the larger world and a sense of himself as being so tiny in the world. I believe it comes from a sense of being lost in all the possibilities of life and then ironically from a deeper premonition of loss—that someday even those overwhelming possibilities will be taken away by death and a journey to that huge, amorphous, ethereal blank space called heaven.

Heaven doesn't work for Gavin. And I can't push it too much because it doesn't really work for me, either. As Gavin reminds me, nobody has ever come back to say what it's like. So there is a lingering doubt that fuels the fear that heaven is not real. It is not the truth. It is not enough insurance to cover the loss. No one that we know has definitely collected on the policy.

When I was asked to reflect on dreams and visions in the context of today's readings, to imagine that DAY at the end of time, I felt much like Gavin. The images that have been a part of my life through years of myopic religious instruction—that focused on the future rather than the here and now—surfaced in their ridiculous and incredible pantomime of eternity. It was not a dream; it was a nightmare. And, like Gavin's, it was a nightmare of loss.

That was a visceral reaction. I was stuck in it until I took the time to remember I was not a child anymore and these were no longer my fears. Something the years had given me was a vision . . . a vision of life that really told me everything I needed to know about death and the end of time and the days of glory.

The days of glory, the realm of God, come all the time in moments of death as most of us fear it and in times of great and seemingly irretrievable loss—moments of obliteration at the indiscriminate hand of all the chaotic and unjust and cruel possibilities of life. Death comes when self-recognition is taken away, when the familiar ground we walk evaporates into an invisible abyss, when there is no one or no thing you remember in quite the same way as before. There are so many ways this can happen. Each of you carries the memory or the foreboding of such moments depending on your own sense of being lost and of loss.

The vision I have to offer you this morning is this: that what is lost can be found in that very self that is diminished in moments of darkness, when the sun and moon lose their light and the stars you wished on as a child fall mercilessly from your dreams. It is at that moment when the human One—the true self that has been tortured by the images of life gone awry, stripped of the outer garments of acceptability, crucified by distorted belief systems, and buried by the confounding realities of living death rises to the occasion of grace. For deep, deep down, as one layer of knowing life dies away to another layer, the true Self resides in abundant being. Instead of being lost, the true Self finds itself in the recognition of what is essentially human and ultimately divine. And there is so much light, so much radiant glory, so much peace.

This is not a vision for an apocalyptic end of time; it is a vision for now. If I could give anything to myself, to my son, to you, I would want this vision to be before us, within reach all the time. For once you have seen the light of true Self—the soul—in union with God there can no longer be the fear of loss that drives us to hurt one another so terribly and catastrophically in order to protect the little selves in a childish world, that we sense we are.

I feel the presence of this vision . . . the glorious swelling of the company of true Selves, and I know it to be the truth. It is confirmed each time I am drawn down deep by loss and rise again by grace to discover that you and others are there.

These days when Gavin has his nightmare, I tell him that instead of thinking about death maybe we could just think about living. That doesn't always put him to sleep, but he can't quite argue with it. And someday, when he needs to, he will not be afraid of death anymore. He will be caught up in a mesmerizing vision of the infinite possibilities of life.

THE REVEREND MARY BYRNE HOFFMANN *is an interfaith minister in the Community of the Beloved in Nyack, New York, where she lives with her son, Gavin. She has produced more than twelve television documentaries on spirituality and social issues, including "Search for Spirituality" and "Hope Out of Ashes." She also presents workshops on media literacy to a wide range of audiences across the country—parents, teachers, clergy, and youth. Ms. Hoffmann is a graduate of Union Theological Seminary in New York City. She is a Roman Catholic by tradition and a "roaming Catholic" by necessity.*

Standing on the Promises of Love

On Faith

MATTHEW 11:28; LUKE 11:9–10; PSALMS 46:1

(This sermon was transcribed from an audiotape.)

JUST for a moment I want to leave a few words with you on this Pride Sunday. Two and a half years we've been here, and we've been through a lot of things. And God has blessed us. We started with a few, and we became many. We developed programs and a choir and ministries; we have all these things going on. And every Sunday we do an affirmation, we do a libation, and the choir sings. If you come to LIT (Liberation in Truth, Unity Fellowship Church) you kind of have a sense of what's going to happen, every Sunday. And we like that. We like knowing what's gonna happen when we go to church. I mean when you pay to go out, you don't go to a club that you know is going to be stinky. You go to a club where you know that the music is going to be good—maybe you'll see some nice-looking women, nice-looking guys, you know. So you go for what you know.

At LIT we go for what we know. We know when we come in, Spirit is going to be here. But the thing that I want to ask you this afternoon is, What do you hold on to? If we do the same thing every single Sunday just about, and Spirit moves a little differently but basically you do the same thing, there's a danger in getting used to it, and you can begin to recite things. You know a deacon is going to pray. You know I'm going to do my little thing down the aisle—the affirmation—some people move their mouths as I'm saying it. So my question is, For spiritual people like us, living in a world that does not like us, living in a world where we suffer and go through many things that are out of our control, what do we hold on to?

If I would use a theme today, it would be Standing on the Promises of Love. If all else fails, you can stand on the promises of love. There's an expression that says, stand for something or you'll fall for anything. You've got to be solidly planted in some belief. Otherwise you'll fall for just about anything. And this afternoon that's what I want to give to you, just a few scriptures you can stand on.

Standing on the Promises of Love. Matthew, the eleventh chapter, the twenty-eighth verse, says, "Come unto me all ye that labor and are heavy laden, and I will give you rest." That's the King James version. The New International Version says, "Come to me all you who are weary and burdened and I will give you rest." The Living Bible says, "Come to me and I will give you rest all of you who work so hard beneath the heavy yoke." New Revised Standard: "Come to me all you that are weary and are carrying heavy burdens and I will give you rest." Four different versions of one scripture. Truth never changes. The promises of God never change. You can say it in Spanish, you can say it in Chinese, you can say it in English, you can say it in Swahili, you can have fifteen different versions of the same scripture, but what's liberating is the truth in it. It says when you get tired, come to me, the Lord, the Spirit of Love, and I, I will give you rest.

Another scripture says, "Ask and it will be given to you, seek and you will find it, if you knock on the door, it will be opened to you," unconditionally. It didn't say you had to have any specific kind of dress or specific kind of lifestyle, or specific look. It says, all you have to do is ask. Just tell me what you want, and it's yours. The promises of Spirit are true. That's what Liberation in Truth is all about. The liberation is in the truth. And we can find some truths in the Bible. We can find some truths in the Qur'an. We can find some truths in all of those spiritual books. There's some truth in it. That's what liberates—the truth. Say it any way you want. Howl it, rap it, sing it, quote it . . . any way . . . you can vogue it! If it's true, it's going to liberate you. Standing on the Promises of Love.

Coming every week, every Sunday, "Hey, how are ya?" we say. "This is Liberation in Truth, and we are having a good time." Monday morning is bad. Something hits you. Now if you really had a good time at church you may still be going on that little extra . . . like, "It's all right, now you can throw it at me, 'cause I had a good time yesterday." Tuesday . . . just a little bit weaker. Trying to remember what happened, but it's . . . By Wednesday, it's over. I don't even remember what happened in church. Over. Finished. Done. Beat down. Something about Wednesday, that middle-of-the-week day. If you can get past Wednesday, you can make it to Friday. The song that Leslie sang, the choir sang, on Sunday and Monday you were still hearing it, and you will probably remember that Reverend Holland preached, or Deacon Kimberly preached, and somebody testified, and Tuesday it's still ringing in your head. But by Wednesday, it's totally different. Over. What do you hold on to? The Promises of Love.

The winds come, and the waves come, and the storm is rough. And yes, your boss is gonna get on your nerves—guaranteed. Somebody's gonna get on your nerves; that's a guarantee. Somebody. Your momma, your daddy, your lover, your child, your best friend. Somebody's gonna work your nerves during the week. And if all you got is a jump and a shout, I'm telling you, by Wednesday it's gonna be gone. Stand on the Promises.

Another scripture says that God is our refuge and strength. This is one I like: Psalms, forty-sixth chapter, first verse. "A present help in times of trouble. So we need not fear, even if the world blows up and the mountains crumble into the sea. Let the oceans roar and foam, let the mountains tremble, there is a river of joy flowing through the city of our God." God is the refuge. God is the strength. Not the songs of the Voices of Liberation. They're wonderful! They feel good, and you can take some of it. But it's the Spirit of the Lord that you got to stand on. You got to stop and think when it gets rough, and Spirit says, "I'll never leave you nor forsake you." Now your best friend promises to be with you, but Spirit says, "I'll never leave you nor forsake you." God is your refuge, and God is your strength. When it gets rough, other people start running. When things get tough, they say the tough get going? Say it how it is! "Sister, I'm with you, but you know what? You're on your own." "Brother, you fine over there, but I can't help with that stuff. Call me when it's over." God, God, God, God, *God* is our refuge. God is our strength. The Spirit of the Lord, the all-powerful spirit of love; that's what's gonna make you different. When the church is full and we got the rockin' going on, there's so much energy up in here that when you walk in the door, you can feel it. People who don't dance, all of a sudden, their feet start tappin'. And some folks are acting real cool, but there's something about walking into Liberation in Truth. When people are up in here, everybody gets moving.

But when there's only a few folks in church, when you're needed to pull ahead, when you can't look around to Sister So-and-So, you know, the church lady, who's always guaranteed to have something to say no matter what. You know she'll say, "Jesus, ah!" "Joy, ah!" "Peace, ah!" the *lit* church lady. We know she's got it 'cause she got a testimony. Spirit raised her up when she was lying down, and the doctor said, "Sister, call your family. We can't do nothing else for you." The Spirit of the Lord lifted her, and she gonna shout it like nobody else shouts. But what happens when she ain't shoutin'? What happens when the choir can't really get a tune together for you? When they've tried, but they're goin' through it, and they need your help? What happens then? What do you do? What do you pour on? What I'm saying to you is that it's the promises of love that can help you in those moments. You can stop and think about how it was rough, and you didn't know how you were gonna make it, but you waited for the Lord. Like Isaiah said in the fortieth chapter, "They that wait on the Lord will be lifted up on eagles' wings." It doesn't say to wait on your girlfriend. Or to wait on Bishop So-and-So. Or to wait on your momma to get there. Or if your lover comes through, it doesn't say, "They that wait on their lovers," no.

Scripture says, "They that wait on the Lord." Wait on the Lord. Their strength is gonna be renewed. Sometimes now, you keep on waiting when you're down and it feels like "Lord, it's the eleventh and a half hour. Now they said I need this by a certain time. And I believe in you, Lord, but it's getting a little hairy here. I ain't trying to be homeless, Lord. I mean, come on, I been praying and I'm trying to do the right thing, Lord. I did my tithes, I was shouting on Sunday, and when they called for prayers I gave my little prayer. Come on, Lord, I need you here. It's getting a little rough at the eleventh and a half hour."

Wait on the Lord, Spirit says, and I'll renew your strength. I'm gonna lift you upon eagles' wings, and you will run and not get weary.

Oh, it was a long walk today. It was a long walk at the Gay Pride March. We started at Fifty-fourth Street and Fifth Avenue. And we thought when we were at Fifty-fourth Street, that we had to get all the way to Christopher Street, and you know, at first it was cool. Oh! All these people! It's wonderful! We're excited! By the time we got to Thirty-ninth Street, I said, now this *was* cute. I don't have to break down now. In the Twenties we were singin' these songs like: "I'm Blessed 'Cause God Says I'm Blessed!" We started dragging by Twenty-something, but we hung in there. We got all the way to Christopher Street. We made it.

Scripture says that when you get tired and it's rough, don't look to the ground, don't look to the right, don't look to the left, don't listen to that friend who's saying, "Girl, I told you to give up. I told you, you might just as well give up, and go ahead and do what you used to do before. You know how to make that money. I know you stopped doing that, but you need the money."—Spirit can lift you out of that . . . "And I know it wasn't good for you, but maybe you'll pick up a good deal of money. Brother, go for it. Who's gonna know?"—Spirit says, "They that wait on the Lord, their strength will be renewed." If you run a little bit and get tired you may have to start walking. We were marching, but we kept going, pouring water, doing libations in the street. It was hot, but we kept going. Had to walk a little slower, but we kept on going. Some people held on to other people, and Spirit says that when you're tired, I'll send somebody to lift you up, lift you up on eagles' wings—you know, with the big giant wings. Beautiful. You ever see them take off? Their wings lift up and they're so strong and they soar through the air.

Spirit says, all you got to do is wait. Learn fifteen scriptures? Fast for forty days? Wear that long dress down to your knees and all white for a month? No. Just wait on the Lord, and the Lord will renew your strength. There is a song that says that when nothing else, nothing, nothing, *nothing* else can help you, just wait on the Lord. My point is this: that when nothing else can help, when you have no desire to change, because this is who you are, when people talked about us, gave up on us, when nothing else could help, when everybody else gave up on you, it was love, it was the love of God, it was the *love of God* that said it's all right. You don't have to change your clothes. I don't care if you cover up your head. I don't care if you wear pants. I don't care if you wear a dress. You're in need. Come to me. My arms are open wide. Nothing else could help. Love lifted me. Standing on the Promises of Love.

When you get the phone calls from people saying, "Oh, I saw that church. It's not gonna last. God is gonna burn it down." People are very convicted in their beliefs. And it saddens me to think that this comes from a group of people who supposedly exemplify Jesus Christ, people who are supposedly followers of Christ who think that because I don't talk like them, and because I don't believe what they believe, I'm an abomination. I'm no good. My children can't even play with their children.

The God that I serve, when nothing else could help me, didn't put me down. She didn't condemn me. He didn't say I was never gonna be anything. Didn't say that I was just an old so-and-so and had to get rid of her. Spirit loves me and said it was all right. These are the things that we need to hold on to. The promises. Don't forget the thing that brought you here. The thing that drew you in. The difference. The reason why you left the other church. It's the liberated message. It's the scripture that says that you can come as you are. And if you don't feel like dressing on Sunday, you can still come. Standing on the Promises, the Promises of Love.

When you're in love with somebody . . . and I'm almost done . . . you know, you make these great commitments. "Oh, baby, it's so wonderful, and I want to be with you for the rest of my life. The way you kiss. Oh yes this is it! I'll never look at another person, baby! You the one!" Promises, commitment. "This brother is God, and I know he's it." And you hold on to that. A few months later? A few years later, it's all past. "I know what I said about her . . . but oh, no . . . she's the one . . . I want to give my all to *her*, and be with *her!*" "I know you married me last year, but *he's* the one!" The promises, the commitments, are like holding sand in your hands. And we mean well. But we're human beings. And the way you feel today may *not* be the way you feel tomorrow! You may mean well, but you could be lonely, and she was wonderful in the dark. It was oh so special and oh so sweet, but when you saw her in the morning . . . oh! "How do I get out of this one that I was getting ready to commit the rest of my life to? How do I get rid of her?"

As human beings, we may think we can stand on our own promises; but no, we stand on the Promises of Love. God was the same yesterday. God is the same today. God is the same in the Pentecostal church. God is the same in the temple. In the synagogue. In the streets. In the clubs. God is the same. Now people change hair colors, and people change faiths, and they change their partners, too. But God, but God, *but God*, Hallelujah, but *God*, never changes. Hold on to the promises. Hold on to the Promises of love. Take them in. Chew them up. Swallow them. Let them digest. So that when you can remember nothing else, all of a sudden, the promises will come up. "But she said she'd never leave me." "He said that he'd stay always." "Nobody else understands." "Nobody else can deal with it." "I tried to explain it, and I've confused myself." "But she said she'd never leave me—she'd stay always." That's not what you can hold on to. Stand on the Promises of Love. Momma's good, and Momma's wonderful, but Momma's not God. Momma's gonna make some mistakes. Your partner will make some mistakes. Your best, best, best buddy will hurt you sometimes. So hold on to the promises. Hold on to the Promises of Love. Stand on the Promises of God.

THE REVEREND JACQUELYN D. HOLLAND *is founder and pastor of Liberation in Truth Unity Fellowship Church in Newark, New Jersey. The daughter of a minister, she was raised in the Pentecostal tradition in North Carolina. She had not felt free to praise the God of her understanding openly as a lesbian until she joined the Lavender Light Black and People of All Colors Lesbian and Gay Gospel Choir in 1992. She became assistant pastor at Unity Fellowship Church of New York City, then went on to found Liberation in Truth UFC in Newark in 1995, which, giving all praise to God, is flourishing today. A former public school teacher, she received a B.A. from Hunter College and is attending the Theological School of Drew University in the M.Div. program. She lives in New York City.*

Dr. Ada María Isasi-Díaz

Women of Revolutionary Integrity

On Resistance

EXODUS 1:15–21; MARK 7:24–30; MATTHEW 15:21–28

THIRTY years ago I was working in Lima, Peru, among the poor of that city. One Sunday evening I visited a nearby church and was struck by the sight of a huge banner that the people had made. It hung across the back of the church and said: *La Palabra de Dios Tiene Fuerza y Da Vida* (the word of God has strength and is life-giving). Little did I know then how deep an impression this saying and the way that community lived it out was to have in my life. The banner I read that night has seeped into the depth of my mind and my heart and has become an intrinsic part of the way I approach scripture.

The texts from the scriptures that I find life-giving and strength-giving are the ones that sustain me and comfort me in my struggle for justice and liberation precisely because they challenge me. These two stories are the texts that have become meaningful and that I have studied, prayed over, and discussed with other women. The story about the midwives, Shiphrah and Puah, and the one about the Syro-Phoenician woman who challenged Jesus are just this kind of text for me. They are like old friends that are always revealing new understandings about the world, about *la lucha* (the struggle for justice), about our God, and about myself. They are two pearls of a great price, and that is why I want to share them with you today.

The three women in these stories teach us much. We find them in situations that are different but have important common elements: the women are powerless. Like women throughout the ages, like women today (especially Latina women and other racial-ethnic women) there stand Shiphrah, Puah, and the Syro-Phoenician woman facing men who have power over life. Also, in both stories the women are engaged in preserving life, in bringing healing to children, in creating a future for their communities. What motivates them is not personal gain but the good of those for whom they care. And, finally, the women keep their objectives in mind at all times.

In the case of Shiphrah and Puah—the midwives who are ordered by the pharoah to kill all male Hebrew babies—the text does not make clear if they themselves are Hebrew or if they are Egyptians dedicated to the Hebrew women. What is clear is that their job is to enable life. Notice how the text contrasts them to the pharaoh. Here they are, women whose job it is to help give life; there he is, having the power to order them to kill. How often in the world today, among my own Latino people, I see those bent on life who have less power, face those who have more power, and are bent on death. I see mothers bent on bringing up their children in the face of drug dealers. I see women who want to be their own persons faced with husbands, boyfriends, or lovers who abuse and demean them. I see us, Latinas who want to make a contribution while preserving our identity, facing the power of a society that insists we must accommodate, that we must betray ourselves and Americanize if we want to survive and move ahead.

As powerless people facing a powerful system, as powerless women facing power-wielding men, what are we to do? The women in today's texts—our foremothers—help us to see how to proceed.

Face-to-face with the pharoah, what can Shiphrah and Puah do? Can they argue with him? Can they chide him and tell him they are not going to do what he is telling them to do? No, they cannot, and so they seemingly submit. Now, many think that to submit is a sign of weakness, but the fact is that for many submission is a strategy for survival. I know many Latina women who appear submissive outwardly, but they are not weak. They are towers of strength, with more inner power than a volcano. Their outward submission is a way of buying time, of ridding themselves of the oppressor at least for a while in order to regroup and figure out a way to disobey in order to survive.

When Shiphrah and Puah reenter the scene they have to face an angry pharoah, but they are ready for it. Their task was to bring to light new life (the Spanish for "birthing" is *dar a luz*, to bring to light). They are not going to allow him to pervert that, no matter how powerful he is. So we have this wonderful scene of these two women making fun of the pharoah, telling him that the Hebrew women were so strong that they gave birth before the midwives could arrive. These two seemingly submissive women are now victorious. Every time I get to this point in the story, I want to give Shiphrah and Puah a standing ovation.

Now, before I sermonize about the Syro-Phoenician woman, let me tell you a little bit about this story. Jesus has withdrawn to Tyre and Sidon. This region is beyond the northern boundaries of his country, and he has gone there not to teach or to carry out his mission but rather to rest. The disciples, who also want to rest, ask Jesus to send the Syro-Phoenician woman away. And Jesus does try to send her away. Twice. His argument is the same both times: I was sent only to the house of Israel.

The Syro-Phoenician woman's situation is somewhat different from but also much like that of the midwives. Here is a reticent Jesus who wants to be left alone. Here is a Jesus guarded by male disciples who are embarrassed by the woman and want to get rid of her. But she keeps her goal in mind: My daughter is sick and I need you, Jesus, to heal her. The disciples are not able to quiet her, and Jesus' insistence that she, her daughter, and their problem were of no concern to him do not make her give up. She begs.

To beg is not at all unusual for oppressed people, including racial/ethnic people in this country, including Latinos and Latinas *in this country*. I have learned from my mother and many other Latinas, I have learned from the homeless, the hungry, the poor, that there is nothing dishonorable in begging. The objective is survival; the objective is to live today. And, for the oppressed, to insist on living today is an enormous act of hope. To insist on living today is to hope that tomorrow things will be different. So the Syro-Phoenician woman begs. She throws herself at Jesus' feet and she begs because she wants her daughter to have a tomorrow.

To beg is not to surrender: begging is a strategy for survival; it is a way of gaining time to change the situation. Begging speaks of a not-giving-up attitude; it is an act of self-determination.

Jesus is not kind to her. The picture we have here of Jesus is not a nice one. In harsh and even unfair terms he turns her down: It is not right to give the food of the children to the dogs, he tells her. Biblical scholars have been so perplexed by the harshness of Jesus' reply that they have tried to "fix" his reply, to ameliorate its harshness. Some scholars have gone to great pains to show that the word that Jesus used for dog meant "puppy," and that his use of the word did not denigrate the woman. I have always insisted that whether it means puppy or not, if it has four legs and a tail and it barks, it's a dog. And that is what Jesus called that woman's daughter.

But harsh denigration did not stop her. Jesus hoped that his strong answer would make her leave, but that was not to be the case. She finds a way to keep up the struggle and uses his rebuke to engage him in a dialogue. Her need was too big for her to give up. Her comeback was the best one possible: Even the dogs eat the crumbs that fall from the master's table.

Her willingness to go all the way for the sake of her daughter is so strong that Jesus acquiesces. It is the only time in the scriptures that we see Jesus changing his mind. It is a woman who calls Jesus to see things differently, to understand that he had been sent not only to the house of Israel. It is a woman who calls Jesus to be converted, and Jesus listens. He tells her: Because of what you have said, because of your arguments, your feistiness, your insistence (because of the lip you've given me, the young people would say today) your daughter has been cured.

The Matthew account has "spiritualized" the story, and the author of Matthew has Jesus saying "because of your faith." Sure, the Syro-Phoenician woman had faith. But it was her arguments, her wit, her intelligence, her insistence that brought forth Jesus' conversion and her daughter's cure.

These women were important in their communities. Their actions had immense repercussions, and they were remembered. Most of the stories about women in the Hebrew scriptures are about nameless people. The oppressed all look alike to the oppressors; our names are not important. But when it comes to Shiphrah and Puah, their names are remembered. Without them no Exodus would have been possible. Their conversations with the pharaoh foreshadow the conversations of Moses and Aaron with the pharaoh. Their intelligent resistance, bravery, and valor were rewarded with numerous progeny of their own and also with a people, Israel, from whom the Messiah was to be born.

And though the Syro-Phoenician woman's name has not been preserved, there is no way that her actions will be forgotten. Out of her need she engaged Jesus, and Jesus was converted. Faced with her insistence he came to realize that his mission was to the whole world and not only to the house of Israel.

My sisters and brothers, let us look carefully at the women in these stories. Let us understand that for them, as for those of us who belong to minority groups in this country, *la vida es la lucha* (to struggle is to live). Survival is a day-to-day struggle that requires commitment. But let us also understand that *la lucha*, the struggle, the commitment to survive, is both a never-ending task and the source of our hope and strength.

The word of God says to us today: Resist obliteration, resist death, struggle to hope for tomorrow, struggle to live. The word of God calls us today to be clear that to struggle for life is to do the will of God and that to struggle for life often requires of us revolutionary integrity: commitment to life, disobeying oppressive and unjust authorities, oppressive religious structures and religious authority. Revolutionary integrity is about living the life that is given to us by God, even if we have to struggle to live fully with every ounce of our being.

Along the road, sisters and brothers, may we learn from Shiphrah, Puah, and the Syro-Phoenician woman. As we praise them for being women of revolutionary integrity, let us pray that we can also be people of revolutionary integrity.

Born and raised in Cuba, DR. ADA MARÍA ISASI-DÍAZ *is currently Associate Professor of Ethics and Theology at Drew University. For the past twenty years, she has worked to elaborate a Mujerista Theology—a Hispanic women's liberation theology. Her most recent publication is* Mujerista Theology: A Theology for the 21st Century, *published by Orbis Press. A Roman Catholic, she is the former Associate General Secretary and Director of Program for Church Women United. She is often invited to lecture and preach on issues of justice, Latin American culture and theology, and women-centered theologies in the United States and abroad. Recently, she has taught in the Philippines and in Cuba. She lives in Fort Washington Heights, New York City.*

THE REVEREND BARBARA LUNDBLAD

God's Homecoming

On Homelessness

JOHN 14:23-29

T HERE is a man in my neighborhood who is known by his first name to almost everybody. His name is Emmett, and for as long as most people can remember, Emmett has lived on the streets. Long before the newspapers wrote stories about street people, Emmett was one. His memory is that it started when his mother died and his brother got rid of their apartment, but he can't be clear on the year. With the first hint of cold weather, Emmett is at the door of our church almost every day and night. By now, most folks at the church know his life story which he narrates in a monotone voice without stopping for breath, the minute that you say hello. "I used to work at the Metropolitan Art Museum, and then I was a bank teller until some guys jumped me downtown and now I can't work. I got 86.3 on the civil service exam. I had a girlfriend once in Staten Island, and I took her to the movies. My brother lives in New Jersey, and he took me to Burger King for Thanks-giving. He has two nice boys . . ."

And there is lots more. Always the same, though sometimes in a different order. I can almost recite it now by heart like an old Christmas piece from the Sunday school play.

One night, late and very cold, I let Emmett in to sleep on the bench in the church narthex. Later, when I went to turn out the lights, I heard him talking to himself, talking to no one except the darkness. The same, long litany, his life history, a broken record, played and replayed. But then in the middle of a para-graph, between the civil service exam and the girlfriend in Staten Island, something that was not usually there, as though the record got unstuck: "Thank you, Jesus, for this warm house. It's so cold outside."

He didn't skip a beat but went right on to Staten Island and his brother in New Jersey, and I stood there in the darkened stair-well as though I'd had a visitation from an angel. Or from one of those strangers who came to Abraham and Sara's tent looking for something to eat. "Thank you, Jesus, for this warm house. It's cold outside."

And Jesus said, "Those who love me, will keep my word, and my Father will love them, and we will come to them and make our home with them." For the winter, it seemed that God had come to be at home with us in Emmett. It was not that we loved so very well . . . but Emmett had come to live with us and he became our teacher. His very presence taught us something about God's long-ing to be at home on the earth.

His teaching began in earnest around Thanksgiving time. Several fifth-graders of our parish had come to church to bake communion bread as part of first communion preparation. When our session was over, the talking and the baking, they got ready to leave for home. But Emmett was fast asleep on their jackets. They had thrown them on the bench, forgetting it was his bed! No one said, "Oh, yuck!" (Although they might have thought it, for Emmett looked very scraggly that day. His face, always raw and red in the cold, was bleeding because he had tried to shave.) Instead, the fifth-graders wanted to make Emmett something to eat. So we went to my kitchen . . . they found some canned corn beef and some cheese to make sandwiches on two English muffins. A few chips and two Granny Smith apples. It took quite a while since each one wanted to do something, but finally they put the lunch in a bag and were off to the narthex. Gently, one of them said his name, "Emmett." He woke with a start that made them jump back. Then, they handed him the brown bag. He took it with thanks and began to tell them about his job as a bank teller and the guys who jumped him downtown. Quietly, they retrieved their jackets and started for home while he was still talking. They knew he'd still be talking when they saw him again. When their parents asked them what they learned about communion, it was Emmett's lunch they talked about. It is not a bad understanding of holy communion, of Christ's real presence. God making a home with us in the breaking of bread, in the sharing of a lunch.

Every now and then Emmett joins us for communion, usually standing over to the side, not quite knowing if he should or could come to the altar. He waits over by the piano, standing quietly until I come to him. "Emmett, the body of Christ broken for you." Sometimes, he comes into the middle of the service and sits near the back. Or he walks to the very front during the sermon or the prayers and calls out, "Hello, Barbara." "Hello, Emmett," I answer him, and we go on, but we are never quite the same. His presence with us is the story, the word, the teaching. At Christmas time, someone bought him a flannel shirt and warm socks, all wrapped up for one of the family. We have not been quite the same since he arrived.

I do not mean to be sentimental about homeless people, or to say that God purposely makes people homeless to be teachers for the rest of us! Nor do I claim that Emmett is really Jesus in disguise, a character from a storybook, a poor peasant or a simple shoemaker knocking at our door on Christmas Eve to test our response. But at the very least Emmett has become for me and for our congregation a parable of God and Jesus making a home with us. The experience of acceptance and love, the sharing of shirts and socks and simple lunches, the reaching beyond ourselves and our own friends to someone who simply appeared in our midst, has helped us to see our church building as Jesus' warm house. It has awakened us to the notion of God longing to be at home here, with the children of earth: ". . . and we will come to them," Jesus said, "and make our home with them." We had not thought much about God looking for a home. Hadn't we usually heard it the other way around? That someday God would take us to be at home with him? "In my Father's house are many mansions," Jesus said. "I go to prepare a place for you."

For now, it is we who are called to make a place for God, and to believe that God longs to make a home with us here on earth. Of course, we can't do it by ourselves, for we are limited in our vision of whom we'll bring home. But the promise Jesus made to the disciples is the promise that continues to come also to us: ". . . the Counselor, the Holy Spirit, whom the Father will send in my name, the spirit will teach you all things and bring to your remembrance all that I have said to you . . . And now I have told you before it takes place, so that when it does take place, you may believe."

Such visitations of the Spirit are perhaps rare among us. And they come in ways we do not expect, often quieter and smaller than we had hoped for. Like Elijah, we have been waiting for the earthquake and the mighty wind . . . but the Spirit comes to us in a still, small voice. Or a prayer in the darkness. "Thank you, Jesus, for this warm house. It's so cold outside."

The Spirit's visitation will empower us to be more than sentimental. Emmett has not been with us so much in recent days.

The weather is a bit warmer, but the real reason is that Emmett now has a home of his own. He has a room now because lots of people in our neighborhood—church people, college students, and others of goodwill—staked a claim on a city-owned building. There was nothing sentimental about it. In a city where hundreds of single-room hotels have been converted into luxury housing, driving tenants into the streets, these folks went for reverse gentrification! They turned a six-story apartment building into a single-room hotel. Fifty-five formerly homeless people now call the building "home." "Come and see my room," they beckoned with excitement when the building opened in January. They each have keys and a bed. They take turns working at the front desk. It will take lots of hard, unsentimental work to make homes for those still on the streets . . . for fifty-five out of twenty thousand in our city it is just a small beginning. It's not much.

Except when at least one of the fifty-five is part of your family. We have been blessed with Emmett's presence among us . . . sitting on the bench in the narthex every Sunday morning, sleeping on our jackets, asking if we have any good books he can read. Now and then he comes by with his life story and a few new twists . . . like wondering why the weather has been so changeable and don't we think it's because there are too many scientific experiments? He still promises to give the church a lot of money when he wins the lottery.

Emmett has been with us, reminding us all that it's so cold outside . . . outside the embrace of loved ones and community, in vast cities and in small towns, so cold without anyone who cares if you're ever at home. "Those who love me will keep my word," said Jesus, "and my Father will love them and we will come to them and make our home with them." Thank you, Jesus, for this promise. It's so cold outside. **AMEN.**

THE REVEREND BARBARA LUNDBLAD *is Associate Professor of Homiletics at Union Theological Seminary in New York City. An ordained minister in the Evangelical Lutheran Church of America, she was formerly the pastor of Our Savior's Atonement Lutheran Church in New York City. A nationally known preacher, she teaches and leads workshops throughout the country for numerous women's, church, and educational gatherings. She has been heard on the Protestant Hour Radio Series. Raised in the land of Garrison Keillor, she makes her home in New York City.*

KATHLEEN NORRIS

Annunciation

On Mystery

My only rule: If I understand something, it's no mystery.
—Scott Cairns, "THE TRANSLATION
OF RAIMUNDO LUZ: MY GOOD LUCK"

If God's incomprehensibility does not grip us in a word, if
it does not draw us into his superluminous darkness, if it does
not call us out of the little house of our homely, close-hugged
truths . . . we have misunderstood the words of Christianity.
—Karl Rahner, POETRY AND THE CHRISTIAN

ANNUNCIATION" means "the announcement." It would not be a scary word at all, except that as or of the Christian mysteries, it is part of a language of story, poetry, image, and symbol that the Christian tradition has employed for centuries to convey the central tenets of the faith. The Annunciation, Incarnation,

Transfiguration, Resurrection. A Dominican friend defines the mysteries simply as "events in the life of Christ celebrated as stories in the gospels, and meant to be lived by believers." But modern believers often trust in therapy more than in mystery, a fact that tends to manifest itself in worship that employs the bland speech of pop psychology and self-help rather than language resonant with poetic meaning—for example, a call to worship that begins: "Use this hour, Lord, to get our perspectives straight again." Rather than express awe, let alone those negative feelings, fear and trembling, as we come into the presence of God, crying "Holy, Holy, Holy," we focus totally on ourselves, and arrogantly issue an imperative to God. Use this hour, because we're busy later; just send us a bill, as any therapist would, and we'll zip off a check in the mail. But the mystery of worship, which is God's presence and our response to it, does not work that way.

The profound skepticism of our age, the mistrust of all that has been handed to us by our grandfathers and grandmothers as tradition, has led to a curious failure of the imagination, manifested in language that is thoroughly comfortable, and satisfyingly unchallenging. A hymn whose name I have forgotten cheerfully asks God to "make our goals your own." A so-called prayer of confession confesses nothing but whines to God "that we have hindered your will and way for us by keeping portions of our lives apart from your influence." To my ear, such language reflects an idolatry of ourselves, that is, the notion that the measure of what we can understand, what is readily comprehensible and acceptable to us, is also the measure of God. It leads all too many clerics to simply trample on mystery and in the process say remarkably foolish things. The Annunciation is as good a place as any to start.

I once heard a Protestant clergywoman say to an ecumenical assembly, "We all know there was no Virgin Birth. Mary was just an unwed, pregnant teenager, and God told her it was okay. That's the message we need to give girls today, that God loves them, and forget all this nonsense about a Virgin Birth." A gasp went up; people shook their heads. This was the first (and only) gratuitously offensive remark made at a convention marked by great theological diversity. When it came, I happened to be sitting between some Russian Orthodox, who were offended theologically, and black Baptists, whose sense of theological affront was mixed with social concern. They were not at all pleased to hear a well-educated, middle-class white woman say that what we need to tell pregnant teenagers is, "It's okay."

I realized that my own anger at the woman's arrogance had deep personal roots. I was taken back to my teenage years, when the "demythologizing" of Christianity that I had encountered in a misguided study of modern theology had led me to conclude that there was little in the religion for me. In the classroom, at least, it seemed that anything in the Bible that didn't stand up to reason, that we couldn't explain, was primitive, infantile, ripe for discarding. So I took all my longing for the sacred, for mystery, into the realm of poetry, and found a place for myself there. Now, more than thirty years later, I sat in a room full of Christians and thought, *My God, they're still at it, still trying to leach every bit of mystery out of this religion, still substituting the most trite language imaginable. You're okay, the boy you screwed when you were both too drunk to stand is okay, all God chooses to say about it is, it's okay.*

The job of any preacher, it seems to me, is not to dismiss the Annunciation because it doesn't appeal to modern prejudices but to remind congregations of why it might still be an important story. I once heard a Benedictine friend who is an Assiniboine Indian preach on the Annunciation to an Indian congregation. "The first thing Gabriel does when he encounters Mary," he said, "is to give her a new name: 'Most favored one.' It's a naming ceremony," he emphasized, making a connection that excited and delighted his listeners. When I brood on the story of the Annunciation, I like to think about what it means to be "overshadowed" by the Holy

Spirit; I wonder if a kind of overshadowing isn't what every young woman pregnant for the first time might feel, caught up in something so much larger than herself. I think of James Wright's little poem "Trouble," and the wonder of his pregnant mill-town girl. The butt of jokes, the taunt of gossips, she is amazed to carry such power within herself. "Sixteen years, and / all that time, she thought she was nothing / but skin and bones." Wright's poem does, it seems to me, what the clergywoman talks about doing, but without resorting to ideology or the false assurance that "it's okay." Told all her life that she is "nothing," the girl discovers in herself another, deeper reality. A mystery; something holy, with a potential for salvation. The poem has challenged me for years to wonder what such a radically new sense of oneself would entail. Could it be a form of virgin birth?

Wondering at the many things that the story of the Annunciation might mean, I take refuge in the fact that for centuries so many poets and painters have found it worthy of consideration. European art would not have been enriched had Fra Angelico, or Dante Gabriel Rossetti for that matter, simply realized that the Annunciation was a form of negative thinking, moralistic nonsense that only a modern mindset—resolutely intellectual, professional, therapeutic—could have straightened out for them. I am glad also that many artists and poets are still willing to explore the metaphor (and by that I mean the truth) of the Virgin Birth. The contemporary poet Laurie Sheck, in her poem "The Annunciation," respects the "honest grace" that Mary shows by not attempting to hide her fear in the presence of the angel, her fear of the changes within her body. I suspect that Mary's "yes" to her new identity, to the immense and wondrous possibilities of her new and holy name, may provide an excellent means of conveying to girls that there is something in them that no man can touch; that belongs only to them, and to God.

When I hear remarks like the one made by the pastor at that

conference, I am struck mainly by how narrow and impoverished a concept of virginity it reveals. It's in the monastic world that I find a broader and also more relevant grasp of what it could mean to be virgin. Thomas Merton, in *Conjectures of a Guilty Bystander,* describes the true identity that he seeks in contemplative prayer as a "point vierge" at the center of his being, "a point untouched by illusion, a point of pure truth . . . which belongs entirely to God, which is inaccessible to the fantasies of our own mind or the brutalities of our own will. This little point . . . of absolute poverty," he wrote, "is the pure glory of God in us."

It is only when we stop idolizing the illusion of our control over the events of life and recognize our poverty that we become virgin in the sense that Merton means. Adolescents tend to be better at this than grown-ups, because they are continually told that they don't know enough, and they lack the means to hide behind professional credentials. The whole world confirms to them that they are indeed poor, regrettably laboring through what is called "the awkward age." It is no wonder that teenagers like to run in packs, that they surround themselves with people as gawky and unformed as themselves. But it is in adolescence that the fully formed adult self begins to emerge, and if a person has been fortunate, allowed to develop at his or her own pace, this self is a liberating force, and it is virgin. That is, it is one-in-itself, better able to cope with peer pressure, as it can more readily measure what is true to one's self, and what would violate it. Even adolescent self-absorption recedes as one's capacity for the mystery of hospitality grows: it is only as one is at home in oneself that one may be truly hospitable to others—welcoming but not overbearing, affably pliant but not subject to crass manipulation. This difficult balance is maintained only as one remains virgin, cognizant of oneself as valuable, unique, and undiminishable at core.

What may trouble modern people most about this concept of virginity, and the story of the Annunciation itself, is what I find most inspiring; there's no room in the story for the catch-22 of sexual liberation. It was not uncommon, in the 1960s, for young men to insist that their girlfriends seek medical treatment for "frigidity" if they resisted sexual intimacy. In many cases the young women were reasoning in a mature fashion, doubting that they were ready for sex, at fourteen or seventeen years of age, and wondering if their boyfriends were as ready as they pretended to be. In doing so, they were regarding sexual intercourse as a major rite of passage, one that would foster but also require a deepening maturity and emotional commitment, and they had the good sense to wonder if it might not be a good idea to become more their own person before sharing themselves so intimately with another. The remedy for this pathology? Birth control pills, of course. These girls were not well served by doctors, or well-meaning clergy who told them not to worry, it's okay.

We all need to be told that God loves us, and the mystery of the Annunciation reveals an aspect of that love. But it also suggests that our response to this love is critical. A few verses before the angel appears to Mary in the first chapter of Luke's Gospel, another annunciation occurs; an angel announces to an old man, Zechariah, that his equally aged wife is to bear a son who will "make ready a people prepared for the Lord." The couple are to name him John; he is known to us as John the Baptist. Zechariah says to the angel, "How will I know that this is so?" which is a radically different response from the one Mary makes. She says, "How can this be?"

I interpret this to mean that while Zechariah is seeking knowledge and information, Mary contents herself with wisdom, with pondering a state of being. God's response to Zechariah is to strike him dumb during the entire term of his son's gestation, giving him a pregnancy of his own. He does not speak again until after the child is born and he has written on a tablet what the angel has said to him: "His name is John." This confounds his relatives, who had expected that the child would be named after his father. I read Zechariah's punishment as a grace, in that he could not say anything to further compound his initial arrogance when confronted with mystery. When he does speak again, it is to praise God; he's had nine months to think it over.

Mary's "How can this be?" is a simpler response than Zechariah's, and also more profound. She does not lose her voice but finds it. Like any of the prophets, she asserts herself before God, saying, "Here am I." There is no arrogance, however, but only holy fear and wonder. Mary proceeds—as we must do in life—making her commitment without knowing much about what it will entail or where it will lead. I treasure the story because it forces me to ask: When the mystery of God's love breaks through into my consciousness, do I run from it? Do I ask of it what it cannot answer? Shrugging, do I retreat into facile clichés, the popular but false wisdom of what "we all know"? Or am I virgin enough to respond from my deepest, truest self, and say something new, a "yes" that will change me forever?

KATHLEEN NORRIS *is an award-winning poet and the author of* Amazing Grace: A Vocabulary of Faith, The Cloister Walk, *and* Dakota: A Spiritual Geography, *as well as three volumes of poetry, the most recent of them* Little Girls in Church. *A recipient of grants from the Bush and Guggenheim foundations, she has been in residence twice at the Institute for Ecumenical and Cultural Research at St. John's Abbey in Collegeville, Minnesota, and has been, for ten years, an oblate of Assumption Abbey in North Dakota. She and her husband, the poet David Dwyer, live in South Dakota.*

Reprinted from Kathleen Norris, Amazing Grace *(New York: Riverhead Books, 1994), 71–77.*

Vanessa Ochs

Tamar

On Subversion

I F you read the kind of family saga fiction that gets made into TV miniseries—I don't, because all I have to do is call home and say, "Ma, what's up?"—but if you do read sagas, or if you read Shakespeare, you know that sometimes, just as the main story is starting to get interesting, you get diverted by a subplot. When you see a subplot coming, you can't help but wonder—is this here just to distract me, or is there important information I'm supposed to pick up?

Just when the Joseph story starts to get juicy, just when he gets sold to Potiphar in Egypt and you want to know what's going to happen next, a chapter-long subplot intrudes about Joseph's brother Judah and his daughter-in-law, Tamar. Not a typical subplot duo. What would be the scenario: murder? jealousy? Certainly not a love interest. Curious indeed.

The story of Judah and Tamar, because it intrudes upon the

popular Joseph story, is easy to overlook. It's not the stuff of Hebrew school Bible storytelling, either. Savvy as kids are now, onanism and incest taboos still don't make it into the elementary school curriculum. Certainly, my own Hebrew-school teacher, Mrs. Feinblum, who loved having us do wall-sized construction paper murals of Bible stories, would have nixed this one. But among adults, the story is also typically glossed over, in the name of good taste and modesty. And that's a pity. Because in the Judah and Tamar story, we see a Jewish woman—a viable role model— using a subversive and unconventional creativity to preserve her line and restore justice and personal rights in a world that had denied her them.

Let's overcome our squeamishness and stop averting our eyes when we reach this significant part of the Genesis narrative. Let's see it not as a distraction but as a powerful source of information.

Let me retell the story then, which is unusual enough, and then, to complicate matters, let me tell the story paying particular attention to Tamar: what we hear about her and what we don't. Let me read behind the lines, both of the Torah text itself and of the commentaries through which we conventionally know this story.

We've already been introduced to Judah; his name is mud. True, he did tell his brothers they shouldn't kill Joseph—he was, after all, flesh and blood—still, as a big brother, Judah hardly set the best example. He had the same idea our own children fleetingly consider but rarely carry out: he was ready to sell his pesky kid brother to the first bidder. So even before Judah and Tamar enter the limelight, we think poorly of Judah. He is the deceiver, the one who dipped Joseph's coat in the blood of a kid and used that as evidence to prove to his father that Joseph was killed by a beast. Keep that in mind: the deception, the blood of a kid.

In any story, there are limited outcomes for bad guys. You may find out the bad guy is just as bad as you thought he was from the start, or you find out you misjudged him and he has a heart of gold. If he starts out a loser, he may change and improve. Possibly, that change will come about independently, or through the influence of another character. Sometimes it's a matter of positioning the bad guy to see the light. That, too, keep in mind.

Judah marries and has three sons: Er, Onan, and Shayla. He finds a wife for Er, and this is Tamar. She appears out of the woodwork. Unlike other biblical wives-to-be, she neither is discovered at a well nor is celebrated for having offered a thirsty traveler a drink. She just appears. Should we like her, dislike her, root for her? The text gives us none of the conventional clues that force us to get involved or engaged with a character. She's a walk-on, an extra.

We learn from the Torah that Tamar's husband, Er, was wicked in God's eyes, and God put him to death. The scenario is cryptic. Whatever he did, he got zapped. Let me assume that not everyone here is versed in Jewish methods of Torah study, so a word of explanation. This is precisely the kind of passage that makes our commentators take note. Rashi (a famous commentator on the text) asks what we're all wondering but are afraid to ask, because we think it must be so obvious that everyone else, learned in Torah or wise in the ways of the world, knows but us. What, asks Rashi, did Er do? The same thing that brother two, Onan, did. He failed to have the conventional relationship with Tamar that would provide an heir.

Rashi even weaves in a little Dr. Ruth: Er feared that if he made his wife, Tamar, pregnant, her beauty would be compromised. Not that Er wasn't keen on preserving Tamar's beauty for her own sake, but for himself. He would not compromise her desirability. Nowadays, he'd be advised to pursue short-term therapy with Masters and Johnson. He would not be sentenced to death.

What did Tamar think? What did she feel? We don't know. There are no clues. I'd guess she'd have preferred that her husband had been illuminated and rehabilitated rather than snuffed out. Rashi explores the psychology of Er; he doesn't search to round out Tamar. So we have to do that, because the absence of Tamar's psychology in the texts is just as much an irritant to us as the absence of Er's psychology was to Rashi.

Let's imagine that Tamar followed a conventional social pattern: she wanted a child, and without one she was disappointed. According to the custom of levirate marriage, introduced here for the first time in Torah, Tamar is given brother number two, Onan, as a husband after the death of her first husband so she might produce an heir in her husband's name. But Onan, knowing that the child he would have with Tamar would not count as his own heir but as his deceased brother's, also finds reason to prevent Tamar from conceiving. And he dies, too. In both relationships, there is nothing Tamar can do. She is powerless. We assume she is guiltless and lacking in agency, for nothing—nothing—in the text leads us to believe otherwise.

Judah sends Tamar back to her father's house. She is by no means a free woman. She is told that she's being put into cold storage until brother number three is ready for levirate marriage. It is clear to us, just as it is clear to Tamar, that no marriage will take place. At this point, the story could end and we'd draw an easy moral from it: Judah and his sons are bad news. But then, out of the blue, we witness active engagement on Tamar's part. After Judah's wife dies, he and a friend go off on a business trip to Timnah to look after his sheep-shearing interests. Somehow, and we don't know how, Tamar hears about this trip ("It was told," the text reads). Tamar sees, almost literally, a window of opportunity. She tosses off her mourning clothes and veils and wraps herself so thoroughly that she's disguised, then heads for a spot at the crossroads to Timnah, Petach Eynayim, it's called, the entrance of a place called Eynayim—but literally translated, *petach eynayim* means the opening of the eyes. With open eyes, certain things become clear. It is a place for insight.

By then Judah's son number three had clearly grown up and

Tamar could see that Judah had no intention of giving up his last son to this apparently cursed woman. At Petach Eynayim, the place where eyes are open, Judah does not see through Tamar's disguise. He takes her to be a prostitute, a harlot, and he propositions her. Think for a moment of Tamar's psychic burdens. She has lost two husbands and has implicitly been blamed for their deaths. She thinks that she has no choice but to act as a prostitute and even to risk death if Judah sees through her disguise. We know more about Tamar now. She is a person who can bear pain and she is a person who isn't crippled by her pain. Instead, pain moves her to action.

Tamar sees an outcome many steps away. Would she have created this scheme if she couldn't anticipate how the future would unfold? Tamar, who sees that she must act independently and plot her way to a fulfilled destiny, makes a deal with Judah. For her services, in the future she'll take a kid (goat) as payment, but for the present, she wants as collateral three items of Judah's personal belongings, things that can be identified as his: a seal ring, a cloak, and a staff.

In biblical times, it seems that either you were barren or you were wildly fertile. Presto, Tamar conceives. She returns to her father's home and slips back into her mourning clothes. When Judah sends his friend to deliver the kid and retrieve his seal ring, cloak, and staff, the markers of his identity, no one has ever heard of the harlot of Petach Eynayim because she doesn't exist. In some respects, she is a figment of Judah's imagination, which makes Judah nervous. He remembers deceiving his father with the blood of a kid, and now, he fears, he is the one deceived.

Three months pass, and Judah hears that Tamar, his daughter-in-law who has given him more then enough trouble, has gotten herself pregnant and has done so through harlotry. A *shanda*, a shame. And she, who was supposed to have been in chaste, cold storage. This was not yet the age of "innocent until proven guilty," so Judah commanded that Tamar be brought forth to be burned (that being the proper death for a priest's daughter who had fallen to harlotry, Rashi explains).

Tamar is tactful. She presents the seal ring, the cloak, and the staff and sends a message to Judah. These things belong to the father of my child. A lightbulb goes on. What does Judah see, what is his insight? Or rather, what has Tamar made Judah acknowledge? He exclaims, *Tzadka mimeni,* she is more righteous than I because I didn't give her Shayla, my son. A happy end for all. Judah gets to redeem himself, and Tamar gets twins. But the risk to her reputation, to her life, was enormous in carrying out such a plan.

I have a friend in Jerusalem, a poet named Linda Zisquit. She once told me she was obsessed with the story of Tamar—so much so, that she named a daughter Tamar. Zisquit explains why: Like Judah, Tamar is also deceptive. She pushes deception to the limits. But she manages to do so within the system of Torah ethics, by pushing law and stretching convention to the limits. By the letter of the law, Tamar did nothing wrong. But, in effect, with the future of Jewish survival as her concern, she took that law into her own hands. Had she asked for permission no one, I assure you, would have given her a *hecksher,* a seal of rabbinical approval. Tamar is too confusing for the guardians of the system, as she models subversiveness and subterfuge. Sometimes I think Tamar is a matriarch with no matriarchal status because she didn't look to others to find out what was acceptable—she made that call herself.

A *shanda,* my mom would call it—Tamar perpetrated a *shanda*—but what else could she have done, knowing what was at stake? To give birth, physically and spiritually, actively and intellectually, to the line of King David and, eventually, as tradition holds, the Messiah. (Specifically, Tamar's son Perez will be an ancestor of Boaz, Ruth's husband, who will be the great grandfather of King David.)

Did Tamar have any other alternative in her quest to restore justice? Tamar Frankiel, the author of *The Voice of Sarah: Feminine Spirituality and Traditional Judaism,* thinks so: Tamar . . . "appears to have been from a significant family; eventually she, or her father, could have used legal means to force Judah to marry her to Shayla." But she didn't pursue those alternatives. Why?

Frankiel answers: "Perhaps she feared Judah would have resisted her direct attempts to gain her marital rights. . . . [thus] . . . she bypassed what would appear to have been the more normal legal and social routes. In a sense, she played the part he gave her; a woman of strange and dangerous sexual powers, she took on the disguise of a harlot."[1] And in that disguise, she redeemed her personal power. She saw justice being undone and saw how it could be restored.

Tamar didn't wait for the tide to turn, or for her pain to subside. Bypassing the normal social system, she acted. This has always been the stuff of heroes. But I assure you, it makes many nervous to learn that this fierce independence, this willingness to risk all and act, is also the stuff of heroines.

VANESSA OCHS *teaches Anthropology of Religion and Judaism at the University of Virginia, in Charlottesville. Formerly a professor at Colgate, Yale, and Hebrew University, she has been a Senior Fellow at the National Jewish Center for Learning and Leadership (CLAL) and director of their National Resource Center. She is also a director of the International Committee for Women at the Wall, which strives for women's equality in prayer in Israel, and has written extensively for newspapers and magazines such as the* New York Times, Newsday, *and* Redbook, *and is the author of* Words on Fire: One Woman's Journey in the Sacred *and* Safe and Sound: Protecting Your Child in an Unpredictable World. *Her latest book explores new Jewish rituals. She lives in Charlottesville, Virginia.*

THE REVEREND ALTAGRACIA PEREZ

Abundant Life

On Choice

LUKE 14:26–27

(This sermon is transcribed from an audiotape.)

I'M sure, after listening to the lesson this morning, you're thinking to yourself, "Well, I'm not sure I understand what it is that Jesus is asking of us." In order to make more clear the lesson that we have read as the gospel this morning, I want to point out the passage from the book of Deuteronomy. In this passage, we see that Moses went before the people of Israel and told them what the Lord commanded him to tell them. He was not thinking on his own, out of his own authority, but was speaking under the authority of God, and he was sharing God's words with them. And the Lord said, "I have set before you this day, life, and good, death, and evil."

I would dare say that this day the Lord has set before you the same choice. You have a choice between life and good, and death and evil. God, with all of his majesty, does not take our power of choice away from us. He has given us the power to make a decision about which way we will be. What do you choose? And how will you experience the rest of your life?

If we love the Lord our God and follow His commandments, we are promised life. It is in the scriptures; we are promised life. It's not just that we'll keep breathing. It's not that quick. It's not that clear. It's not that if we decide to turn away from God we immediately drop dead of a heart attack, either. (Though I'm not telling you that it won't happen. Don't go out and say, "Well, she didn't say I was going to die of a heart attack, so I'm going to have a good time!") What I'm saying is that the image is not always clear with the followers of Moses. Here we have a description of what people will receive as part of life. They will receive a land in which they can live and multiply, a land where they receive much blessing. It will be a place where they can fully live an abundant life. That is the kind of life that God offers to us as well: a life that is abundant, a life that is full, a life in which we can experience love, hope, and joy. And we can choose between life and good, and death and evil.

I often say that just because people are walking around eating, sleeping, working, and breathing does not mean that they are living, or that they are choosing life. That's just existence. In fact, I would argue that many people, if not most people today, are only existing. They go from day to day, working to pay their bills, taking care of their children because they have to, doing whatever they have to do, just to live to the next day. They go to work and try to figure out how they can do the least amount of work and still get paid and still get to keep their jobs.

For some of you, the American dream is about getting over and not getting caught, as opposed to living abundantly. What God promised the people of Israel then, and what God promises you here today, is not that kind of life. It's not just barely scraping by. It's not just living another day. That is not the choice that God gives us.

If we choose to turn away from God and worship other idols, we are choosing death. In Moses' day Baal was worshiped, along with all the other idols of the people in the land. Today it's money, and power, and greed. If you don't believe me, just look around. Maybe you don't even have to look that far. Look around and see how people are living. Those people who think it's so great just to get over are the same people who can't wait to have a six-pack and not just a beer, to have a pint and not just a drink, and to have as many other drugs as they can possibly get their hands on just so they can relax, sleep, and get ready for the next day. If it's so great, having the ability to get over, if it's so great, having all the money that you want, if it's so great, striving after the gods of this world, then why is it that people are so miserable? Why is it they have no joy in their lives? Why is it they experience no peace? Why are they constantly in turmoil, feeling troubled and anxious? Why is Prozac making such a great impact? Why is it that everybody is looking to be on medication, whether or not they're suffering from depressive illness? I would argue that it's because they have chosen evil and have chosen death.

Today, you, too, are faced with a choice. And the choice is not simple. Sometimes, when people tell me, "Oh, I wish the church could always be this full," or, "I wish that we could fill every single pew on every single Sunday," I am quick to remind them that many are called, but few are chosen. Jesus did not do some sort of mass rallying where he gathered tons and tons of people who decided to follow along and do what he said. Jesus called people to a real life. But real life entails real pain, as well as real joy and hope and peace. And so faced with that truth, people will often choose death, choose evil, and choose just to get by. They think the cost is too much.

Choosing life and good, choosing love, is costly. And let me tell you that, first of all, love is not a feeling. Love is always a decision. It's always a decision about whom you choose to commit your life to. It's always a decision about getting up at two o'clock in the morning to feed the children that God has given you. It's always a choice to raise your children in the fear of the Lord, even if it's not fashionable or hip to do so. Love is always about choice. And given that choice, God is very clear whom you are to choose.

In today's gospel lesson, we hear Jesus saying something that sounds outrageous:

> If any one comes to me and does not hate his own father and mother and wife and children and broth-ers and sisters, yes, and even his own life, he can-not be my disciple. (Luke 14:26-27)

How can it be that Jesus would want me to hate my mother, my father, my husband, my wife, my sister, my brother, my son, my daughter? How can that be? Isn't God a loving God?

The word that is used here for *hate* is not the word that we would necessarily use. This Semitic word is better translated as *if you love something less than*, or *if you love something more than.* If you love something more than me, Jesus says, put it away. If you love God less than you love your mother, your father, your brother, your sister, your son, your daughter, then you are not worthy of him and you are not a disciple. If you love anything in this world more than you love God, then you are lost. You have made your choice, and your choice may not seem evil, but because it is the lesser good, it is *not* the good. Whoever does not bear his own cross, and come back to Me, cannot be My disciple, Jesus says. If you love your own life more than you love the Lord, you are not choosing to be His disciple.

Why is that? Because even though God, in the form of Jesus, tried to summarize in a little, simple way what it is He calls us to do, we still forget. When asked, What is the greatest com-mandment? Jesus was very clear. Love the Lord your God with all your heart, with all your mind, with all your soul, and with all your strength. And this is really the greatest and most important commandment. Within this commandment everything else is taken care of. Then, thank God, the lesson from this morning is not surprising to us. If we love anything or anybody more than we love God, then we are not loving Him with all our heart, and mind, and soul, and strength. It's very clear. The choice is very clear.

What happens when we make that choice? What happens when we choose good? I don't know if you have ever had the experience of standing up for something that you knew was right. What was the reception you received from the people around you? What did it look like? Did everybody come up to you and say, "Oh, good going, that was really important?" Did people pipe up in the middle of the situation and say, "I agree with you, this is wrong." Or, "I agree with her, we shouldn't have done this." I doubt it. Usually what happens is that you're standing there, all by yourself, standing up for truth, standing up for what is right, and nobody says a word. And you experience all the focus, all the uncomfortableness, all the difficulty, and you die a thousand little deaths, while you're standing there, for justice and truth. And then if you're lucky, after the situation passes, in private down the hall, in the bathroom by the water cooler, somebody will come and say, "You know, I agree with you. It was true. They shouldn't have done it, that was wrong." But when it was time to take a stand, you were standing alone.

Jesus knew that. He knew that standing for truth, standing for justice, standing for life would often, if not always, cost us a great deal. We would experience ourselves as if we were on the cross. He knew that, for he had decided to live His life, consistently and at every moment, seeking God's word and standing for truth, for God's truth. And you know how that story ended. You know what He got then. What makes you think that you will suffer any less?

Now this is not a popular message. You know, folks in church don't like to hear how if they stand for what's right, if they stand for truth and for justice, they're going to suffer. Nobody likes that, but it's the truth, and I have to tell you the truth. I don't know when I'll see you again. I can't run from this; you must know that God sets before you a choice. You can choose life, choose what's good, or you can choose what is evil, choose death.

When we're choosing life, we're not always positive about what it is, what is right and good, or what is death. So, wait a minute—life is when it's right, and death is when it's evil—but we're not always positive what those situations look like. But often, we do know. The situations where you don't know, I encourage you to pray for the gift of insight and God will help you to discern what is right. In all of those gray situations I suggest that you read the scriptures. I suggest that you come to Bible study and learn what the word of God teaches you about what is right and what is wrong. I suggest you do these things, but you can start where you want to.

There are many things that you know are right, and that you often stay quiet about. You've seen people teasing others. You've seen people putting down other people and destroying their dignity. And you may have even joined in and laughed. You have seen the injustices of the workplace. You have seen what management does to workers and what workers try to get away with from management. You see it. And yet, you stay quiet, because after all, that's the way it is. You've seen situations in which people assault and attack people because they're black, because they're brown, because they're white, because they're yellow, red, gay, sick, whatever. Whatever the situation might be, you've seen it happen. And what do you do? Do you stay quiet and allow a creature that God created from love to experience humiliation? And while you were supposed to stand up for Jesus, did you say nothing?

Today you are called to make a choice. I suggest to you that you choose good and you choose life. You can't take this at face value; you have to live it to know it. But the truth is that we know how the story really ended. Yes, Jesus stood for truth, and he was crucified. But he was also resurrected having conquered death forever, never again to be a respecter of death. He chose to live in the way that he was commanded to live. If you choose good, and you choose life, you may experience uncomfortable situations. You may be embarrassed, you may have a hard time. You may even be persecuted. But the truth is that the promises of God are also faithful. You will stop just existing from day to day and seeing a world destroying itself all around you. You will stop being sad and feel empowered. You will begin to live, and not just merely exist. And it won't be for a little while. You will have a big life, an abundant life, in which God will bless you at every turn. If you choose good, and you choose life, it may not be easy, but it will always be worth it. What is the point of living if you don't really live? What's the point?

And so this morning I put this choice before you, and invite you to rededicate your life, so that you once again decide that you will choose life. And I promise you, that the blessings that you will experience will be more than you can ever imagine.

THE REVEREND ALTAGRACIA PEREZ, STM *is the rector of the Church of Saint Philip the Evangelist in Los Angeles, California, an historically black church that has become a bilingual, multicultural parish. Dedicated to community outreach, the church has a senior citizens center, a food bank, and an after-school program, which was featured in* Newsweek *magazine. As an activist working with young people and their families, Mother Perez has designed and implemented programs for the Pilsen Catholic Youth Center, a gang-prevention agency in Chicago. She has also served as Diocesan Coordinator of Youth Ministries in the Episcopal Diocese of Chicago, and eventually became Provincial Coordinator of Youth Ministries for the Episcopal Church Center in New York City. Actively involved in the fight against HIV/AIDS since 1985, she is a member of President Clinton's Advisory Council on HIV/AIDS and co-chair of the Racial Ethnic Populations committee. Mother Perez holds a B.S. in Educational Psychology from New York University and an M.Div. and an S.T.M. (Master of Sacred Theology) from Union Theological Seminary. She is married to Carlos Rafael Alvarado and has two daughters and two stepdaughters. She lives with her family in Los Angeles.*

A Charge to the Sisterhood: Love Yourself

On Self-Love

MARK 12:30-31

THE Presbyterian women's symbol reminds me of the relationship between self, God, and neighbor described in the gospel of Mark: "Love the Lord your God with all your heart, and with all your soul, and with all your mind, and with all your strength . . . and love your neighbor as yourself." The chain circle, consisting of different-sized links, symbolizes the diversity; the broken chain the brokenness of our world. But within the circle I also see a triangle shaped like the front of a pyramid. The highest point represents God. A line extends from God to self forming the left side of the triangle, from God to neighbor forming the right side, and from self to neighbor forming the base. When all three lines are connected, a loving three-way relationship exists among self, God, and neighbor. When one line is broken, the whole relationship suffers.

When the text commands us to love God with all our heart,

soul, mind, and strength and to love our neighbors as ourselves, the assumption is that self-love is already present and can, in turn, be extended to the neighbor. But given our human brokenness, especially among women, can we assume the presence of self-love?

Let's start by asking the question "What is the self?" According to Genesis 2:7, God formed Adam from the dust of the ground, breathed into his nostrils the breath of life, and he became a living soul. Therefore the term *self* refers not only to the mind, which is the faculty of reasoning, and to the heart, which some scholars describe as the seat of the intellect and the point of contact with God[1] but also to everything that constitutes personhood. "Love God with all your heart, all your soul, all your mind, and all your strength."

How do we come to love ourselves? According to Julia Boyd, author of *In the Company of My Sisters,* our self-esteem is determined by the core personal beliefs we form about ourselves over the years.[2] She explains that everyone is born with a healthy self-esteem, which positive messages from the outside world reinforce. However, if we are repeatedly exposed to negative messages, we internalize them and they become part of what we believe about ourselves. This produces an unhealthy self-esteem. The only two messages necessary for a person to develop healthy self-esteem are "I am lovable" and "I am worthwhile." Self-love, then, is the perception of one's self as being lovable and worthwhile. Perhaps it is because God creates humans with a healthy self-esteem that the text assumes that Israel already knows how to love self.

Boyd knows about unhealthy self-esteem firsthand. When she was ten years old, her aunt, an experienced beautician, told her, "Julia, I'm going to do your hair. When I'm through with you, you're going to look like a princess." When her aunt finished her hair, she handed Julia the mirror. What a disappointment! Yes, her hair was curled, and the shiny curls hung down around her face, but her face was still black! Who ever heard of a black princess! The only princesses she ever saw were in the white cast of characters in fairy tales. She knew nothing of the African kings and queens from whom she was descended. She had expected to be transformed into Snow White, complete with the seven dwarfs.

Think about this, sisters and brothers. By age ten, she had already learned to despise her blackness. Many of us can relate to this because not only blackness but everything associated with being African is despised and devalued by the dominant American culture. Such devaluing constitutes what Engelbert Mveng, an African Jesuit priest, calls anthropological poverty. It is a type of impoverishment that despoils human beings not only of their resources but also of their identity, history, ethnic roots, language, culture, faith, creativity, dignity, pride, ambitions, and right to speak.[3]

For women, this impoverishment includes our female identity. Womanhood is devalued and women are assigned all sorts of negative stereotypical images, many of which we internalize, allowing them to shape our self-perception. The sisterhood also receives many messages that are directed at us as women of African descent. In her book *Spirit Speaks to Sisters,* June Gatlin asks:

> What are you allowing to come into your brain? Is your brain inviting and receiving ugly, hostile images and impressions? Is your consciousness generating diseased thinking? Are you listening to words that are power filling or are you relaying negative programming?[4]

> When you look into the mirror, who do you see? Do you find yourself making judgments about your appearance based on concepts of beauty which have nothing to do with you or your culture? Are you allowing your physical attributes to distort your thoughts about what beauty is?[5]

A year or so ago Oprah Winfrey had a woman on her show who said she wore makeup and a wig both day and night. She had been married for fifteen years, and her husband had never seen her without makeup and a wig. Several men on the same show were growing bald, and they also wore toupees around the clock. The point of the show was to help these women and men build up enough self-esteem that they could remove the props and still feel good about themselves.

Self-care says something about our self-love. Sisters and brothers, how do you treat yourselves? Do you go for annual checkups or do you wait for symptoms? Do you exercise regularly? Look at the kinds of food, drinks, and other substances you put into your body. Look at the books you read and the music you listen to— Do they send a positive or a negative message? Do you spend time with God for daily meditation or do you pray on the run? All these things contribute to our physical, emotional, and spiritual well-being and shape our perception of others.

Self-love is an obedient response to God's command. It is also the basis, if not the prerequisite, for loving neighbors. How can one love neighbor as self if one does not love self? It determines not only how we treat ourselves but also influences the message we send to others about how we want to be treated.

Martin Luther King, Jr., taught that love of neighbor is possible through *agape* love, which he defines as the love of God operating in the human heart.[6] It enables us to love our neighbors not because they love us, or are nice to us, but because they are created in the image of God.[7] If *agape* love enables us to love others because they are created in the image of God, it can enable us to love ourselves who are also created in God's image. King saw *agape* love as God's willingness to go to any length to restore community. If we accept it, God's love is strong enough, and wide enough, and deep enough, and enduring enough to form this three-way love triangle between self, God, and neighbor. But in order to experience the transforming power of this love, we must enter a personal relationship with God. We have to know God for ourselves.

Earlier this year, a student from Union Seminary invited me to Beth Israel Medical Center to respond to theological papers written in a Clinical Pastoral Education class. I listened intently as these future pastors and rabbis struggled with the whole notion of evil and suffering and a God of love. Some had experienced suffering in their families, in their ministries, and in their communities. Their postures ranged from confrontation with God to feelings of anger and abandonment. One young man felt that he had gone as far as he could go, and he had neither the inclination nor the strength to do anything else until he heard from God for himself. Like David from Psalm 35, he asked, "How long, O Lord, how long?" How long will you stand on the sidelines looking on before you come to my rescue?

We all struggle with why a God of love allows human suffering. But what is more important for our purposes is the way these students were "in relationship" with God. The quality of their relationship gave them the freedom to ask their questions and to be honest with God about their emotions.

In relationship with God, we begin to understand the goodness of God and to see ourselves as created in the image of God. We understand that, despite the enemy's attempt to obscure it, the image of God resides within us and with it self-love. Not even the devil can stamp it out! We understand that much of the pain that enters our lives is the result of human evil, not a lack of God's love. We understand that God never abandons us. God does come to our rescue, and no matter what happens, we can still declare that God is good! Hallelujah! This is when we experience the love of God!

The Presbyterian Women's Mission Statement affirms women in all their diversity: age, size, nationality or ethnic background, and physical and mental ability. Whether we are young, old, or middle-aged; whether we are short or tall, big or small; regardless of class status or intellectual ability; regardless of race or gender, God still loves us, and we ought to accept one another.

I want to commend you women on the work you have already done. It is praiseworthy that you were serious enough to write out a mission statement and create such a meaningful symbol. Your commitment to justice and inclusivity is impressive, and your theme, "Seeding the Sisterhood," suggests that you have something worth passing on to younger generations of women. You have already begun to sow the seeds among them. However, I urge you to include self-love in the legacy you leave to the sisterhood. I charge you to love yourself. Self-love means self-acceptance. It also means striving to be your best self despite others' perceptions of you.

Self-love must not be confused with narcissism, which is self-absorption. Whereas narcissism leads to selfishness and apathy toward the neighbor, self-love leads to love of neighbor. Some of us perceive self-love as a barrier to loving others, but it is not. The commandment is to love others "as self." Loving self does not mean we love others less; it means we learn how to love them more.

Seeding the sisterhood with self-love must also mean sharing our insights with brothers. Whether they support or oppose us, we pass it on. How do we do this? By the way we relate to them. If we want the brothers to respect us, we must respect ourselves and them. If we want them to show us love, we must love ourselves. Love is like the word of God, alive and active. Love empowers. Love brings happiness and joy. An inactive love is dead and therefore worthless. If we want to be affirmed, we must affirm ourselves and one another. If we want support, we must support one another. Nobody ought to do more for us than we do for ourselves!

Let us join hands with our sisters and brothers nationally and internationally. Let us appreciate our differences and the diversity of our gifts while honoring what we share in common. We must explore ways we can pool our resources to take the personal, social, and political actions required to stamp out anything that denigrates our humanity and fills us with self-contempt. We cannot afford another generation of men and women filled with self-hate. If indeed we are free, why should we become prisoners of other people's hate or our own?

Self-hate makes us turn on ourselves and one another. If we are forgiven, let us forgive ourselves. Jesus can deliver us from pain and transform us into effective workers for God. Listen, we have enough social and political factors against our survival as a people. We cannot afford to participate in our own destruction. To love God with all our heart, soul, mind, and strength and to love neighbor as self is the most comprehensive response we can give.

The two great commandments cannot be separated. Can we be in a right relationship with God without loving neighbor? Can one truly love God and neighbor without loving self? I leave you with this charge: "Love yourself."

THE REVEREND DR. ANNIE RUTH POWELL *is Seminary Pastor and a professor at Union Theological Seminary in New York City. An ordained minister in the African Methodist Episcopal Church, she holds M.Div. and Ph.D. degrees from Union. She is the executive director of the Christian Community Learning Center, a house church ministry focused on inreach and outreach. A health activist, particularly in the areas of breast cancer, she has also taught and done research on issues of domestic violence. With Jacquelyn Grant, she is currently working on the Bricks Without Straw project, doing research on women in the African Methodist tradition. A native of North Carolina, she currently resides in New York City.*

THE REVEREND DR. BONNIE ROSBOROUGH

Rachel's Consolation

On Grief

ISAIAH 63:7-9; MATTHEW 2:13-23

MIDST the angels, bending low, and the shepherds, and the Magi, adoring where the infant redeemer lay, we find Rachel: so disconsolate, so brokenhearted that her grief cannot be addressed. Who is she, this Rachel for whom there is no consolation? And why does St. Matthew include her in his story of Jesus' birth?

Who is Rachel? We first learn of Rachel in Genesis, where she is identified as one of the great matriarchs of Israel. She is the wife of Jacob, and the mother of Joseph and Benjamin, who, after having suffered the shame of barrenness for years, very pointedly dies in childbirth, "in travail and hard labor," as the text bluntly puts it. This Rachel, mother of her nation, is remembered in Israel's story as a woman of great sorrow and great pain.

A second Rachel is found one thousand years later, in Jeremiah, after Israel had been conquered and her citizens driven into exile and slavery or imprisoned in Babylon. Here, Rachel is portrayed again as weeping, this time for the defeat of her people and the eradication of her culture. She wailed so bitterly for the loss of her homeland and its freedoms that Jeremiah wrote that there was no solace for her, no comfort, no balm. And it is this Rachel, for whose grief there was no sufficient address, whom Matthew cites in his nativity story. As far as Rachel was concerned, Herod's hateful massacre of the innocents of Judea was an event so horrific that efforts to explain it were futile and attempts to pacify or assuage had to be refused. There could be no brief for such brutality! Or as Emily Dickinson wrote, "To relieve the irreparable degrades it."[1]

Who is Rachel? She is a woman of sorrow who confronts the reality of human suffering and refuses to have its reality diminished by attempts to mollify or relieve.

And why does Matthew include her in his story of Jesus' birth? Rachel is here, I think, as testimony to the fact that there is stuff in human life that is so awful it cannot be addressed with human speech, or repaired with reassuring words. Rachel is here at the manger, refusing consolation, because the stuff of her experience—the abuse and murder of her children, the tyrannies of human oppression, the calamities of nature—is the sort of stuff that platitudes and bromides cannot explain or remediate. This stuff is so awful that human speech fails. And Rachel's refusal to be consoled, to have her suffering "made better," is testimony to the fact that such suffering is anathema, blasphemy, abomination. Only God's word can speak to it. Matthew's claim in placing Rachel's testimony in the story of Jesus' birth is that God's word, incarnate in Jesus Christ, addresses what human speaking cannot. There is no earthly consolation for Rachel; only heaven, the divine word, can convey hope for her situation.

Here, in Bethlehem, Rachel anticipates Calvary; and in the birth, she is witness to the resurrection, when God's final word, a "yes" profound enough to address whatever horrific stuff living and dying can present, is powerfully heard through all eternity. God speaks when human tongues must fall mute, and Rachel is witness.

As such, on this cusp of a new year, Rachel encourages us, my friends, to refuse human explanation for that which is not right and must not be justified, relieved, or condoned. I am thinking now of the stuff of Rachel's life that is also the stuff of ours: the abuse and murder of our innocents, for example; the brutal oppression of the Chinese, Burmese, Rwandans, Kazakhs, and the list goes on and on; or calamities like the fire this week in Mandi Dabwali, India, where no explanation on earth is sufficient and no earthly consolation adequate.

As Christians, my friends, our hope is not in human terms— human wisdom and prowess—but in Christ, where heaven and earth meet and the consolation of hope is in God's Word spoken for our lives—spoken to our lives—and the life our world.

THE REVEREND DR. BONNIE A. ROSBOROUGH *is the pastor of the Broadway United Church of Christ in New York City and Adjunct Professor at Union Theological Seminary. She was a founding member of AIDS Interfaith New York and is active in issues of housing and homelessness. A native of Maine, she is a graduate of the University of Maine at Orno and Union Theological Seminary, and received her D.Min. from Hartford Seminary. She lives on the Upper West Side of Manhattan with her husband, novelist John Batchelor, and their two children, Sam and Anna.*

This meditation is indebted to *Not Every Spirit: A Dogmatics of Christian Disbelief*, Christopher Morse (Valley Forge: Trinity Press International, 1994).

MAXINE SILVERMAN

Leaving the Bed Unmade

On the Sabbath

EXODUS 20:9

ERE we are again. Lucky us.

I look forward to Kabbalat Shabbat. I like to be right here, at sundown, as day evens out to the mysterious and usually comforting dark of night.

Because for me, it is in these quiet, evening moments that our congregation shines. We're not a neon shul, all flash and dash. In the intimate moments of teaching, of reaching out to each other, of prayer, B'nei Yisrael shines with the luster of pearls.

The seeds for my comments tonight were planted last spring in the Shavuot Tikkun conducted by our rabbi and cantor. As you remember, we studied various commentary dealing with the mitzvot of communal prayer and Shabbat observance.

Rabbi Hoffman presented this lesson from Mechilta Yitro. "'Six days you will labor and do all your work'" (Exodus 20:9).

But is it possible for a person to do all his work in six days? Rather one should rest, as though all his work were finished."

Does the phrase "as though all work were finished" resonate for you as it does for me?

I don't know if it's possible for a person to do all of *his* work by Shabbat, but I do know for sure a person doesn't finish all of *her* work in six days.

Gender semantics aside for the moment, let's rest *as though* all of our work has been finished.

All week, but especially on Friday as Sabbath approaches, I run around like the proverbial chicken with its head cut off, trying to finish up the work, hurrying, hurrying. But on Friday afternoon, I put that ole chicken in a pot, add an onion, and a carrot. While it simmers I attack last-minute tasks, set the table, and just before I light the candles, I take off my watch and step out of time *as though my work were done.* Enough, it is time to stop. And the blessing of it is, for me, it's not my decision. It's a mitzvah, a commandment, and that makes it easier for women, and other compulsives, whose work has no clear-cut beginning, middle, and end.

Candles, wine—blessings over both—the food, the children. And tomorrow morning when I wake up, I will leave my bed unmade. Notice the language is positive, the tone triumphant, rather than the guilt tinged "I didn't make my bed." If anyone shakes his or her finger at my unmade bed, I can just say—"speak to HaShem." I leave my bed unmade, and later that Shabbat morning, when I put on my tallis, I kiss each end of the blessing on the atarah, and wrap the tallis around me. Mine is soft gray wool. I hold it over my head like a tent or a chupa, and it falls around my shoulders and down my back and I stand there. It's one of the few times the entire week when I'm really alone, for although my children are old enough that they no longer follow me into the bathroom, our poodle often does.

So I cherish that time enveloped in my tallis. There, in that pristine privacy, I can say those words that my heart desires and my soul requires. The air inside that tallis changes. First of all it's no longer air, it's breath. It warms with the energy of healing and the presence of the Shekinah. Wrapped in layers of warm breath and soft gray wool and when you emerge, who knows who you will have become.

Stop.

As though your work is done. Shabbat Shalom.

MAKING my bed is a subject for consideration that predates my observance of Shabbat and my wearing a tallis. If the seeds of my remarks about Shabbat rest were planted in Rabbi Hoffman's Shavuot tikkun, then the choice of leaving my bed unmade—of all the work I could choose to mention specifically—the choice of leaving my bed unmade has its roots in childhood, mine, and in my relationship with my mother, who taught me the domestic art of making one's bed (and lying in it). As part of our morning routine, before breakfast on school days, my sisters and I dressed and made our beds. When we grew a bit older, my older sister made my father's bed while he showered and dressed and I made my mother's bed, while she cooked our breakfast. I had a hard time getting up in the morning; I was always the last one up and dressed, the last one at the breakfast table, the last one out the door for school. You will not be surprised when I say I had a hard time making my bed, let alone my mother's, and I had a hard time with her because of it.

She was particular about domestic chores, that they be done well, and was clear that our doing them had nothing to do with getting allowance. My sisters and I learned to set the table and wash dishes, to make the beds, to dig weeds in the yard, because we would need to manage our own households one day and because each member of our family should help with the work of maintaining the family. We got an allowance to teach us how to manage money. Now, as a parent, these make sense to me, good sense. As a child and a middle daughter, the distinction mattered not at all and was, in fact, a lesson lost in my resentment of her expectations. If the beds were not made to her satisfaction, she pulled the blankets and sheets down and we had to do it again. And again. And sometimes again. My older sister learned quickly to make her assigned beds right and was done with it. On to scrambled eggs or oatmeal. I learned it was nigh on to impossible for me to give in to what seemed, to me, unreasonable and arbitrary rules. There were mornings I made that bed three and even four times—until she gave up because we would all be late for school. I was stubborn and a master of the art of leaving just enough wrinkles to satisfy us both.

At college I managed to find roommates who tolerated my side of the room. When I was on my own, I gloried in not making my bed at all, for days and even weeks at a time. So there! Until I had a very small studio apartment in Manhattan, where the bedroom, living room, study, and kitchen were one. I did make my bed then, out of necessity, choosing luxurious sheets as a palliative. I chose for the spread a shimmering ivory quilt. Once when I babysat for the daughter of a friend, she gazed admiringly at that quilt and asked, "Are you a movie star?" I confessed that I was.

When I married and had children, I found myself unconsciously adopting many of my mother's ways and consciously avoiding others, but by that time making the bed had ceased to be so fraught and burdensome. For that, I thank my friend's daughter. My own children have learned that a sure way to stir me up, ah my mother's sweet revenge, is to burrow under the covers of a freshly made bed. The nuances of bed making, you see, continue to accumulate.

It is easy to discern, without the help of an analyst, why my first decision about observing Shabbat would be to leave my bed unmade. I love it! Even as I write these words I feel intense pleasure. All week long as soon as I get up, good daughter that I am,

I make the bed, now with kavanah, and on Shabbat, with kava-nah, I rest.

One Sunday as we rushed to get out the door, the boys to Hebrew school, my husband and I to morning minyan, I realized that I had not made the bed. Oh well, I thought, just this once I won't. But habit and Lord knows what else were stronger, and I returned to the bedroom. As I folded the blanket under the mat-tress I had an insight so strong I stopped, the mattress lifted up, just stopped. The understanding was so powerful I couldn't move. Let me, if I may, share it with you. If I observe Shabbat, in part, by leaving my bed unmade, then making it all week is also part of that observance. All week long I make the bed so that leaving it unmade becomes significant, becomes holy, the fulfillment of a mitzvah. I leave my bed unmade and if anyone wags his or her fin-ger at my unmade bed, I can just say—speak to HaShem.

There is a part of Kabbalat Shabbat service that talks about ennobling the workweek by resting on Shabbat. I had never un-derstood it before, not really, I had never taken it into my con-sciousness by taking it into my body. Standing there with the mattress lifted and everyone shouting at me to hurry was a scene from my childhood with a twist. A saving twist of meaning, of re-framing, a saving grace.

For at that moment when I fully comprehended the relation-ship between work and rest, between Shabbat rest and the other six days of the week, I felt a sensation throughout my body like standing in the shower with the water streaming all over. I expe-rienced something rushing over me, and the hair on the back of my neck rose up on end.

I have felt that thoroughly shaken and joyous only a few times in my life, when I fell in love with my husband, when my sons were born, and when my husband surprised me by saying he wanted to convert to Judaism. (I fell in love all over again.) So I stood there with that uplifted—and uplifting—mattress. I under-stood, at a level of meaning below language, when I cease from my work on Shabbat, that "work" means more than earning a living and feeding the family. It means that all the days are lived in anticipation of Shabbat. My friend Ellen has since told me that in traditional Hebrew the days of the week are named by their distance from Shabbat. Sunday is Yom Reeshon l'Shabbat or one day after Shabbat, Monday is Yom Sheni l'Shabbat or two days after Shabbat, and Friday, oh Lordy, Friday is Yom Shishi l'Shabbat, only one day away.

SHABBAT is the only day with her own name.

In the Sabbath morning service at the conclusion of the Amidah, the central prayer of the service, personal prayers may be added. The Siddur, or prayer book, offers an example and an alternative. On page 441, the alternative expresses the impact of Shabbat on the other days of the week. We read:

> Grant me the privilege of the liberating joy of Shabbat, the privilege of truly tasting the delight of Shabbat. May I be undisturbed by sadness, by sorrow, or by sighing during the holy hours of Shabbat. Fill Your servant's heart with joy, for to You, O Lord, I offer my entire being. Let me hear joy and jubilation. Help me to expand the dimensions of all Shabbat delights. Help me to extend the joy of Shabbat to the other days of the week, until I attain the goal of deep joy always. Show me the path of life, the full joy of Your Presence, the bliss of being close to You forever. May the words of my mouth and the meditations of my heart be acceptable to You, O Lord, my Rock and my Redeemer.[1]

B'nei Yisrael, Lord only knows, there are many other opportunities, in addition to leaving the bed unmade, that extend the joy of Shabbat to the other days of the week if we are alert to them. Lord only knows . . .

Since it is the place for personal prayer, I would add my thanks for finding myself in a community where I can express these personal thoughts and feelings in safety, for the opportunity of redeeming the task of making my bed from the morass of adolescent struggle and elevating it, transforming it in the mitzvah of Sabbath rest.

Dear God, give us strength that we may be generous, work that we may be strong, and may we, Your people Israel, always find our way to the path of life that You have shown us.
SHABBAT SHALOM.

A poet by trade, MAXINE SILVERMAN *has also written essays, fiction for children, and d'vrei Torah, commentary on the weekly Torah delivered during Shabbat morning services. "Leaving the Bed Unmade" was given during an evening Shabbat service. Her work has appeared as a chapbook of poetry* (Survival Song) *and in journals and anthologies. She teaches writing workshops, is a master gardener, sings in an interfaith community choir, and maintains long-distance friendships. Whatever the form or forum, she depends on the* kavanah *(prayerful intention) of* tikkun olam *(repairing the world). With her husband and two sons, she lives in the Hudson River Valley.*

THE REVEREND DR. JOANNE MARIE TERRELL

How Low Can You Go?

On Solidarity

LUKE 7:36–50

D O me a kindness: Look at your neighbor. No, I mean look at your neighbor. Really see your neighbor. See your brother or sister again for the first time. Look deep into his or her eyes, beyond the mask that we all wear to try to protect ourselves. Don't let them duck or dodge—you know, the way we all do when we are hiding some-thing—some past transgression or present indiscretion, some fear or failure we would rather forget. And while you are really seeing your neighbor, your brother or sister, perhaps for the first time, let them see you. It is, perhaps, more difficult than you thought.

Now, I want to tell you a story about something that hap-pened to me when I was in my first year of seminary in New York City. I was living in the dormitory and I was very active in the seminary community. Already, I had a reputation for being a pretty good singer. One night, and this was early in the semester, the telephone rang, interrupting my studies. It was the student minister of a church in Brooklyn. She made a request of me that I will never forget. She asked me to sing a solo at the funeral of a woman whom I did not know. This woman, whose name was Darlene, had died of a drug overdose. Immediately, something within me objected to this request. First of all, I did not know the woman. Second, being the countrified southerner that I still am, I had never heard of any such thing, hiring someone to sing at a funeral! I wondered what it was like to be so alienated from yourself that even in death they could not find among your friends someone who would do something for you like the request that was made of me.

And third, although I did not admit this to myself until long after I had hung up the phone, I felt morally superior to Darlene, because I was a Christian and I would never do something as sinful as taking drugs. A strong part of me really wanted to say no. But something else in me, something stronger, would not let me say no. So I said, in my own pious way, "I'll have to pray about it."

All night long I wrestled with my feelings. I felt smug and I felt guilty. I felt pain for Darlene and I despised her, too. I prayed over and over again, "Lord, what would you have me to do?" Finally, the Lord answered in a vision that flashed quickly before my eyes. It was a scene of the woman who anointed the feet of Jesus, who washed them with her tears and dried them with her hair. I could hear the voice of Jesus saying, "She to whom much hath been forgiven, the same loveth much." Instantly, I recognized that this woman was Darlene. But in that same instant, I was also exposed to my own hypocrisy. I knew that, as much as I have required forgiveness in my life, I, too, was the woman in the vision, and that realization brought me into a sisterly relationship with the woman whom I didn't even know, a woman whose addiction got the better of her and caused her to lose her life. And even though I have never been addicted to drugs, I knew that I, too, was and

am afflicted with that very human capacity we all have for grab-
bing and grasping at the things we think we need.

Although I am at times discouraged, I desire, as we all desire,
to "make it" in this life, to "be somebody" in the eyes of others,
to excel in my chosen profession. That is why I am here today. My
résumé is ample testimony that I have, for a long time now, been
engaged with the question we all ask of ourselves from time to
time, "How high can I fly?" As Americans conditioned by competition and by material and social comforts relative to the rest of
the world, we want to know that it is all right to strive, to push
for wealth and fame, for distinction among our fellow human beings on personal, local, national, and even international levels. We
want to know that it is all right to get the many things we may
not really need but that we want in order to satisfy our egos and
our desires. There is nothing intrinsically wrong with that. But the
Word of God reminds us that "wisdom is the principal thing.
Therefore, get wisdom, and with all your getting, get understanding."

At times, though, it seems that we are altogether possessed by
the spirit of competition, rather than the Spirit of God, or wisdom. We even enter into "spiritual competition" with our sisters
and brothers in the family of God, sometimes even daring to judge
others as sinners, ourselves as saints, holding up our contributions
as something great at the same time that we belittle others.

How much, then, does Simon in today's gospel lesson remind
us of ourselves! Simon was a Pharisee. Like you and me, he was
religious, if not spiritual. Like some of us, he had a little money,
he was able to entertain guests in his home. Like some of us,
Simon had a reputation for being somebody.

The woman in our lesson, on the other hand, is described as
a sinner. The text does not state what kind of sins she supposedly had committed, but Luke does not leave much to our imagination. Her brazen appearance at Simon's house, the action of
exposing her hair, her ardent kissing of Jesus' feet, and Simon's

silent ruminations about her actions and the effect they would have on a "real" prophet lead us to the conclusion that she was a member of the world's oldest profession—she was a prostitute.

Now, from the beginning, prostitution has been poor young women's means of "making it" in the world, and it has become poor young men's means of "making it" in our postmodern, dog-eat-dog world. Whatever money a prostitute makes is hard earned. Like all prostitutes, the woman in our text had no reputation. She didn't even have a name! All she had was a broken heart and a contrite spirit, and I know for myself that "God is near to those who are of a broken heart, and saves such who are of a contrite spirit." Although the profession is well utilized, often by those who are well respected in their communities, it is so easy to dehumanize the downtrodden, like the homeless, teenaged parents, and drug addicts in our midst. But do you know what? It becomes harder to dehumanize the downtrodden once we remember that we, too, are made from the dust of the ground.

Obviously, the woman in our text knew something about the Lord, because when she learned that Jesus was at Simon's house she made her way there, even though she was an uninvited guest, at least for this dinner party. She brought an alabaster jar of ointment, a rather expensive item, to anoint the feet of Jesus. She was so emotionally overcome that she began to cry and to express her appreciation to Jesus for what he had already done for her. Jesus did not dehumanize her. In his acceptance of her ministrations, in his affirmation of her worth as a human being, he rehumanized her!

I HAVE to testify that you don't know like I know what He's done for me! One day when I was lost, He picked me up and turned me around . . . When my mother died, brutally murdered in the prime of her life, Jesus held this fifteen-year-old child together with the glue of His love and His blood! When the storms of my life raged, when I was used and abused by people I trusted and loved, Jesus affirmed and continues to affirm my worth as a human being, regardless of what others say or think or try to do to me. Thank God, Jesus has rehumanized me. And when I was thirsty, when I was hungry for things that could not and did not satisfy, He who is the living water, He who is the living bread gave me what I needed. So, like the woman in our lesson, I come this morning bearing a gift to the Giver of life, the gift of myself.

BUT in his heart, Simon despised the woman's gift, and he despised her tears, and secretly, he despised Jesus, and challenged Jesus' authority as a prophet on the grounds of what he knew that woman to be. He couldn't even see that an act of faith, an act of love was being performed, as improper as it might have seemed or as crude as it might have been. Sometimes, we Christians are just like Simon, when, in the spirit of competition, we disdain the gifts of others and puff ourselves up with vain thoughts about our own greatness. But don't you see that when we despise the gift, we despise the Giver? When we despise the acts of love, the acts of faith, when we despise the tears of our sisters and brothers, we, too, are guilty of despising the Lord. If we confess that we love God, yet despise our sisters and brothers in our hearts, we are liars and the truth is not in us!

SISTERS and brothers, the name of the game in the life of a Christian is not competition; the name of the game is *love*. I want to suggest to you today that the relevant question in your life and in my life as Christians is not "How high can you fly?" or "How high can I fly?" The relevant question is rather "How low can you go?"

I am not suggesting that God wants us to continue in sin whatever sin has meant in our lives. I am not suggesting that God does not want you to have the things you desire. On the contrary, we are the children of God, made in God's image and in God's likeness, and we have a right and a responsibility to be all that we can be. But that has less to do with wealth, fame, and material things than it has to do with utilizing the gifts and callings of God. It has to do with the kinds of relationships we can have with each other and with God when we open our eyes and our hearts to see each other as we really are.

Considering the times and the ways we have all been so much less than what we can be, it is truly amazing that God loves us so. If only we could behold ourselves in the same light in which God beholds us, perhaps we would be a little more merciful, a little more loving to ourselves, and to our sisters and brothers. Jesus simply wants us to remember that, like the sinner woman, we, too, were once strangers; we, too, were once far from the peaceful shore, and even now, we, too, stand with the sinner woman in the need of grace.

Jesus exonerated the woman. He said to her, "Your sins are forgiven." Her love, which was measured by her service, was the evidence that she had been changed. The question "How low can you go?" therefore, should serve as a reminder to us that, before we look around, we ought to look within, and when we look around again it ought to be in order to see whom we can raise up, rehumanize, and restore to his or her rightful status as a child of God!

I selected this passage from the gospel of Luke, and I know that at first glance it does not seem very flattering to women, especially church women, who are frankly fed up with being despised as Jezebels and harlots, incompetent to pastor churches and to preach the Word of God! But I also know that down through the years, women from every station in life—and let's face it, some men, too—have known what it means to be poor and hungry, to cry tears that cannot be comforted, and to be considered outcasts from our communities and even our families. We have all known what it means to sink so low, to go so low, burdened by the sin within us and the oppression around us, that it took nothing less than the hand of God to raise us up. Luke's gospel, including the sinner woman's story, tells us that God is not indifferent to our situations. That God is not indifferent to our tears. That God does not despise our acts of love nor our acts of faith. God is willing to forgive us our sins and to deliver us from evil. That Christ Jesus is able to save "from the guttermost to the uttermost." That Christ Jesus is ready to empower us for service.

The lesson in Darlene's story taught me that Jesus sees me as I am and loves me just the same. And now I have a secret to tell you: He sees *you* as you really are and loves you just the same. But more than that, he sees you as you can be, the potential you, the you you are becoming, the you you want to be. If we are serious about seeking his image in the faces of our brothers and sisters, can we afford not to be as gracious to the people around us?

Sisters and brothers, I want you to remember that the relevant question in your Christian walk is not "How high can you fly?" but "How low can you go?" If you would but humble yourselves, in due time *God* will exalt you.

Consider the woman with the issue of blood. She said, "If I can just touch the hem of his garment, I know I'll be made whole." Jesus said, "Somebody touched me, for I perceive that *power* is gone out of me." And he said to that woman, "Daughter, your faith has made you whole. Go in peace." Daughters of God, your faith can make you whole. Brothers, consider the beggar Lazarus, lying at the gate of the rich man, desiring to be fed. The dogs licked his sores. Lazarus died. The rich man died; in hell he lifted up his eyes. Lazarus was carried by the angels to the bosom of Abraham. You see, God exalted him, and God will exalt you, too. Consider the woman with a spirit of infirmity and a double-bent back. She couldn't even lift herself up. She was in that condition for eighteen long years. But one day, Jesus came by. He told her, "Woman, you are *loosed* from your infirmity. Immediately, she was made straight, and began praising God. Sisters and brothers, *you*, too, are loosed from *your* infirmities!

Consider Jesus, who, though he was in the form of God—"light from Light, very God of Very God, begotten, not made—though he was in the form of God, he did not count equality with God a thing to be grasped, but he emptied himself, made himself of no reputation." How low can *you* go? Jesus humbled himself, poured himself out on the Cross, the blood came streaming down. Jesus went down into the nether regions of hell—how low can you go? Yet there in hell, he "led captivity captive" and gave gifts to men and women. Now God has highly exalted him and has given him a name that is above every name, that at the name of Jesus, every knee should bow—male knee, female knee, black knee, brown knee, red knee, yellow knee, white knee—every knee should bow, of things in heaven, of things in earth, and of things under the earth.

Do you know what this means, Church? Jesus does not despise your tears. If you are oppressed by sin and evil, take it to the Lord in prayer. If you made your bed in hell, he has already been there. You and you and you are loosed from your infirmities! I am loosed from my infirmities! Your sins and my sins are forgiven. Give God the praise, and go in peace. Serve one another and serve the Lord. If you want to know how high you can fly, consider the question "How low can you go?" **AMEN.**

THE REVEREND DR. JOANNE MARIE TERRELL *is an ordained elder in the African Methodist Episcopal Zion Church. A native of Springfield, Massachusetts, she graduated from Rollins College in Winter Park, Florida, and holds a M.Div., M.Phil. Philosophy, and Ph.D. from Union Theological Seminary in New York City. Currently serving as an associate minister at the Greater Walters African Methodist Zion Church in Chicago, she has also served as Assistant Pastor of the Mt. Hope AME Zion Church in White Plains, New York. An assistant professor of ethics and theology at the Chicago Theological Seminary, she is the author of* Power in the Blood? The Cross in the African American Experience. *Reverend Terrell is a member of the American Academy of Religion, the Society of Biblical Literature, and the Society for the Study of Black religion, and also serves on the board of directors for Women, Ministry and the City. She lives in Chicago, Illinois.*

Dr. Ann Ulanov

The Dread of the Good

On Good and Evil

MATTHEW 2:16–18

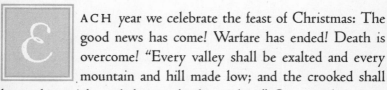 ACH year we celebrate the feast of Christmas: The good news has come! Warfare has ended! Death is overcome! "Every valley shall be exalted and every mountain and hill made low; and the crooked shall be made straight and the rough places plain." Our search is over. God has come: "For unto us a child is born, unto us a son is given; and the government shall be upon his shoulder: and his name shall be called Wonderful, Counselor, The mighty God . . ." (Isaiah 9:6).

And three days after Christmas, in the middle of Christmastide, our liturgical calendar marks the slaughter of the innocents. Herod, realizing that he had been outwitted by the Magi, became furiously angry. He ordered the massacre of all the boys two years old and under in Bethlehem and its entire neighborhood. . . . Then what was said by the prophet Jeremiah was fulfilled: "A cry was heard at Rama, sobbing and loud lamentation: Rachel bewailing her children, she would not be comforted because her children are gone" (Matthew 2:16–18).

Next to the Christmas image of mother and child—the child who in his birth brings joy, grace, and love—are placed the images of other mothers holding small bloody corpses, dead children savaged by hate, killed by envy and blind fury. Goodness and evil are not far apart. We see one in the light of the other. One child is born; other children die. One mother receives the infant to her breast; other mothers bury their infants in the cold ground.

Wars still go on. Death continues to rob us of our loved ones. Hatred makes its force felt, and our own unrecognized animosity is loosed into the world. In this community of people who are believers in God and in Christ—or long to be—we know the ever-present force of evil in our midst, the destructive effects of paralyzing fear, the temptations to suicide, the fear that turns to manipulation, the urge simply to disrupt and destroy, the emptiness that turns away from filling up to persist in emptiness.

IN our world illness and madness continue, suffered especially strongly at Christmas. Depression, despair, and crushing isolation overcome many persons at the time of year when we sing of hosts of angels heralding our savior's birth. In the midst of joy, for many there is only dark misery. In the midst of the revelation of the godhead, there is, as with Herod, a savage fury, a perilous gnashing and tearing to pieces of new life by a tortured soul.

Opposites lie beside each other—the birth of Christ revealing the grace and the good, saluted by the release of a killing hate, of envy so great that if it cannot have the good for itself alone it will kill the good and prevent everyone from having it. This kind of envy, this terrible fear of the good, is an enactment of our dread of the good. It is a refusal to receive the gift as it is given.

How often at Christmastime are we swept up into giving

gifts, gifts that we buy or make for family and friends? How often do we neglect to receive the gifts given to us—really to take to ourselves the feelings behind the presents others give us? We forget and find ourselves unable to receive God's gift to us of love and grace.

Our failure to receive is not just one of neglect. Often it stems from an active refusal, a stolid impenetrability, a resistance to the rearrangement of our lives and our perception of our lives, by the breaking in of God's goodness upon us. Like Herod, we will not take this rearranging of our principalities and powers. We reject putting God's goodness before what we value as good—before our causes and ambitions, our plans for getting a degree or tenure, for our school, for our world. These values of ours must come first. We refuse God's good. We will smash it if necessary, and try to blot it out to secure our meager position in the world.

In dreading the good, we are not the only ones who suffer from refusing what God would give us. Others suffer, too, from our refusal to receive the good. The slaughter of the innocents—these are the real innocent bystanders of our world—new life, young life, killed off before it has matured or perhaps even lived at all. We all have children of our own—our own new insights and new possibilities, our hopes and wishes, our secret plans for the future. These bits and pieces of our lives promise new life, life still to be lived, much as children see hope for the future. It is this new, not yet strong life, this possibility for being, that is slaughtered in our refusal to receive God's gift, in our preferring our own order over what God offers.

When such smashing envy as Herod's is let loose into the world, when such adamantine refusal to open and receive what is given is joined with the impulse to destroy what is given, then all young life in our surroundings is threatened. Children wilt in an atmosphere of hate; new imaginations are throttled at birth by a savage insistence on one way and one only. Nothing can get through to consciousness from the unconscious when such intense fear and desire to control are dominant. Young life, the innocent bystander, suffers terribly from such dread of the good. Unwillingness to receive God's gift works terrible suffering, gratuitous suffering, the very definition of unnecessary pain.

If the first way we resist God's gift is to put our need for power in place of it, as Herod did, the second way we fail to take the goodness offered is to sentimentalize it. For example, any mother of a young child is easily tempted to identify with this story, to feel how she herself could not be comforted if her child, an innocent bystander, was slaughtered because of someone else's hate and dread of God and the good. Such a story is simply insupportable if it is read with identification. For then we are saturated by the suffering welling up inside us, and we cannot help thinking of all those times when children—and not just one's own—have been innocent victims of others' greed, prejudice, and evil. We remember then those who starve, those who are denied the possibility of a life, of free choice, and of self-realization. In such meditations our emotions often overwhelm us and we feel we cannot survive them. The fact of evil threatens to obliterate us.

But this turmoil of emotions often turns out to be something less than significant feeling. It may be sentimentality instead of true feeling. We are led then to ask that indignant question so many of us have asked, are asking, will always ask: How can there be a God who lets this sort of suffering happen? What kind of love permits wars, concentration camps, Hiroshima, the slaughter of innocent children?

How quickly we imagine it would have been better had there never been a God or an incarnation if all those children had to be slaughtered because of it! We fall into our own dread of the good and transfer Herod's action onto God. Doing so, we become Herod, feeling in ourselves a maniacal need to hunt down and stamp out the good. Sentimentality is not true feeling at all, but simply undifferentiated emotion mixed with aggression. We move from drowning in undifferentiated suffering to telling God what God should be and should not be, should permit and should not. We identify with the Matthew story and read it as our own personal story, failing to receive the tale the text is narrating, the instruction it would give us. We assert, instead, our own moral, our own lesson, which becomes a lecture to God on right behavior. On the one hand, such sentimental identification is not tough enough to survive—we are overwhelmed and drowned in misery. On the other hand, such sentimental identification is not soft enough to endure—it turns into its own brittle shoulds and should-nots.

What both this false toughness and false softness miss is the free gift of God's self in Christ. The scandal of love is freedom. You may respond as you will. There is never control or dictation. God permits us to be as we are, to respond as we will. God does not create evil but permits it in the world. When we refuse the gift—the free gift of love—we do not want God to be permissive, but in control. Spare us this suffering! Take it away! Do not allow it!

We cannot identify with this story. We cannot become one with any of its protagonists without suffering badly and fruitlessly. But God can become one with us with impunity. We need to read the text—not as our personal story—but as a story addressed to us as human persons, to instruct us, to inform us, to make us learn from it. What do we learn?

We learn to move out of unconscious identification with the slaughtered innocents and with the parents who see only the evil. We learn to give up our own dear children to God's care. We come to see all of life resting in God's hands. Our refusal to see this is what lets loose so much of the world's murderous fears and attacking hatreds. We learn to care for all that is given us for as long as it is given us—our children, our health, our loved ones, our sanity, our work, and to feel how threatening this can be.

When goodness takes on human flesh, when total incarnation of goodness as a human person occurs, we feel a tremendous power. We know that it is the most differentiating force that exists. When love comes in this way into its most exultant being, it marks itself off from all that is not love, distinguishes itself clearly from nonlove. When goodness is articulated in the flesh, it identifies evil more clearly than ever before. When light floods into darkness, we really see darkness. We see the invincible power of goodness in the light of evil.

What is not permitted us is to identify with darkness and become overwhelmed by the forces of nonlove. What is not permitted us is to become so filled with evil's horror that we fail to see the goodness it outlines so firmly. This is what the story of the slaughter of the innocents teaches. It is a hard teaching, but one much needed in our time of violence. The story shows us the threats, the terrors that happen to the Herods of the world—and to the piece of Herod that exists in all of us.

Goodness constellates evil. It performs a central ontic function, creating the precondition for consciousness of evil. Christ is born, and the effect is radical. That incredible birth in our midst rearranges all human life violently so that those who refuse its new truths—every time they refuse its new truths—must resort to violence to destroy the force of the event.

Goodness makes us see that evil is really there, however negatively, as the privation of being, defiantly unable to receive being, refusing it, preferring unconscious sentimental identification to a conscious tough seeing of what is there, preferring dread of the good to taking it into ourselves. Evil, when acknowledged, illuminates the good, points to it, witnesses to its powerful effect.

The presence of God alone makes visible to us the presence of evil. Then we can cope with it and deal with it. Now we can dare to touch it and find ways to deal with it. When evil remains a mere privation, an absence only, we cannot deal with it; all we

can do is fall into it. But in the light of Christ we can really acknowledge it without sentimentality; we can see it for the ugly
force that it is, the horror that refuses the good and murders others with that refusal.

The genius of scripture in placing the story of the slaughter
of the innocents so close to the Christmas nativity anticipates the
insight of twentieth-century depth psychology. It tells us that
without facing and acknowledging evil—evil outside us and evil inside us—we cannot find our own goodness, the good that is ours
and no one else's, the good that comes to us in the light of the
evil with which we are now equipped to deal.

In the birth of Christ we are reborn, taken out of childhood
into a tough, realistic maturity, prepared to see that evil really does
attack the good and does not hesitate to crucify it. Such a seeing
prepares a way in our wilderness, where a rough mixture of good
and evil gives us the great choice freely to consent to the good now
given us in its most resplendent and tangible form, in the fleshi-
fication of love that we celebrate in both these feasts—the feast of
the Nativity and the feast of the slaughter of the innocents.

We see evil in all its power, but we know that good is not
overcome. In the light of evil the invincible power of God's goodness shines forth. It survives even the evil risen up to crush it.
Goodness seen in the light of evil remains a constant love, love
freely offered, a goodness intact, wholly itself, wholly present,
coming toward us in this Advent time to be received into ourselves.
God waits on us, given us for the taking, too good to be true, yet
unmistakably true, beyond words and yet the Word itself—the first
and the last. Nothing ends or begins the way we expect. Evil is
not banished, yet goodness prevails. GOD BE PRAISED.

DR. ANN ULANOV, M.DIV., PH.D., L.H.D., *is the Christianne Brooks Johnson Professor of Psychiatry and Religion at Union Theological Seminary in New York City. A psychoanalyst in private practice, she is a supervising analyst and faculty member of the C. G. Jung Institute in New York City. With her husband, Barry Ulanov, she is the author of* Religion and the Unconscious; Primary Speech: A Psychology of Prayer; Cinderella and Her Sisters: The Envied and the Envying; The Witch and the Clown: Two Archtypes of Human Sexuality; The Healing Imagination; Transforming Sexuality: The Archetypal World of Anima and Animus; *and, by herself, she is the author of* The Feminine in Christian Theology and in Jungian Psychology; Receiving Woman: Studies in the Psychology and Theology of the Feminine; Picturing God; The Wisdom of The Psyche; The Female Ancestors of Christ; The Wizards' Gate; *and* The Functioning Transcendent. *An Episcopal laywoman, she lives in New York City and Connecticut.*

ALICE WALKER

FROM *Anything We Love Can Be Saved*

On Inherited Religion

THE church I attended as a child still stands. It is small, almost tiny, and made of very old, silver-gray lumber, painted white a couple of decades ago, when an indoor toilet was also added. It is simple, serene, sweet. It used to nestle amid vivid green foliage at a curve in a sandy dirt road; inside, its rough-hewn benches smelled warmly of pine. Its yard was shaded by a huge red oak tree, from which people took bits of bark to brew a tonic for their chickens. I remember my mother boiling the bark she'd cut from the tree and feeding the reddish-brown "tea" to her pullets, who, without it, were likely to cannibalize each other. The county, years later, and without warning, cut down the tree and straightened and paved the road. In an attempt to create a tourist industry where none had existed before, they flooded the surrounding countryside. The fisherpeople from far away who whiz by in their pickup trucks

today know nothing about what they see. To us, they are so un-
connected to the land; they appear to hover above it, like ghosts.

The church was donated to our community in 1866, after the
Emancipation Proclamation, by the daughter of the slave owner.
It is "ours" only for as long as services are held there. Few young
people have remained interested in the church, and so it has been
kept going by one or two elderly women. I have supported their
effort to keep the church open by responding to whatever modest requests for assistance they have made. I do this because I respect these old women, and also because I recognize them as the
keepers of a personal heritage that is very dear to me. The cemetery with virtually all of my relatives, including grandparents and
parents, is just across the way, as is the vetch-covered space where
the first consolidated school for black people in our community
used to stand—a school my father was instrumental in erecting. I
find myself once or twice a year sitting on the church steps, peek-
ing into the windows, or just standing in the yard, remembering.

What I remember is playing tag and hide-and-go-seek with my
cousin and best friend, Delilah.* She was radiantly black, funny,
and fleet of foot, and her mother dressed her in airy, colorful summer dresses and patent-leather shoes, just the way my mother
dressed me. Perhaps she had more pigtails; I had bigger bows. In
winter we wore identical maroon-colored snowsuits, which served
us well in the uninsulated church, which was then, and still is,
heated by a potbellied stove. We would grow up and lose touch,
and she would barely escape a violently abusive marriage, about
which I would hear only after the fact. I remember my father hud-
dled with other men outside under the trees, laughing. My mother,
scrubbed and shining, smiling. We were all on our best behavior;
even my incorrigibly raucous brothers, who, only at church, managed to be both neat and quiet.

*Delilah is not her real name.

Because we were Methodists and sang mostly standard hymns, the singing wasn't all that great. I loved it, though, because I liked singing with others—still do—and I was, even as a small child, humbled by the sincerity in the voices of everyone. After we sang any kind of song together, there was nobody in the congregation I didn't love.

Perhaps the singing had been even more arresting a hundred years earlier; legend had it that the former slave owners would stop their buggies underneath the red oak to listen. Sometimes professional gospel singers came down from Atlanta and "turned the place out." They were undisputed queens in their shiny red or blue robes: They shouted at God as if they knew Him personally and also knew He was hard of hearing. The black stuff around their eyes, which began to run and smear the moment they began to sweat, was strange to us, as was the fact that they wore, and wiped off, more lipstick in an afternoon than my plain, country-beauty mother would own in her life.

My mother, in addition to her other duties as worker, wife, and mother of eight children, was also mother of the church. I realize now that I was kind of a little church mother in training, as I set out for the church with her on Saturday mornings. We would mop the bare pine floors, run dust rags over the benches, and wash the windows. Take out the ashes, dump them behind the outhouse, clean the outhouse, and be sure there was adequate paper. We would sweep the carpeting around the pulpit and I would reverently dust off the Bible. Each Saturday my mother slipped a starched and ironed snowy-white doily underneath it.

One season she resolved to completely redo the pulpit area. With a hammer and tacks and rich, wine-dark cloth she'd managed to purchase from meager savings, she upholstered the chairs, including the thronelike one in which the preacher sat. She also laid new carpeting. On Sunday morning she would bring flowers from her garden.

There has never been anyone who amazed and delighted me as

consistently as my mother did when I was a child. Part of her magic was her calm, no-nonsense manner. If it could be done, she could probably do it, was her attitude. She enjoyed being strong and capable. Anything she didn't know how to do, she could learn. I was thrilled to be her apprentice.

My father and brothers cleared the cemetery of brush and cut the grass around the church while we were inside. By the time we were finished, everything sparkled. We stood back and admired our work.

Sister Walker, my mother, was thanked for making the church so beautiful, but this wise woman, who knew so many things about life and the mysteries of the heart, the spirit, and the soul, was never asked to speak to the congregation. If she and other "mothers" and "sisters" of the church had been asked to speak, if it had been taken for granted that they had vision and insight to match their labor and their love, would the church be alive today?

And what would the women have said? Would they have protested that the Eve of the Bible did not represent them? That they had never been that curious? But of course they had been just as curious. If a tree had appeared in their midst with an attractive fruit on it, and furthermore one that they were informed would make them wise, they would have nibbled it. And what could be so wrong about that? Anyway, God had told Adam about the forbidden fruit; He hadn't said a word directly to Eve. And what kind of God would be so cruel as to curse women and men for eating a piece of fruit, no matter how forbidden? Would they have said that Adam was a weak man who evaded personal responsibility for his actions? Would they have pointed out how quickly and obsequiously he turned in his wife to God, as if she had forced him to eat the fruit rather than simply offered him a bite? Would they have said Adam's behavior reminded them of a man who got a woman pregnant and then blamed the woman for tempting him to have intercourse, thereby placing all the blame on her? Would they have said that God was unfair? Well, He was white, His son was white, and it truly was a white man's world, as far as they could see.

Would they have spoken of the God they had found, not in the Bible, but in life, as they wrestled death while delivering babies, or as they worked almost beyond, and sometimes beyond, capacity in the white man's fields? I remember my mother telling me of a time when she was hugely pregnant and had an enormous field of cotton, twenty-five or thirty acres, to chop, that is, to thin and weed. Her older children were in school, from which she refused to take them, her youngest trailed behind her and fell asleep in the furrows. My father, who was a laborer, dairyman, and chauffeur, had driven the bosslady to town. As my mother looked at the immense acreage still to be covered, she felt so ill she could barely lift the hoe. Never had she felt so alone. Coming to the end of a row, she lay down under a tree and asked to die. Instead, she fell into a deep sleep, and when she awakened, she was fully restored. In fact, she felt wonderful, as if a healing breeze had touched her soul. She picked up the hoe and continued her work.

What God rescued my mother? Was it the God who said women deserved to suffer and were evil anyway, or was it the God of nonjudgmental Nature, calming and soothing her with the green coolness of the tree she slept under and the warm earth she lay upon? I try to imagine my mother and the other women calling on God as they gave birth, and I shudder at the image of Him they must have conjured. He was someone, after all, they had been taught, who said black people were cursed to be drawers of water and hewers of wood. That some people enslaved and abused others was taken for granted by Him. He ordered the killing of women and children, by the hundreds of thousands, if they were not of his chosen tribe. The women would have had to know how little they and their newborns really mattered, because they were female, poor, and black, like the accursed children of Hagar and of Ham, and they would have had to promise to be extra good, obedient, trusting, and so forth, to make up for it.

Life was so hard for my parents' generation that the subject of heaven was never distant from their thoughts. The preacher would gleefully, or so it seemed to me, run down all the trials and tribulations of an existence that ground us into dust, only to pull heaven out of the biblical hat at the last minute. I was intrigued. Where is heaven? I asked my parents. Who is going to be there? What about accommodations, and food? I was told what they sincerely believed: that heaven was in the sky, in space, as we would later describe it; that only the best people on earth would go there when they died. We'd all have couches to lounge on, great food to eat. Wonderful music, because all the angels played harp. It would be grand. Would there be any white people? Probably. Oh. There was not one white person in the county that any black person felt comfortable with. And though there was a rumor that a good white woman, or man, had been observed sometime, somewhere, no one seemed to know this for a fact.

Now that there's been so much space travel and men have been on the moon, I wonder if preachers still preach about going to heaven, and whether it's the same place.

The truth was, we already lived in paradise but were worked too hard by the land-grabbers to enjoy it. This is what my mother, and perhaps the other women, knew, and this was one reason why they were not permitted to speak. They might have demanded that the men of the church notice Earth. Which always leads to revolution. In fact, everyone has known this for a very long time. For the other, more immediate and basic, reason my mother and the other women were not permitted to speak in church was that the Bible forbade it. And it is forbidden in the Bible because, in the Bible, men alone are sanctioned to own property, in this case, Earth itself. And woman herself is property, along with the asses, the oxen, and the sheep.

I can imagine some latter-day Jezebel in our community (Jezebel apparently practiced a Goddess-centered pagan religion, one of those the God of the Old Testament is always trying to wipe out) having the nerve to speak up about being silenced. And the smugness with which our uninspiring and indifferently trained minister, Reverend Whisby, might have directed her to a passage from the New Testament that is attributed to Saint Paul: "Let women keep silence in the churches." He would run his pudgy finger underneath the sentence, and she would read it and feel thoroughly put down. For God wrote the Bible, she would have been persuaded; and every word, even every word about murdering the suckling babies of your enemies and stealing all their worldly goods, was Truth.

I remember going with my mother to get water from the spring. What is a spring? Many will ask, just as I did. It is a place in the earth where water just bubbles up, pure and sweet. You don't ask for it, you don't put it there. It simply appears. There was one down the hill from our house, in a quiet grove of trees. Someone years before had put a piece of a terra-cotta culvert around it, with a notch in the lip for overflow. We'd dip our battered buckets into the shallow well, always careful to spot where the crawfish might be hiding, and perhaps sit for a minute before trudging back up the hill. How on earth did the crawfish get in there? I'd ask. They are always in healthy springs, was the answer. Yes, but why? I don't know, that's just the way it is.

But why is that the way it is? Where did they come from: There were no other crawfish for miles around. I never saw them in the creek, for instance, where my brothers and I waded. This was a mystery that was not explained by my mother's final exasperated "God brought them."

I was happier with my father's explanation: "Well, you see, these crawfishes used to live over 'round Buckhead, but it just got too goldarn hot on account of all them fires the lumber company makes cleaning up the slag . . . so they held a crawfish convention, kinda like our revivals, and they resolved to move east. So they traveled and they traveled and one day they came to this place where there was this pretty little girl sitting looking down in the water. And you know crawfish love to be looked at, so . . ." In fact, neither of my parents knew how the crawfish got into the spring.

On the one hand, I could strain to imagine a large white man in a white robe—unfortunately, real-life white men in robes belonged to the Ku Klux Klan—lovingly carrying two tiny crawfish down the hill to place them in our spring, or I could fantasize about the stouthearted crawfish pioneers leaving Buckhead with their Sears Roebuck catalog suitcases, crawfish-size.

The water we collected had many uses. We drank it; we washed dishes, clothes, and ourselves with it. We watered our livestock and my mother's vegetable and flower gardens.

Because of the criminal exploitation inherent in the sharecropping system—in which the landowner controlled land, seeds, and tools, as well as records of account—sharecroppers were often worse off than slaves, which was the point. Sharecropping was the former slave owners' revenge, against black people for having attained their freedom. It's no wonder that under such complete subjugation and outright terrorism, which included rape, beatings, burnings, and being thrown off the land, along with the entrenched southern custom of lynching, people like my parents sought succor from any God they were forced to have. The idea that as descendants of Africans and Native Americans and Europeans—Scottish and Irish—on both my mother's and my father's side, they might have had their own ancient Gods, or that as free human beings they might choose a God uniquely perceived by themselves, never entered their minds, except negatively. The "heathen" from whom they were descended knew nothing of salvation, they were warned in church, and any God except the one in the Bible was just another illusion produced by Satan, designed to keep them out of heaven. Satan: always described as evil; in color, black or red. African or Native American? Never admitted to be also a son of God, made also in the image of his creator, just the shadow side of him. And yet everyone in our family and in our church understood instinctively who Satan was. He was the other side of "the son of God" we always saw in the white people around us. Never did we see "Jesus" among those who insisted we worship him. Only Judas, and every day.

"Pagan" means "of the land, country dweller, peasant," all of which my family was. It also means a person whose primary spiritual relationship is with Nature and the Earth. And this, I could see, day to day, was true not only of me but of my parents; but there was no way to ritually express the magical intimacy we felt with Creation without being accused of, and ridiculed for, indulging in "heathenism," that other word for paganism. And Christianity, we were informed, had fought long and hard to deliver us from that. In fact, millions of people were broken, physically and spiritually, literally destroyed, for nearly two millennia, as the orthodox Christian Church "saved" them from their traditional worship of the Great Mystery they perceived in Nature.

In the sixties many of us scared our parents profoundly when we showed up dressed in our "African" or "Native American" or "Celtic" clothes. We shocked them by wearing our hair in its ancient naturalness. They saw us turning back to something that they'd been taught to despise and that, by now, they actively feared. Many of our parents had been taught that the world was only two or three thousand years old, and that spiritually civilized life began with the birth of Jesus Christ. Their only hope of enjoying a better existence, after a lifetime of crushing toil and persistent abuse, was to be as much like the long-haired rabbi from a small Jewish sect in a far-off desert as possible; then, by the Grace of His father, who owned heaven, they might be admitted there, after death. It would be segregated, of course, who could imagine anything different? But perhaps Jesus Christ himself would be present, and would speak up on their behalf. After all, these were black people who were raised never to look a white person directly in the face.

I think now, and it hurts me to think it, of how tormented the true believers in our church must have been, wondering if, in heaven, Jesus Christ, a white man, the only good one besides Santa Claus and Abraham Lincoln they'd ever heard of, would deign to sit near them.

ON Saturday night everyone in my family bathed from head to toe, even though this meant half a day spent carrying pails of water up a steep hill. The water was heated in the big black washpot in the yard. On Sunday morning we rose, washed our faces, had a hearty breakfast, and went off to church. As the smallest, I was bathed by my mother, dressed by my mother, fed by my mother, and wedged into the front seat of our secondhand blue-and-cream Packard between my mother and my father. They had worked hard all week, for the landowner's benefit; this was their only time of pleasure, of rest, other than an occasional Saturday-night film at the local picture show. We spent most of the day in church, listening to the minister, who stood on the carpeting my mother had laid and read from the Bible I had dusted. Sometimes there were wonderful stories: Daniel in the Lion's Den. The Three Wise Men. David and Goliath. The Life of Christ. (Everybody loved Jesus Christ. We recognized him as one of us, but a rebel and revolutionary, consistently speaking up for the poor, the sick, and the discriminated against, and going up against the bossmen: the orthodox Jewish religious leaders and rich men of his day. We knew that people who were really like Jesus were often lynched. I liked his gift for storytelling. I also loved that, after Moses and Joshua, he is the greatest magician in the Bible. He was also, I realized later, a fabulous masseur, healing by the power of touch and the laying-on of hands. Much later still I learned he could dance! This quote from the Acts of John, from the Gnostic Gospels, is worth remembering: "To the Universe belongs the dancer. He who does not dance does not know what happens. Now if you follow my dance, see yourself in me.") But basically, according to the scriptures: We had sinned. (I did not know then that the root of the word "sin" means "to be.") Woman was the cause. In our life we must suffer just because we existed. Worthless, worthless us. Luckily enough, we would die, but only a very small number of us would get into heaven. There was hell, a pit of eternally burning fire, for the vast majority.

Where was hell? I wanted to know. Under the ground, I was informed. It was assumed most of the white people would be there, and therefore it would be more or less like here. Only fiery hot, hotter than the sun in the cotton field at midday. Nobody wanted to go there.

I had a problem with this doctrine at a very early age: I could not see how my parents had sinned. Each month my mother had what I would later recognize, because I unfortunately inherited it, as bad PMS. At those times her temper was terrible; the only safe thing was to stay out of her way. My father, slower to anger, was nonetheless a victim of sexist ideology learned from his father, the society, and the church, which meant I battled with him throughout childhood, until I left home for good at seventeen. But I did not see that they were evil, that they should be cursed because they were black, because my mother was a woman. They were as innocent as trees, I felt. And, at heart, generous and sweet. I resented the minister and the book he read from that implied they could be "saved" only by confessing their sin and accepting suffering and degradation as their due, just because a very long time ago, a snake had given a white woman an apple and she had eaten it and generously given a bite to her craven-hearted husband. This was insulting to the most drowsy intelligence, I thought. Noting that my exhausted father often napped while in church. But what could I do? I was three years old.

When I was in my thirties, I wrote this poem:

SUNDAY SCHOOL, CIRCA 1950
"Who made you?" was always
The question
The answer was always
"God."
Well, there we stood
Three feet high
Heads bowed
Leaning into Bosoms.

Now I no longer recall
The Catechism
Or brood on the Genesis
Of life
No.

I ponder the exchange
Itself
And salvage mostly
The leaning.

It is ironic, to say the least, that the very woman out of whose body I came, whose pillowy arms still held me, willingly indoctrinated me away from herself and the earth from which both of us received sustenance, and toward a frightful, jealous, cruel, murderous "God" of another race and tribe of people, and expected me to forget the very breasts that had fed me and that I still leaned against. But such is the power of centuries-old indoctrination.

We know now with what absolute heartlessness the male leaders of the orthodox Christian Church—not unlike those of orthodox Judaism and Islam—stamped out, generally after robbing them of their land and enslaving them, pagans and heathens, our ancestors and theirs, around the globe: a campaign of such unspeakable cruelty, which has lasted for so long, and which still continues, that few have had the heart to encounter it in art, politics, literature, or consciousness until the present era. If our awareness is beginning to change, it is thanks in large part to feminism and feminist scholarship, and to a resurgent belief in the sacredness of the feminine, which was deliberately erased, demonized, and disparaged in all major religions. But thanks also to indigenous peoples who, though a mere remnant of their former selves, before the invasions of conquerors professing Christianity, have risen up to speak in defense of the ancient Goddess/God of all pagans and heathens, Mother Earth.

IN this connection, Haile Gerima's extraordinary film *Sankofa* has much to teach us. While being photographed, dancing and carefree, inside the walls of a "slave castle" in contemporary Africa, a black fashion model for a white, Western magazine finds herself trapped inside the castle's dungeon, from whose loading tunnels millions of enslaved Africans, from the fifteenth to the nineteenth century, began their soul-shattering journey to the New World. The woman is horrified to discover she has somehow slipped back into the past and is, in fact, one of her own enslaved ancestors. We follow her spiritual development as her own beliefs are denied her and the imprint of Christianity is literally beaten and branded into her flesh. People of color have been so successfully brainwashed to believe that white orthodox Christianity has given us something we didn't already have that we rarely think of what it has taken away. *Sankofa* speaks to this. It also, perhaps for the first time in cinema, graphically depicts the process by which sadists who purport to be Christians have forced their religious ideology on the cultures they destroyed.

· · ·

IN the black church we have loved and leaned on Moses, because he brought the enslaved Israelites out of Egypt. As enslaved and oppressed people, we have identified with him so completely that we have adopted his God. But here is another look at Moses, when God commanded him to make war against the Midianites, although his wife, Zipporah, was a Midianite, two of his children were Midianites, and his kindly father-in-law, Jethro, was also a Midianite.

From the Book of Numbers, Chapter 31:

> 9 And the children of Israel took all the women of Midian captives, and their little ones, and took the spoil of all their cattle, and all their flocks, and all their goods.
>
> 10 And they burnt all their cities wherein they dwelt, and all their goodly castles with fire. . . .
>
> 12 And they brought the captives, and the prey, and the spoil, unto Moses, and Eleazar the priest, and unto the congregation of the children of Israel, unto the camp at the plains of Moab, which are by Jordan near Jericho. . . .
>
> 14 And Moses was wroth with the officers of the host, with the captains over thousands, and captains over hundreds, which came from the battle.
>
> 15 And Moses said unto them, Have ye saved all the women alive? . . .
>
> 17 Now therefore kill every male among the little ones, and kill every woman that hath known man by lying with him.
>
> 18 But all the women children, that have not known a man by lying with him, keep alive for yourselves. . . .
>
> 25 And the Lord spake unto Moses, saying,

26 Take the sum of the prey that was taken, both of man and of beast, thou, and Eleazar the priest, and the chief fathers of the congregation: . . .

31 And Moses and Eleazar the priest did as the Lord commanded Moses.

32 And the booty, being the rest of the prey which the men of war had caught, was six hundred thou-sand and seventy thousand and five thousand sheep,

33 And threescore and twelve thousand beeves,

34 And threescore and one thousand asses,

35 And thirty and two thousand persons in all, of women that had not known man by lying with him.

These miserable, grieving, orphaned young women and chil-dren ended up as sex slaves, concubines, and drudges in the ser-vice of the soldiers and the priests.*

Women have little voice in the Bible, and what voice they do have is given them only to illustrate the deviousness, silliness, un-trustworthiness, and general insignificance of their sex. The only thing that makes them worthwhile is the birth of a son; they ex-pend much of their energy trying to bring this about. In the whole of the Old Testament only Deborah, the judge; Vashti, the dignified wife of a foolish king; Esther, who saves her people; and Naomi and Ruth, the devoted mother- and daughter-in-law, stand out as women of substance. One cannot help but feel empathy for the Jewish women of the Bible, however, who had no rights under the law of Moses—and indeed were told to stand back when he came down from the mountain with the Ten Commandments, which, after all, were not written for them—and were forced to

---

*In the discussion that follows I am indebted to the fabulous Elizabeth Cady Stanton, and her great work, *The Original Feminist Attack on the Bible* (published as *The Woman's Bible, 1895–98*), for her insights and, more particularly, for her attitude.

share their husbands and homes with strange, weeping women ab-
ducted from other lands.

As to why my mother and grandmother rarely spoke of their
spiritual connection to the universe, we have only to read these
verses in Deuteronomy, Chapter 17:

> 2 If there be found among you . . . man or woman,
> that hath wrought wickedness in the sight of the
> Lord thy God, in transgressing his covenant,
> 3 And hath gone and served other gods, and wor-
> shipped them, either the sun or moon, or any of the
> host of heaven, which I have not commanded; . . .
> 5 Then shalt thou bring forth that man or that
> woman . . . unto thy gates . . . and shalt stone them
> with stones, till they die.

This is a God who does not recognize you as His unless you
are circumcised. I don't believe the men in the congregation I grew
up in realized this; they were definitely not circumcised. On the
other hand, reading the Old Testament, and noting how readily
this God would kill you if you were uncircumcised (Zipporah, the
non-Jewish wife of Moses, circumcises one of their "heathen" sons
with a rock before entering Egypt), I am inclined to believe that
the circumcision of women (genital mutilation)—women who
wanted to belong, to be accepted by God—has some of its roots
here. Certainly the slaughter of nine million "witches" over five
centuries in Europe has its root in Leviticus, Chapter 20, Verse
27: "A man also or woman that hath a familiar spirit, or that is
a wizard, shall surely be put to death: they shall stone them with
stones; their blood shall be upon them."

Under this order the "wizards" Moses, Joshua, and Jesus—
especially Jesus, who raised people from the dead and changed

water to wine—would have been burned at the stake in the Europe of the fourteenth through the eighteenth centuries.

It is chilling to think that the same people who persecuted the wise women and men of Europe, its midwives and healers, then crossed the oceans to Africa and the Americas and tortured and enslaved, raped, impoverished, and eradicated the peaceful, Christlike people they found. And that the blueprint from which they worked, and still work, was the Bible.

BAPTISM
They dunked me in the creek;
a tiny brooklet.
Muddy, gooey with rotting leaves,
a greenish mold floating;
definable.

For love it was.
For love of God at seven.
All in white.
With God's mud ruining my snowy
socks and his bullfrog spoors
gluing up my face.

This is the poem of a seven-year-old pagan. The "God" of heaven that my parents and the church were asking me to accept was obscured by the mud, leaves, rot, and bullfrog spoors of this world. How amazing this all is, I thought, entering the muddy creek. And how deeply did I love those who stood around, solemnly waiting to see my "saved" head reappear above the murky water. This experience of communal love and humble hope for my well-being was my reality of life on this planet. I was unable to send my mind off into space in search of a God who never noticed mud, leaves, or bullfrogs. Or the innocent hearts of my tender, loving people.

. . .

IT is fatal to love a God who does not love you. A God specifi-cally created to comfort, lead, advise, strengthen, and enlarge the tribal borders of someone else. We have been beggars at the table of a religion that sanctioned our destruction. Our own religions de-nied, forgotten; our own ancestral connections to All Creation something of which we are ashamed. I maintain that we are empty, lonely, without our pagan-heathen ancestors; that we must lively them up within ourselves, and begin to see them as whole and nec-essary and correct: their Earth-centered, female-reverencing reli-gions, like their architecture, agriculture, and music, suited perfectly to the lives they led. And lead, those who are left, today. I further maintain that the Jesus most of us have been brought up to adore must be expanded to include the "wizard" and the dancer, and that when this is done, it becomes clear that he coexists quite easily with pagan indigenous peoples. Indeed, it was because the teach-ings of Jesus were already familiar to many of our ancestors, es-pecially in the New World—they already practiced the love and sharing that he preached—that the Christian Church was able to make as many genuine converts to the Christian religion as it did.

All people deserve to worship a God who also worships them. A God that made them, and likes them. That is why Nature, Mother Earth, is such a good choice. Never will Nature require that you cut off some part of your body to please It; never will Mother Earth find anything wrong with your natural way. She made it, and She made it however it is so that you will be more comfortable as part of Her Creation, rather than less. Everyone de-serves a God who adores our freedom: Nature would never advise us to do anything but be ourselves. Mother Earth will do all that She can to support our choices. Whatever they are. For they are of Her, and inherent in our creation is Her trust.

We are born knowing how to worship, just as we are born knowing how to laugh.

And what is the result of decolonizing the spirit? It is as if one truly does possess a third eye, and this eye opens. One begins to see the world from one's own point of view; to interact with it out of one's own conscience and heart. One's own "pagan" Earth spirit. We begin to flow, again, with and into the Universe. And out of this flowing comes the natural activism of wanting to survive, to be happy, to enjoy one another and Life, and to laugh. We begin to distinguish between the need, singly, to throw rocks at whatever is oppressing us, and the creative joy that arises when we bring our collective stones of resistance against injustice together. We begin to see that we must be loved very much by whatever Creation is, to find ourselves on this wonderful Earth. We begin to recognize our sweet, generously appointed place in the makeup of the Cosmos. We begin to feel glad, and grateful to be here.

ALICE WALKER *won the Pulitzer Prize and the American Book Award for her novel* The Color Purple. *Her other bestselling novels include* Possessing the Secret of Joy *and* The Temple of My Familiar. *She is also the author of two collections of short stories, three collections of essays, five volumes of poetry, and several children's books. Her books have been translated into more than two dozen languages. Born in Eatonton, Georgia, Walker now lives in Northern California.*

This exploration of Walker's spiritual quest was presented at Auburn Theological Seminary, New York City, in April of 1995.

RABBI MARGARET MOERS WENIG

God Is a Woman and She Is Growing Older

On God

HO or what is God? Where shall we look for God's presence? Our sages and philosophers are by no means unanimous in their response. But they do concur on one matter: Who or what God truly is is ultimately unknowable. God is the Hidden One, the one who conceals His face, or the Infinite, Unmeasurable One—unknowable, unfathomable, indescribable.

Yet, these same sages dare to try to capture our people's experience of God in images we do know, can comprehend. The Kabbalists went as far as to sketch God's form: the Primordial Man. Each of God's attributes, associated with a specific part of his body: head, arms, legs, torso, even male genitals. Midrashim give us images of God weeping at the sight of Egyptians drowning; bound in chains forced into exile with His people; laying tefillin each weekday morning; and studying Torah with Moshe

Rabbenu. Our liturgy shows us God as an immovable Rock, as a shield, as the commander of a host of angels, as a shepherd, and, on the Days of Awe, the machzor focus upon the images of God as father and God and King.

But all these images are metaphors, allusion—not meant to be taken literally, merely meant to point us toward something we can imagine but never really see. So, tonight I invite you to imagine God along with me. Tonight I invite you to imagine God as a woman, a woman who is growing older.

God is a woman, and she is growing older. She moves more slowly now. She cannot stand erect. Her hair is thinning. Her face is lined. Her smile no longer innocent. Her voice is scratchy. Her eyes tire. Sometimes she has to strain to hear. God is a woman and she is growing older, yet she remembers everything.

On Rosh Hashanah, the anniversary of the day on which she gave us birth, God sits down at her kitchen table, opens the Book of Memories, and begins turning pages, and God remembers.

"There, there is the world when it was new and my children when they were young . . ." As she turns each page, she smiles, seeing before her, like so many dolls in a department store window, all the beautiful colors of our skin, all the varied shapes and sizes of our bodies. She marvels at our accomplishments: the music we have written, the gardens we have planted, the skyscrapers we have built, the stories we have told, the ideas we have spun.

"Now, they can fly faster than the winds I send," she says to herself, "and they sail across the waters which I gathered into seas. They even visit the moon which I set in the sky. But they rarely visit me." There, pasted into the pages of her book, are all the cards we sent to her when we did not bother to visit. She notices our signatures scrawled beneath the printed words someone else has composed.

There are pages she would rather skip. Things she wishes she could forget. But they stare her in the face and she cannot help but remember: her children spoiling the home she created for us, brothers putting each other in chains. She remembers seeing us racing down dangerous roads—herself unable to stop us. She remembers the dreams she had for us that we never fulfilled. And she remembers the names, so many names, inscribed in the book, names of all the children she has lost due to war and famine, earthquakes and accidents, disease, and suicide. And God remembers the many times she sat by our bedsides weeping that she could not halt the process she herself set into motion. Tonight, Kol Nidrei night, God lit candles, one for each of her children, millions and millions of candles lighting up the night, making it bright as day. Tonight God will stay awake all night turning the pages of her book.

God is lonely tonight, longing for her children, her playful ones, Ephraim, her darling one. Her body aches for us. All that dwells on earth does perish, but God endures, so she suffers the sadness of losing all that she holds dear.

God is home tonight, turning the pages of her book. "Come home," she wants to say to us, "Come home." But she won't call. She is afraid that we will say, "No." She can anticipate the conversation: "We are so busy," we'd apologize. "We'd love to see you but we just can't come tonight. Too much to do. Too many responsibilities to juggle."

Even if we don't realize it, God knows that our business is just an excuse. She knows that we avoid returning to her because we don't want to look into her age-worn face. She understands that it is hard for us to face a God who disappointed our childhood expectations: She did not give us everything we wanted. She did not make us triumphant in battle, successful in business, and invincible to pain. We avoid going home to protect ourselves from our disappointment and to protect her. We don't want her to see the disappointment in our eyes. Yet, God knows that it is there and she would have us come home anyway.

What if we did? What if we did go home and visit God this Yom Kippur? What might it be like?

God would usher us into her kitchen, seat us at her table, pour two cups of tea. She has been alone so long that there is much she wants to say to us. But we barely allow her to get a word in because we are afraid of both what she might say and we are equally afraid of silence. So we fill an hour with our chatter; words, words, words. Until, finally, she touches her finger to her lips and says, "Sha. Be still, Shhh."

Then she pushes back her chair, "Let me have a good look at you." And she looks. And in a single glance, God sees us as both newly born and dying; coughing and crying, turning our head to root for her breast, and fearful of the unknown realm that lies ahead.

In a single glance she sees our birth and our death and all the years in between. She sees us as we were when we were young: when we idolized her and trustingly followed her anywhere; when our scrapes and bruises healed quickly; when we were filled with wonder at all things new (a new dress, a driver's license, the new feeling in our body when we first allowed a friend to touch it). She sees us when we were young, when we thought that there was nothing we could not do.

She sees our middle years when our energy was unlimited. When we kept house, cooked and cleaned, cared for children, worked, and volunteered—when everyone needed us and we had no time for sleep. And God sees our later years: when we no longer felt so needed; when chaos disrupted the bodily rhythms we had learned to rely upon. She sees us sleeping alone in a room that once slept two. God sees things about us we have forgotten and things we do not yet know. For nothing is hidden from her sight.

When she is finished looking at us, God might say, "So tell me, how are you?" Now we are afraid to open our mouths and tell her everything she already knows: whom we love, where we hurt, what we have broken or lost. We are afraid to speak now, or we might begin to cry.

So we change the subject. "Remember the time when . . . ,"

we begin. "Yes, I remember," she says. Suddenly we are both talk-ing at the same time, never completing a sentence, saying all the things the cards never said:

"I'm sorry that I . . ."

"That's all right, I forgive you."

"I didn't mean to . . ."

"I know that, I do."

"I was so angry that time."

"I'm sorry that I ever hurt you, but you wouldn't listen to me."

"You're right, I wouldn't listen. I should have. I know that now, but at the time I had to do it my way."

"I know." She nods. "I know."

We look away from her now, our eyes wander around the kitchen. "I never felt I could live up to your expectations," we say.

"I always believed you could do anything," she answers.

"What about your future?" she asks us. We don't have an an-swer because we do not want to face our futures. God hears our reluctance and understands.

After many hours of sitting and drinking tea, when at last there are no more words to say or to hear, God begins to hum. And we are transported back to a time when our fever wouldn't break and we couldn't sleep, exhausted from crying but unable to stop. She picked us up and held us against her bosom and supported our head in the palm of her hand and walked with us. Then God reaches out and touches our arm, bringing us back from our nos-talgia, bringing us back to the present and to the future. "You will always be my child," she says, "but you are no longer a child. Grow old along with me. The best is yet to be, the last of life for which the first was made."

We are growing older as God is growing older. How much like God we have become.

God holds our face in her two hands and whispers, "Do not be afraid. I will be faithful to the promise I made to you when you were young. I will be with you. Even in your old age I will be with you. When you are gray-headed still I will hold you. I gave birth to you, I carried you, I will hold you still. Grow old along with me."

Our fear of the future is tempered now by curiosity: understanding that the universe is infinite, unlimited possibilities are before us still. Though the sun rises and sets just as the day before, no two days are the same. We can greet each day with eagerness, awakening to wonder: What shall I learn today? What can I create? What will I notice that I have never seen before?

It has been a good visit after all. Before we leave, it is our turn to take a good look at her. The face that time has marked looks not frail to us now—but wise. We understand that God knows those things only the passage of time can teach: that one can survive the loss of a love; that one can feel secure even in the midst of an ever-changing world; that there can be dignity in being alive even when every bone aches. God's movements do not seem slow to us now, but strong and intent, unlike our own. We are too busy to see beneath the surface. We speak too rapidly to truly listen. We move too rapidly to feel what we touch. We form opinions too quickly to judge honestly. But God moves slowly and with intention. She sees everything there is to see, understands everything she hears, and touches all that lives.

Now we understand why we were created to grow older: each added day of life, each new year makes us more like God. Rise before the aged and see the grandeur in the faces of the old. We rise in their presence as we would rise in the presence of God, for in the faces of the old we see God's face.

Looking at her now, we are overwhelmed. This aging woman looks to us like a queen. Her chair a throne, her housedress an ermine robe, and her thinning hair shines like jewels on a crown.

On Yom Kippur we sit in the house of prayer, far from home, holding books in our hands like pages and pages of greeting cards bound together, thousands of words we ourselves have not written. Will we merely place our signatures at the bottom and drop the cards in the mailbox?

God would prefer that we come home. She is sitting and wait-ing for us as she has waited every Yom Kippur, waiting very pa-tiently until we are ready. Kol Nidrei night God will not sleep. She will leave the door open and the candles burning, waiting patiently for us to come home.

Perhaps this Yom Kippur we will be able to look into God's aging face and say, "Avinu Malkeinu, our Mother, our Queen, we have come home."

RABBI MARGARET MOERS WENIG *is rabbi of Congregation Beth Am, the People's Temple in Washington Heights, New York City, and Professor of Liturgy and Homiletics at Hebrew Union College—Jewish Institute of Religion. She is also a member of the Interfaith Pastoral Care Service of the AIDS Resource Center. Her sermons have been published in numerous anthologies and journals for Jews and Christians, and she is co-editor, with Naomi Janowitz, of* Siddur Nashim, *a prayerbook. She has been a guest preacher on the Chicago Sunday Evening Club's "30 God Minutes," aired on Chicago Public Television and on the Odyssey cable network. She lives in Brooklyn, New York.*

THE REVEREND DR. TRACI WEST

Mother-Vision

On Justice and Social Transformation

LUKE 1:39-55

I KNOW what you're thinking: "Does this minister have a calendar? This is not the Christmas season! Why are we reading a scripture passage about the birth of Jesus?"

Just give me a chance to explain! First, it's a wonderful story. Why do we have to save it for only one time of the year? Also, this particular story in the gospel of Luke is an especially exciting one. It's my favorite narrative about the conception of Jesus. There are two of them in the New Testament: one is in the gospel of Matthew, and the other is found here in Luke.

In Matthew (in the version of the story that I'm less fond of), the angel comes and speaks to Joseph in a dream. The angel together with Joseph—striving for full mastery of the universe—works out everything about Mary's conception of a child. Mary, the person most directly affected by the pregnancy, is not even introduced into the story until after the baby is born. But in Luke, it's different. There's direct communication between the angel and Mary. Then, touched by the Divine spirit, Mary offers a dynamic prophecy about God's intentions for socially reordering our world. It is a prophecy that must not be skipped over or taken lightly.

So, please tarry with me a while in focusing on the events preceding Jesus' birth (as it is told by the gospel of Luke). This is not merely a warm and fuzzy Christmas tale; neither is it just a story about the conception of Jesus. It's a very provocative story that is centered on a bold and gutsy expectant mother.

I want us to pay attention to the Mary that is depicted here in this narrative. I want to shake us awake to be inspired and challenged by her courage and the assertiveness she displays. Are you ready? Can you handle it?

We may not be ready to accept the real Mary. We're so comfortable with that meek and mild, shy-gentle-little-Mary image that is usually conveyed in the Church. You know the one I mean. The one who has a passive and demure stance. The one who has pale, white skin and folded hands, and eyes that are either averted toward the ground or staring wistfully up at the heavens.

No, I'm here to tell you that when you read your scripture you will find that this passive demeanor is not even remotely fitting of Mary. She was a mouthy woman, not a mousy one! She expressed her faithfulness to God with audacity and fervor.

When the angel comes to tell her that she has been favored by God and will soon give birth to a child, Mary, like the smart woman that she is, interrogates the angel. She asks for a further explanation of how it is possible for her to suddenly become pregnant. After the angel gives further details, then Mary gives her consent. She declares her willingness to participate in this miracle by saying: "I am the Handmaiden of the Lord. Let it be as you have said."

Mary immediately recognizes that this is an extraordinary historical moment. She revels in it as she announces to her cousin,

"My soul magnifies the Lord, and my spirit rejoices in God my Savior . . ."

This mom-to-be does not reflect on the significance of the miracle of her pregnancy by burying her head and timidly batting her eyes. She declares, "God has scattered the proud in the imagination of their hearts, and has put down the powerful from their thrones."

She prophesies. She preaches a specific vision about God's reign here in our world. She celebrates a radical reversal of the present established social and political order. According to Mary, what is presumed to be unshakable and inevitable about who rules and controls, about who "deserves" the advantages and privileges in our society, will be completely overturned by our God.

I told you I wasn't sure you were ready for Mary.

It may be difficult for us to focus on Mary's message for us, because we may be so accustomed to understanding women as fitting into only one of two categories. Too often, we classify women as either good girls or bad girls. So when we make an attempt to listen to Mary's visionary assertions, we may feel confused and think: "Clearly, this is not the submissive, good-little-girl dressed in Madonna-blue we had thought her to be. On the other hand, this aggressive, politically radical woman's soul is magnified by our God, so she can't be a 'bad girl' . . . I don't understand her!" You see, even to begin to grasp the content of what Mary is telling us we have to liberate ourselves from the straitjacket of gender stereotypes.

I know, since we are bombarded with them, that it's very hard to disentangle ourselves from their influence. There was one recent example of this kind of gender stereotyping in the news that I found especially striking. Do you recall some of the media interpretations of Nicole Brown Simpson and how they reinforced these two narrow and polar opposite views of women? If so, did you notice how frequently either one of these two narrow and polar opposite views of women were reinforced when she was described? One national news magazine article about Brown Simpson described her as an ideal mother who was solely dedicated to taking care of her children. She was presented as the perfect mother.

Another article in a similar magazine, written during the same period of time, emphasized the "strong evidence" that Brown Simpson had a lot of "boyfriends" and loved to "party." It was also pointed out that she had a "slick" customized license plate. It was apparent that the authors of this latter "news story" felt that they had located considerable proof that Brown Simpson was morally corrupt.

It never made any sense to me why the press spent so much time trying to fit this particular mom—who suffered such a hor-rific death—into one of two categories of women (a good girl or a bad girl). It was as if they were trying to decide whether or not she deserved to be murdered.

Do you see how this kind of dehumanizing labeling com-pletely distorts our moral compass? We must renounce this ridicu-lous and devaluing "either/or" understanding of women, for it convolutes our perception of the worth and value of our sisters, daughters, mothers, lovers, co-workers, and even of ourselves.

It also leads us to close ourselves off from receiving the gospel from important, God-anointed messengers like Mary. Don't do it! Don't smother Mary and her preaching in an invented "good girl" image. Don't skip over Mary's story and dismiss her prophecy be-cause it's too incongruous with your expectations of women. It would be a grievous mistake to disregard Mary.

Mary calls to us, with her example as well as her words, to be bold people of vision. She urges us to move out of benign accep-tance of status quo injustices. She urges us to see what we can and will be when we heed God's calling.

Push and stretch yourself to hear Mary's prophetic voice over the loud din of current popular sentiment. Our tangible, affirm-ing response to her message is needed now more than ever, for sometimes it seems as though everybody is espousing rhetoric that indicates it's okay to hate, to beat up on, or to castigate certain kinds of people. "They deserve it!" Popular hate speech tells us that poor people deserve to be condemned because they are lazy; gay and lesbian people because they refuse to be like "everybody else"; the racial minorities because they won't stop complaining. And the list goes on . . .

The widespread sentiment is that it's okay to hate and beat up those kinds of people. "Everybody thinks so!" The radio talk show hosts think so. The people who call in to those talk shows agree. The most powerful politicians pronounce that it's the *right* way to think. Even the knowing looks and side comments whispered by our friends, neighbors, and several of our brothers-and-sisters-in-Christ here at church reinforce disdain for and intolerance of "them." This big crowd can appear to drown out any possibility for the realization of the radical vision of God's realm that Mary announces.

Still, as the Church, as the people of God, we are called to behave differently from the loud and angry mob telling us that certain people deserve their lowly or marginalized status. We are urged to view one another through a Divine lens that cancels out your permission to step on or over any part of humanity that does not mirror you and your lifestyle.

Now you will definitely look foolish if you claim the vision that Mary is advocating. You will risk being called a bleeding heart, a nerd, or a liberal. But living out our faith commitment to our God requires us to stand out from the crowd. To genuinely affirm Mary's prophecy is to live in the possibilities for human community; to shape our lives in the "not yet" of God's reign. God desires of us acceptance and imitation of God's own mothering style. We are to love ourselves and one another both for who we are and for who we can be when we wholeheartedly respond to God's call. God said to Jeremiah, "Before I formed you in the womb, I knew you, before you were born I consecrated you, I appointed you a prophet." Indeed, God says to each one of us: "I know the kind of radical, transformative Christian action that you are capable of." Similarly, we should emulate God's style of loving depicted in Isaiah 49, where God is likened to a mother who could never abandon her nursing children. God wants us to know that Her power and vision are ever-flowing, limitless resources for us. Others may not see it or believe in it. But, "You the church, God says to us, you, my children, you must believe in my transformative power."

Be assured that this is not that cheap kind of solace. You might already be more familiar than anyone could want to be with the repulsive, sweet taste of that cheap brand of reassurance. The kind that cruelly irritates rather than helps. When you're feeling alone or rejected with hurt feelings; or when you're ill, weakened by pain, uncertain of what's happening with your body, waiting for doctors or test results; or when you are helplessly enduring the anguish of watching a loved one suffer with a mental or physical illness. It carries the false, simplistic ring of words like "Don't worry," "Look on the bright side"—or "There's always some good that comes out of a bad situation; you just have to find it."

No, the transformative power that I'm speaking about here is not that cheap, superficial kind.

God's transformative power has the kind of potency that nestles in with you directly in the midst of where you are emotionally and spiritually. It may even require more struggle from you. Borrowing phrasing from the Serenity prayer, it may mean accepting some things you don't want to accept or changing in some ways that you don't think you can.

For, let us be mindful that the kind of transformation that Mary preaches about in Luke is far from comfortable change. She tells us:

> God has put down the powerful from their thrones
> and exalted those of low degree; God has filled the

hungry with good things and the rich God has sent
away empty.[1]

This is a formidable message from this young mother-to-be.
When we actually pay attention to the content of Mary's words,
we realize that she is a prophet on behalf of the poor. She pro-
claims God's liberation of marginal and exploited people. This is
our gospel. Yes, my sisters and brothers, one of the most popular
causes among politicians at the state and federal levels at this time
is the cutting of welfare benefits. Democrats and Republicans alike
agree that poor people's entitlement to food and medical care
should be eliminated. The media help support this view by playing into white racist fantasies. They repeatedly depict and refer to
stereotyped images of "lazy" black welfare moms, who are accused of having babies in order to get government checks. Now,
these are mothers that there's almost unanimous cultural permission for us to hate and condemn.

You know the way that some children are spoken of in that
warm, Anglicized voice as "our children," or as "good American
children." Well, it's rare that we hear the children of poor black
and Latina mothers referred to in this manner. These children as
well as their moms, some of whom are themselves actually still
children, are never considered "ours" in popular political postur-
ing. After all, "everybody" thinks it's a good idea to cut off the
spending of "our" tax dollars on prenatal care, nutrition, or baby
formula programs for "those" children. Right?

Of course, in the context of this current political and social climate I sound like a fool telling you that we must listen to a
teenage, unwed, pregnant Jewish girl declaring that God is on the
side of those who are poor and of those who are hungry; God
sends the rich away empty. But this is our gospel!

God calls us to participate in this mother-vision. When we do
so, the common and dehumanizing stereotypes are expunged. We
are able to recognize God's children not only when we look in the

mirror but also in the faces around us, including the ones that don't resemble us at all.

It is certainly not the popular way nor the comfortable way. It means assuming a prophetic stance as a church and as individuals—even sometimes within your own circle of friends or family (including church family).

But let us heed God's call anyway, employing Her mother-vision in our lives and our communities.

Dare to let your soul magnify our God.

Wear God's transformative mother-vision in your thoughts and in your heart. Wrap it around your tongue and let it be heard in the tone of your voice and the words that you choose. Fit that vision on your hands and legs and let it be operative in all that you do.

Be bold and gutsy like Mary as you do so. Confidently trust in God's mothering love: an ever-flowing, sustaining resource for our courage. **AMEN.**

THE REVEREND DR. TRACI WEST *is Assistant Professor of Ethics and African-American Studies at the Theological School of Drew University. She is an ordained elder in the New York Conference of the United Methodist Church and has previously served in parish and campus ministries. She is author of* Wounds of the Spirit: Black Women, Violence and Resistance Ethics *(New York University Press, 1999). Her work in academic, church, and community settings has included particular attention to issues of race, gender, welfare policy, and intimate violence. She lives in Madison, New Jersey.*

Notes

INTRODUCTION

1. Although women had previously completed the full course of rabbinical studies, it was not until 1972 that a woman, Sally Preisand, was admitted to the rabbinate by HUC-JIR (Hebrew Union College and Jewish Institute of Religion). In England, women occasionally preached as early as 1739, when John Wesley appointed Mary B. Fletcher to assume her husband's pulpit upon his death. However, permission to preach and ordination cannot be equated. Ordination confers the authority to handle sacred texts. In Christianity, in the "free church" tradition (communities which have local control over their affairs, unlike the more hierarchically organized sacramental communities, such as Baptist and Congregationalist) women have been ordained for nearly 150 years. Antoinette Brown, a Congregationalist, was the first woman to be ordained, in 1853. See *Women of Spirit: Female Leadership in the Jewish and Christian Traditions,* ed. Rosemary Reuther and Eleanor McLaughlin (New York: Simon and Schuster, 1979), 21, 225-55, 341-42. This volume is an invaluable resource on these matters.

2. See JoAnne Marie Terrell's sermon "How Low Can You Go" in this volume, p. 219.

3. Simone de Beauvoir, *The Second Sex* (New York: Bantam Books, 1952), 585–86.

4. James Hal Cone, *Black Theology, Black Power* (New York: Seabury Press, 1969).

5. An early book that addresses the issues of biblical language from a feminist perspective and articulates the goal of liberating the word from sexism is *The Liberating Word*, ed. Letty Russell (Philadelphia: Westminster Press, 1976).

6. Fifty percent of all rabbinical students on both campuses of Hebrew Union College, New York and Cincinnati, schools of Reform Judaism are women. In *The 1997–1998 Fact Book on Theological Education* (Pittsburgh: Association of Theological Schools, 1998), on the 237 Christian Theological Schools in the United States, including Roman Catholic, mainline Protestant, peace Churches and evangelical and fundamentalist women make up one-third of the total enrollment. However, the statistics for mainline Protestant and non-denominational seminaries are higher, which leads Adair Lumis, a researcher affiliated with Hartford Seminary who has studied women in religion for more than twenty years, to conclude that easily half of the students in these seminaries are women.

7. Mary Daly, in her landmark feminist work *Beyond God the Father* (Boston: Beacon Press, 1973), argues in that all religion simply justifies and rationalizes patriarchy, which is the dominant religion.

8. Marcus J. Borg, *The God We Never Knew* (San Francisco: HarperSanFrancisco, 1997), 71.

9. See Rosemary Radford Reuther, *Sexism and God Talk: Toward a Feminist Theology* (Boston: Beacon Press, 1983) Chapter 2, for an important discussion of the relationship of sexism and God language.

10. Peter J. Gomes, *The Good Book: Reading the Bible with Mind and Heart* (New York: Avon Books, 1996), 20.

11. Ibid., 25.

12. See Elisabeth Schusler Fiorenza, *In Memory of Her: A Feminist Reconstruction of Christian Origins* (New York: Crossroads, 1980), Chapters 1 and 2, and Phyllis Trible, *God and the Rhetoric of Sexuality* (Philadelphia: Fortress Press, 1978) and *Tests of Terror: Literary Feminist Readings of Biblical Narratives* (Philadelphia: Fortress Press, 1984) for ground-breaking discussion of the feminist method and hermeneutics. *The Women's Bible Commentary*, ed. Sharon H. Ringe and Carol A. Newsome (Louisville: Westminster, John

Know Press, 1992), introduction and Chapter 1, provides a useful overview to the various issues for women approaching the task of biblical interpretation.

13. "Lo Contidiario" is a concept taken from my private notes from a course on USA Women's Ethics taught by Dr. Ada María Isasi-Díaz at Drew University in fall 1994.

LAUREN ARTRESS

1. Matthew Fox, *The Illuminations of Hildegard of Bingen* (Santa Fe: Bear and Co., 1985), 6.
2. Ibid., 9.
3. Quoted in Agnes De Mille, *Dance to the Piper* (Boston: Little, Brown, 1952), 44.
4. Stephen Nachmanovitch, *Free Play: Improvisation in Life and Art* (Los Angeles: Jeremy P. Tarcher, 1990), 149.

DOROTHY AUSTIN

1. Leigh Eric Schmidt, *Consumer Rites* (Princeton: Princeton University Press, 1995).
2. Mary Daly, *Beyond God the Father* (Boston: Beacon Press, 1973), 3.
3. Kilmer Myers. For a discussion of Bishop Myers's views, see Emily C. Hewitt and Suzanne R. Hiatt, *Women Priests: Yes or No?* (New York: Seabury Press, 1973).)

HOLLY VINCENT BEAN

1. Annie Dillard, *An American Childhood* (New York: Harper and Row, 1987), 20.
2. Sallie McFague, *Models of God* (Philadelphia: Fortress Press, 1987), 29–57.
3. Anthony de Mello, *The Song of the Bird* (Image Books, 1984).

DONNA BERMAN

1. Cited in Marc Ellis, *Toward a Jewish Theology of Liberation* (Maryknoll: Orbis Books, 1987), 36.
2. See Hans Jonas, "The Concept of God After Auschwitz." *The Journal of Religion*, 67, no. 1, January 1987.
3. Ibid.
4. See S. Daniel Breslauer, *A New Jewish Ethics* (New York: Mellen, 1983) and

Covenant and Community in Modern Judaism (Westport: Greenwood Press, 1984).

5. S. Daniel Breslauer, "Trust in Human Beings Despite Human Evil: Towards a Post-Holocaust Jewish Theology of Covenant," an unpublished paper delivered at the Center for Process Studies at a conference entitled "Process Theology and Evil: The Holocaust Experience," June 1980.

6. Eliezer Berkovits, *Faith After the Holocaust* (New York: Ktav, 1973), 36.

7. Breslauer, "Trust in Human Beings Despite Human Evil," 7.

8. Ibid., 7.

9. Ibid., 6.

10. See Jacob Neusner, "Can Judaism Survive the Twentieth Century?" *Tikkun*, July/August, 1989.

11. See Marc H. Ellis, *Ending Auschwitz: The Future of Jewish and Christian Life* (Louisville: Westminster/John Knox Press, 1994).

12. See Larry Hoffman, "In Search of a Spiritual Home," *Reform Judaism* 23, no. 1, Fall 1994.

13. Cited in Ellis, *Toward a Jewish Theology of Liberation*, 20.

14. See, for example, Sigmund Freud, *The Future of an Illusion* (New York: Norton, 1961).

15. Rabbi Sheldon J. Harr, "The Rabbi—On Love and Loss: One Rabbi's Perspective," *Central Conference of American Rabbis Yearbook*, vol. 103 (Montreal: CCAR, 1993), 62.

16. In Otto Maduro, ed., *Judaism, Christianity, and Liberation: An Agenda for Dialogue* (New York: Orbis Books, 1991), 55.

17. Adrienne Rich, "Through a Keen Lens of Empathy," *Genesis* 2, February/March 1986, 13.

18. Isaiah 58:6–7.

19. Isaiah 58:8–9.

REBECCA EDMISTON-LANGE

1. Annie Dillard, "Total Eclipse," in *Teaching a Stone to Talk* (New York: Harper and Row, 1983), 99.

LAURIE J. FERGUSON

1. Eda LeShan, *Grandparenting in a Changing World* (New York: Newmarket Press, 1993), 173–74.

2. Cited in Anne K. Simkinson, "Freeing the Seed," *Common Boundary*, March/April 1997, 22.

LOUISE GREEN

1. Bishop Desmond Tutu, from a speech given to the All-Africa Church Conference.

ANN HALLSTEIN

1. Cited in Robert Moats Miller, *Harry Emerson Fosdick, Preacher, Pastor, Prophet* (New York and Oxford: Oxford University Press, 1985), 385.
2. Albert Einstein et al., *Living Philosophies* (New York: AMS, 1931), 6.

E. LEE HANOCK

1. Jane Park Huber, "God, Give Us Eyes and Hearts to See," in *A Singing Faith* (Westminster Press 1987).
2. Dorothee Soelle, *Suffering* (Philadelphia: Fortress Press, 1975), 28.
3. Ibid. See critique of Christian masochism, pp. 9–28.
4. Emile Durkheim, *The Elementary Forms of Religious Life* (New York: Free Press, 1915), 13–21, 462–88.
5. Soelle, 32.
6. Jack Reimer, ed., *New Prayers for High Holy Days,* (Media Judaica, 1973).

SUSAN HARRISS

1. Denise Levertov, "Stepping Westward," from *Poems 1960–1967* (New York: New Directions, 1966.)

JOAN E. HEMENWAY

1. Annie Dillard, *Teaching a Stone to Talk* (New York: Harper and Row, 1983).
2. This story was originally published in *Mortal Lessons* by Richard Selzer (New York: Harcourt Brace & Coo., 1974).
3. Used with permission of the Reverend Sandra Belcher, staff chaplain at The Hospital of St. Raphael, New Haven, CT.
4. Alice Walker, *The Color Purple* (New York: Harcourt Brace, 1982), 268.
5. Robert Frost, *In the Clearing* (New York: Holt, Reinhart and Winston, 1962).
6. Marcus Borg, *Meeting Jesus Again for the First Time* (New York: Harper and Row, 1994), 46.
7. Ibid., 48.
8. Tommy Hine, "Skating Solo: A Reflection of the Perfect Pair," in *The Hartford Courant* 2/25/96, 1A.

VANESSA OCHS

1. Tamar Frankiel, *The Voice of Sarah: Feminine Spirituality and Traditional Judaism* (San Francisco: Harper and Row, 1990).

ANNIE RUTH POWELL

1. *Interpreter's Bible Dictionary* (Nashville: Abingdon Press, 1975), 449–50.
2. Julia Boyd, *In the Company of My Sisters: Black Women and Self-Esteem* (New York: Dutton, 1993), 5.
3. Engelbert Mveng, "Third World Theology? What Theology? What Third World?" in *Eruption of the Third World*, eds. Virginia Fabella and Sergio Torres (Maryknoll, New York: Orbis Books, 1983), 220.
4. June Gatlin, *Spirit Speaks to Sisters* (Chicago: Noble Press, 1996), 28–29.
5. Ibid.
6. Martin Luther King, Jr. "An Experiment in Love," in *A Testament of Hope*, ed. James M. Washington (San Francisco: Harper and Row, 1986).
7. Martin Luther King, Jr., *The Strength to Love* (Philadelphia: Fortress Press, 1981), p. 50.

BONNIE ROSBOROUGH

1. Thomas H. Johnson, ed., *The Letters of Emily Dickinson* (Cambridge, Mass.: Belnap Press of Harvard University, 1958), 602.

MAXINE SILVERMAN

1. *The Siddur Sim Shalom* (New York: The Jewish Theological Seminary), 441.
atarah—collar of the tallis (prayer shawl)
Shekinah—feminine aspect of God
kavanah—prayerful intention, mindfulness

TRACI WEST

1. As interpreted by Traci West.